IMAGES
of America

MONTROSE

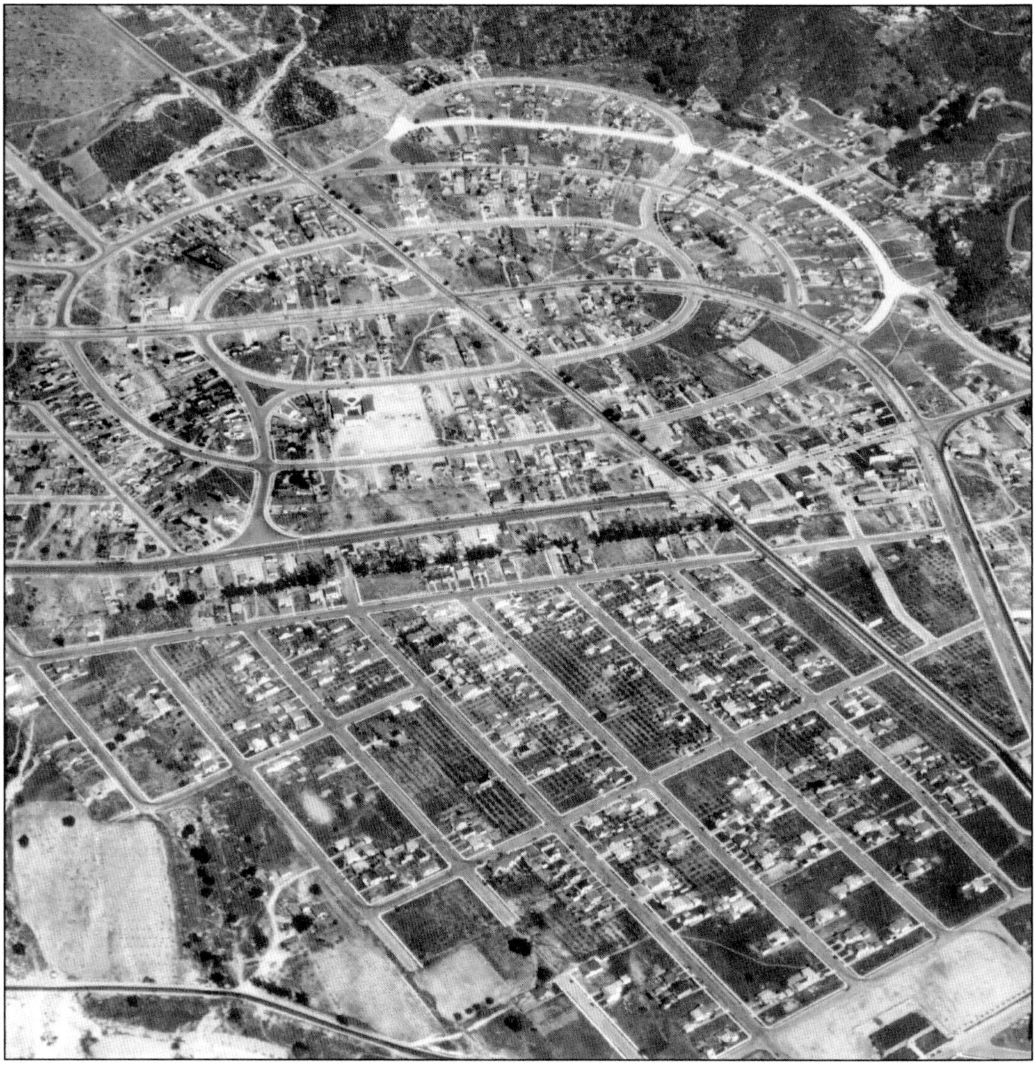

Local historians have long thought that the developers of Montrose laid it out in the pattern of a flower, a "mountain rose" in the foothills of the San Gabriel Mountains, with the "stem" being Verdugo Road (the wide road on the right). The community center was supposed to be at the center of the flower—the intersection of Ocean View Boulevard and Montrose Avenue—but instead formed along Honolulu Avenue, south of the "rose." However, the name Montrose was chosen *after* the streets were laid out. Nevertheless, this Spence Air photograph from 1931 shows the area in "full bloom." (Courtesy of the Benjamin and Gladys Thomas Air Photo Collection.)

On the Cover: The building at the northwest corner of Honolulu Avenue and Verdugo Road has welcomed visitors to Montrose since 1923. It has undergone a number of face-lifts over the years, but it is the same frame under it all. Here is how it looked in the late 1930s. (Courtesy of Kathryn Halford.)

IMAGES
of America

MONTROSE

Robert Newcombe

ARCADIA
PUBLISHING

ISBN 978-0-7385-9634-1

Published by Arcadia Publishing
Charleston, South Carolina

Printed in the United States of America

Library of Congress Control Number: 2012945816

For all general information, please contact Arcadia Publishing:
Telephone 843-853-2070
Fax 843-853-0044
E-mail sales@arcadiapublishing.com
For customer service and orders:
Toll-Free 1-888-313-2665

Visit us on the Internet at www.arcadiapublishing.com

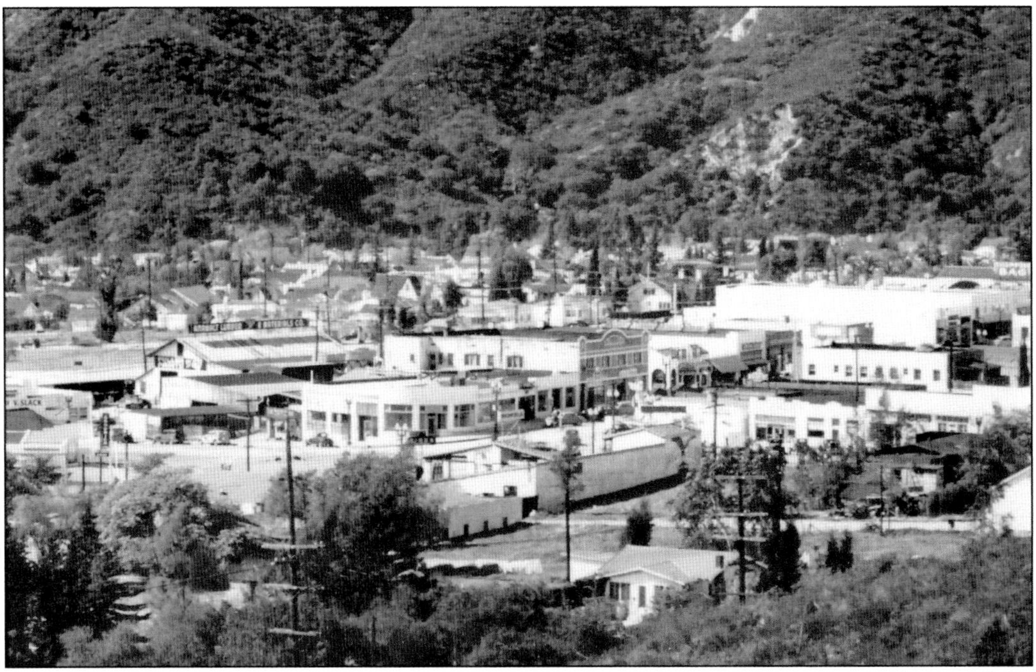

This early 1940s view of Montrose shows the J.C. Penney Building and annex complete, and the empty lot east of them that will become the new Shopping Bag. The Montrose Hotel and the theater are also visible. This photograph was taken from the railroad right-of-way that had been started from Montrose to La Cañada, just above what is now the Indian Springs Shopping Plaza. The line was abandoned before any track was laid, but the right-of-way is still visible above Vons. (Courtesy Glendale Public Library.)

CONTENTS

Acknowledgments

I could not have written this book without the help of my previous collaborator Mike Lawler. He has been a sounding board and font of information and photographs during the entire process, even proofreading chapters from his hospital bed. Mike Morgan has also been a huge help in researching and proofreading; he prodded me to go further in uncovering the truth about how Montrose was named when I was ready to print the legend. John Drayman helped me indirectly in that he was the first (and second, and third) person to give me a walking tour of Montrose. John shared so much information that some of his exact phrases have probably sneaked their way into the book text.

There are many people who helped with bits and pieces of the Montrose story. First, I have to thank Judy Ostrander of the Los Angeles Public Library who helped me determine the source of the "Legend of Montrose." I have to thank Melinda Clarke of the Montrose–Verdugo City Chamber of Commerce who spent almost as much time looking through boxes of old photographs as I did. And I have to thank the following for providing photographs, telling me stories, or just talking to me about Montrose: Thomas Anawalt, Brian Anderson, Henry Baeca, Bob Berger, Wanda Bergstrom, Kelly Callaghan, Mary Dawson, Kirk Gelsinger, Pat Grant, Ken Grayson, John Hammell Jr., Mark Havlik, Chris Humphrey, Amy (Sowers) Jordan, Ray King, Joe McClure, Roberta Medford, John Newcombe, Jessica Palacios, Maureen Palacios, Cynthia Reddon, Jack Roscher, Tom Russell, Kerri (Gelsinger) Scott, Mike Shea, Tim Shepard, John Smatlak, Danielle Smith, and Greg Tomassian.

Finally, I have to thank my wife Debbie and daughter Laura for putting up with me while I "ate, slept (barely), and breathed" Montrose during the time I worked on this. And I have to apologize to my dog Jack for all those missed walks while I was writing.

All photographs are provided by the Historical Society of the Crescenta Valley and the Glendale Public Library unless otherwise marked.

All author royalties go to the Historical Society of the Crescenta Valley.

Introduction

The area now known as Montrose was Tongva Indian territory for centuries. There is evidence that the Tongva had long-term, if not permanent, settlements in the Tujunga and Arroyo Seco areas on the western and eastern edges of the Crescenta Valley, as well as a seasonal settlement in the small canyon known as Indian Springs, just east of present-day Montrose.

When the Spanish arrived in California in the late 1700s, they built missions from south to north, distancing them by one day's ride. The main route between the San Fernando and San Gabriel Missions was through the Crescenta Valley. In 1784, Don Jose Maria Verdugo, a Mexican soldier serving Spain, requested and received the first Spanish land grant, Rancho San Rafael, roughly 36,000 acres that stretched from the San Fernando Mission to the west, the Arroyo Seco to the east, the San Gabriel Mountains to the north, and the Los Angeles River to the south. While this was a huge rancho, Verdugo considered much of the dry, dusty land uninhabitable. Verdugo died in 1831, leaving the rancho to his children, but when California became a state in 1850, recipients of Spanish land grants and their heirs had a difficult time proving ownership. Like many others in their situation, the Verdugos were challenged and forced to pay attorneys with pieces of their land, including the Crescenta Valley. The Verdugo name remains throughout the area, in mountains, parks, and a confusing number of streets.

The first "white American" settler in the area is generally considered to be Theodor Pickens, originally from Kentucky, who arrived in the valley around 1871. He filed a land patent claim and eventually bought 160 acres at the base of the canyon that now bears his name.

In the 1880s, Dr. Benjamin Briggs arrived looking for a healthful climate and bought 2,500 acres of the valley, including Pickens's holdings. Briggs was responsible for turning the area into La Crescenta, including naming it, having a hand in the first church and first school, and building a town center at the intersection of Michigan Avenue (now Foothill Boulevard) and Los Angeles Avenue (now La Crescenta Avenue.) He also laid out many of the north-south streets at angles to lessen the inclines, giving many blocks a parallelogram shape instead of the traditional rectangle. But he never formally incorporated La Crescenta as a city (it still is not today), and the town center eventually became little more than a busy intersection.

The "Legend of Montrose" begins in late 1910 when real estate agent Robert A. Walton of the Holmes-Walton agency teamed with J. Frank Walters to buy about 250 acres of sagebrush from Briggs's daughter Irene Briggs Ward. The story that has been told for decades is that Holmes and Walton held a contest to name their new community and selected "Montrose" as the winner, after the submitter's hometown in Pennsylvania. As the prize, he supposedly won one of the new lots. Interestingly, almost every time this story has been told, the teller includes these two additional embellishments: the name appealed to the many rose fanciers in the area, and it was because of the popular novel *Legend of Montrose* by Sir Walter Scott.

Local historians have recently questioned this story, and while it was tempting to "print the legend," something did not seem right. A search through old microfilm and databases at the Los Angeles and Glendale libraries shed new—actually, old—light on this story but without the definitive answer to the question of what inspired the name.

The first part that is wrong about the story is that Frederick A. Holmes was never involved with the Montrose development; he had sold his share of the company to Walton in 1908. J. Frank Walters was apparently the financier of the project since he bought most of the land. In a story in the *Los Angeles Times* on December 1, 1912, the amount of land involved was updated to 500 acres: "The deal it is stated by those interested, involves approximately $500,000. Nearly $100,000, it is stated, will be expended in improvements."

The second part of the story is not exactly wrong, but if there was a legitimate contest with a real winner, why were the other two bits of information so important that they are always mentioned?

Grace J. Oberbeck was unintentionally responsible for this. In her book *History of La Crescenta-LaCañada*, first published in 1933, she writes that even at that time—only 20 years after the naming, while many involved were still alive—locals were trying to determine where the name came from, and Oberbeck speculated about the source of the name. *Maybe* it was the roses, *maybe* it was Montrose, Pennsylvania, or *maybe* it was because of Sir Walter Scott's novel, but she was not claiming any of these as truths. She wrote at the end of her paragraph, "We think it would be very interesting to know the story of the prized lot."

Here is the story of the "prized lot:" there wasn't one. The first advertisement announcing the contest ran in the *Los Angeles Express* on Thursday, December 5, 1912, with a postmark deadline of December 18 and the winner to be announced on December 24 "as a Christmas Gift to the person who sends the name selected." It was a large advertisement and had details about the new community and the contest. During the next two weeks, two smaller advertisements ran in the *Los Angeles Examiner*, and 10 one-inch advertisements ran in the *Los Angeles Times*. ("Fine Lot or $650 Cash For a Name For Our Townsite. The Holmes-Walton Company.")

On Sunday, December 29, the company took out an advertisement in the *Times* announcing the winner: "Careful examination of thousands of coupons containing names suggested for the wonderfully beautiful Holmes-Walton Company Townsite on the lofty Verdugo–La Crescenta mesa revealed the fact that nine persons had submitted the name "MONTROSE," which was selected by the board of Judges." It said the winning name was picked on Christmas Eve, but the prize was not awarded until December 28. The advertisement listed the names and addresses of the nine (none from the valley) and of the judges, which included Lieutenant Governor Wallace (who lived in a castle in La Cañada). The advertisement said that Homer C. Brown of Los Angeles was the winner and that he chose the $650 cash over the lot. The rules had stated that if more than one person submitted the name chosen, those winners would determine who got the prize. The article did not explain how Brown was chosen by the winners. There was no explanation as to where the name came from or why the judges picked it. But Brown was born in Centre, Pennsylvania, 154 miles from Montrose.

There are two photographs from 1912 that show the name "Montrose" on billboards. Did they really paint the billboards that fast? Or are the photographs mis-dated? Or was the name already picked? One interesting tidbit is that there is a Montrose Street in Los Angeles that dead-ends into Glendale Boulevard in Echo Park. It was under construction in 1911, and Walton would have passed this street every time he made the trip from his office to La Crescenta. Did that play a part in the naming?

No matter where the name came from, Walton laid out the streets in a unique pattern, but the idea that he intentionally carved out a "mountain rose" is questionable. His advertisements never mentioned this, and Walton had already planned the winding streets before he held the naming contest. The pattern looks remarkably like a flower, and it is hard to believe this is coincidental. Perhaps the street layout inspired the name. In any case, Walton did intend for the center of the community to be at the intersection of Montrose Avenue and Ocean View Boulevard, the center of the "rose."

By 1910, a narrow-gauge trolley operated between Eagle Rock and Glendale as far north as Verdugo Park. Having had difficulty selling lots in the area (before calling it Montrose), Walton knew that access by rail was necessary so he and Walters partnered to purchase the line in 1913 and a year later renamed it the Glendale & Montrose (G&M) Railway.

On February 22, 1913, the Holmes-Walton company hosted a huge, heavily advertised public barbecue to attract attention and sell lots in their new development, promising "cool Summer breezes, frostless Winters, pure balmy air and the finest mountain water." Close to 4,000 people attended, and the developer sold more lots that day than he did in the next several years. That date is celebrated as Montrose Founders Day.

In April of that year, the G&M Railway was extended to Montrose, and by the end of the year, the trolley went to La Crescenta Avenue.

The first real commercial building was built by a Los Angeles woman at the southwestern corner of Verdugo Road and Honolulu Avenue. (That one intersection starts and ends with four different streets, mainly because Verdugo Road already existed with a large turn at that point. The east-west portion of Verdugo Road—heading into La Cañada—was renamed Verdugo Boulevard in an attempt to make it less confusing.)

Montrose was not a big success for Walton and Walters, partly due to the United States entry into World War I in 1917, partly due to the influenza outbreak in 1918, and partly due to their inability or reluctance to put as much money into the development as they said they would. Early home builders who were not on Montrose Avenue did not have electricity when their homes were completed. The streets were not paved for several years. The clubhouse was never built. Walton and Walters sold their interest in the G&M Railway in 1916, and their names seem to quietly disappear from Montrose development references in the mid-1910s, replaced in the 1920s by businessmen like Stephen Meyers, Theodore Bellanger, H.F. Anawalt, Monte Friend, and C.J. Reinhard. But the Roaring Twenties brought prosperity to the area, and Montrose blossomed into the community Walton and Walters had envisioned.

Commercial buildings were constructed both along the trolley route on Montrose Avenue and west on Honolulu Avenue. While Walton had expected the main business route to run along Montrose Avenue towards Ocean View Boulevard, residents' legs and lungs had other ideas. Shoppers preferred the leisurely walk along the flat Honolulu versus huffing and puffing up the hill of Montrose. So the business district grew west instead of north, several blocks south of the center of the rose.

At the same time, the trolley line became less important to the growth of the community. At one point commuters had been able to ride from La Crescenta to Los Angeles without switching cars, but the service did not last long because there were not enough riders. The G&M struggled for years, and the service was halted in 1930, a victim of the Great Depression, buses, trucks, and most importantly, the automobile.

Eventually the "westward ho" movement along Honolulu Avenue caused problems for homeowners west of Ocean View Boulevard as they slowly found their properties being encroached upon by businesses. Most families sold their homes, but a few stayed and lived there as late as the 1950s. Some homeowners rented out their houses to businesses. While most of the houses were eventually torn down and replaced with retail buildings, two of the original ones still stand on Honolulu within the shopping park.

Businesses in the early days tended to focus on the day-to-day needs of local residents: pharmacies, food markets, banks, general stores, and clothing stores, but there were also lumberyards, car dealers, hotels, and a movie theater. When "supermarkets" entered the national retail picture in the 1930s, mom-and-pop markets found it hard to compete with the larger chains. A&P, Safeway, Piggly Wiggly, and Shopping Bag moved into Montrose, but even these stores were not large enough to compete with huge, stand-alone buildings, so they eventually left. Pharmacies suffered a similar fate. Though there was a time when many national chains had stores here, most had moved out by the early 1980s.

After World War II, soldiers who had been stationed in Southern California married and moved to places like the Crescenta Valley, causing a building boom. The remaining empty lots were built upon, and much of the wooded and hilly areas were also developed as the demand for housing grew.

From the beginning, residents of La Crescenta relied on the local mountains for their water. As the valley evolved from a rural farming community to a crowded Los Angeles suburb, there was simply not enough water to go around. In the late 1940s, water rationing in the Crescenta Valley became a regular occurrence. The neighboring city of Glendale, which had tried off and on since the 1920s to annex Montrose, had access to water from other sources and offered their services if La Crescenta would become part of Glendale. The majority of residents fiercely opposed this, and the measure was soundly defeated at the polls. Undeterred, politicians in favor of annexation resorted to a new tactic: rather than an all-or-nothing proposition, local neighborhoods were allowed to vote for annexation. Starting in 1951 and continuing for several years, some neighborhoods of La Crescenta voted in favor of annexation while others voted against it, leaving the border between Glendale and unincorporated Los Angeles County (La Crescenta) a confusing, zigzagging jumble. Most of the shopping park was annexed in 1955, but the alley and stores immediately to the north of it are in unincorporated Los Angeles County.

By the late 1950s, most traditional downtown retail districts in the United States were under assault as shoppers abandoned their traditional habits in favor of shopping malls. Montrose was no exception. In 1958, some locals suggested closing Honolulu Avenue to car traffic as had been done in Santa Monica and other cities as a way to spur business. Some politicians even toyed with turning Honolulu Avenue into a truck route to relieve traffic on Foothill Boulevard, essentially destroying the business district.

In 1963, the merchants sent a representative team to Grand Junction, Colorado, to see what that city was doing to reinvent itself, and then again a year later to see how successful it was. They liked what they saw and proposed doing something similar in Montrose. Working with the city of Glendale, the merchants hired local architect Jack H. Simison to redesign Honolulu Avenue. What Simison proposed was radical: remove parking spaces along the street and replace them with curb-outs and landscaping to give the district a more park-like and less urban feel. This was fought heatedly by many merchants, partly because they would have to spend money creating rear entrances to their stores since the plan involved buying homes behind the stores and turning them into parking lots. After much debate, the plan was approved in January 1967 and construction started not long after. (The Montrose Shopping Park Association, though, was not formalized until the following year.) The entire project cost about $300,000 (a huge sum in 1967), with half of it financed by the merchants themselves (almost unthinkable today and rare even then.) As a result, Montrose survived and today owes much of its charm to these forward thinkers, though there are some locals who still think it was a bad idea.

While the "rose" was easy to see from the hills around Montrose early on, as trees grew and taller buildings were constructed, the rose gradually became visible only from the air. The final indignity to it was the construction of the 2 and 210 Freeways in the late 1960s and early 1970s, which pruned off the top petals. State senator Frank Lanterman had fought to prevent the 210 from plowing under the expensive homes in Flintridge, but there was no such champion for the rose. Perhaps that is because Montrose had never independently incorporated, or perhaps it was never really a rose and was not worth saving, or perhaps by then "Montrose" had come to mean just the shopping park.

In its first 100 years, Montrose has grown from uninhabitable sagebrush to an inviting, old-fashioned shopping district that attracts visitors from all over Southern California. As businesses opened and businesses closed, many of the buildings were reused and not replaced, which adds to the charm, especially when combined with the 1967 park-like makeover. The now mature trees, curving road, benches, limited signage, and mom-and-pop stores provide Montrose with pedestrian appeal, something that most modern business districts cannot provide. If City Walk has "eye candy," Montrose has "eye chicken soup."

In the 2000s, many merchants and local residents have expressed concern that Montrose is losing its charm. Many retail stores closed shop and have been replaced by a proliferation of restaurants, beauty salons, and exercise studios. Three franchise operations—Starbucks, Coffee Bean, and Quiznos—opened near each other at the intersection of Ocean View Boulevard and Honolulu Avenue, causing concern that these types of businesses will ruin Montrose. Ultimately, though, the fate of small-town Montrose will be determined by shoppers who will vote with their wallets, lungs, and legs just as they did 90 years ago when they "moved" the center of town two blocks south of the rose.

One

Roots
Montrose Beginnings

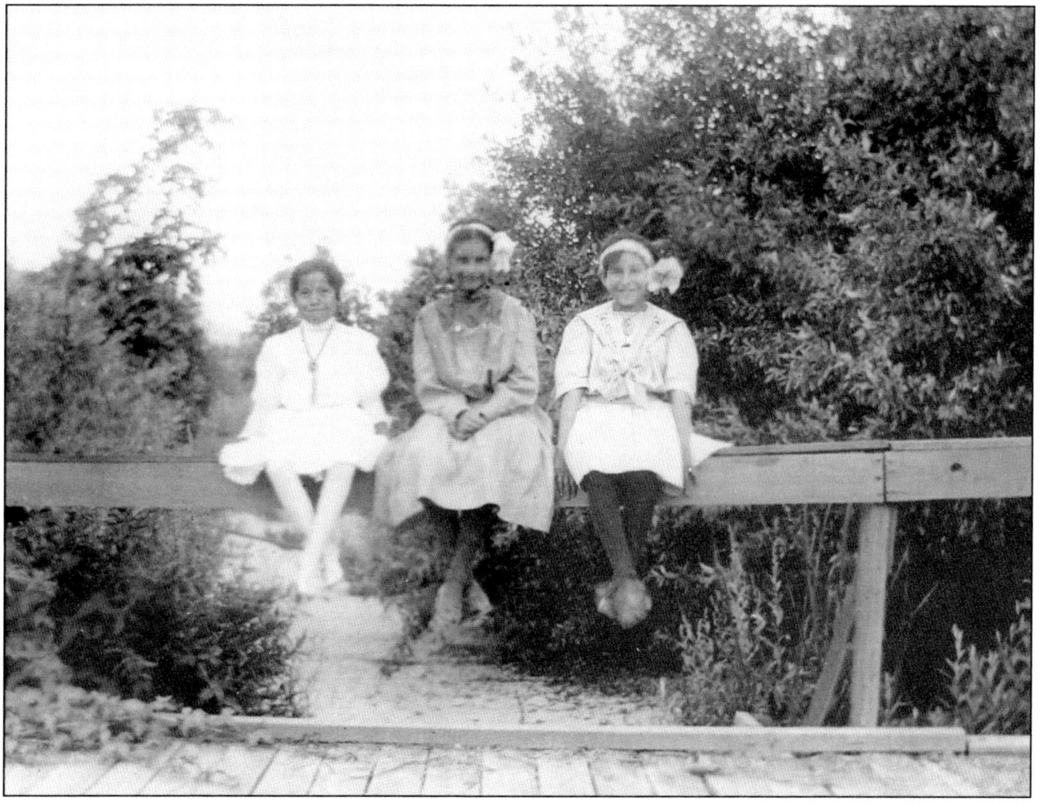

In 1784, Spanish soldier Don Jose Maria Verdugo petitioned for and received a land grant known as Rancho San Rafael, which included all of the Crescenta Valley. The girl on the far right (the other two are unidentified) in this 1890s photograph is Dora Verdugo, the granddaughter of Jose Maria. Dora was an active member of the community and lived here until her death at the age of 102 in 1984. The Verdugo name lives on in many variations throughout Southern California. (Courtesy of John Newcombe.)

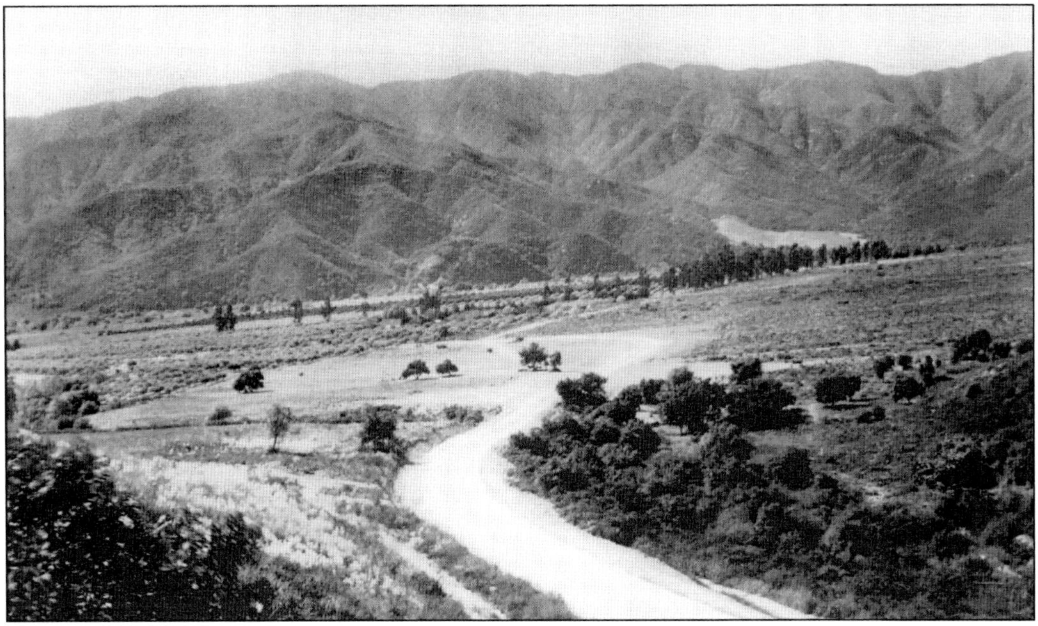

In 1873, investors started work on a route that would significantly cut down the length of the roundabout wagon trip from the silver mines in the Inyo Mountains to Los Angeles by going directly through the San Gabriel Mountains. They widened an existing trail and essentially created what is now Verdugo Road and Boulevard. This photograph from around 1905 faces west along Verdugo Boulevard, showing the curve to Verdugo Road heading south.

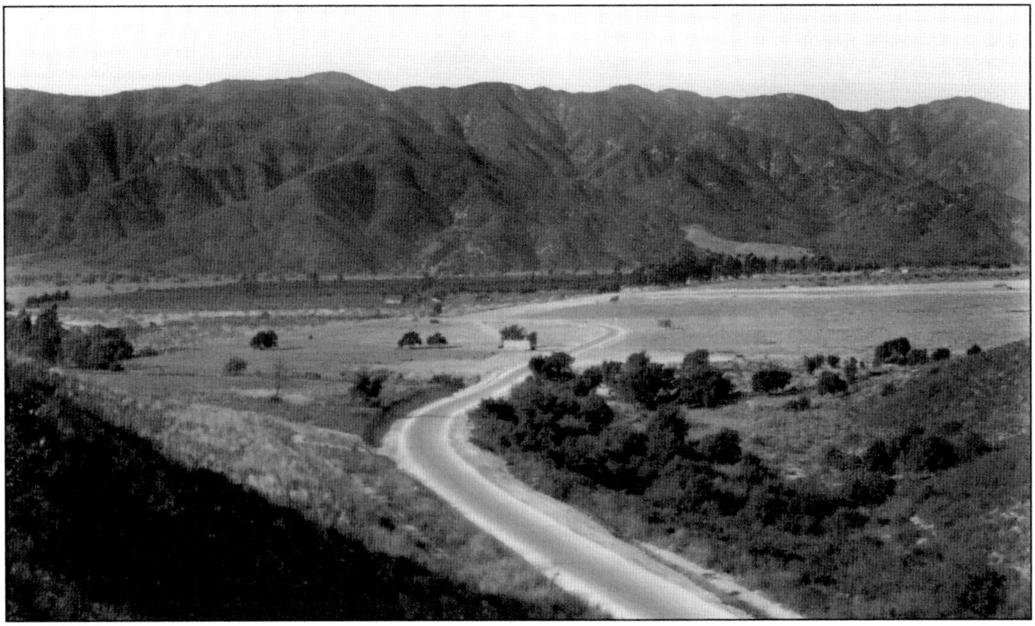

In late 1910, real estate agent Robert Walton of Holmes-Walton and J. Frank Walters bought 250 acres from Benjamin Briggs's daughter Irene and by January 16, 1911, had started selling lots. This photograph from around that time shows the paved Verdugo Road/Boulevard and a billboard (in front of the tree, center) advertising lots for sale from the company, but no mention of "Montrose." (Courtesy of John Newcombe.)

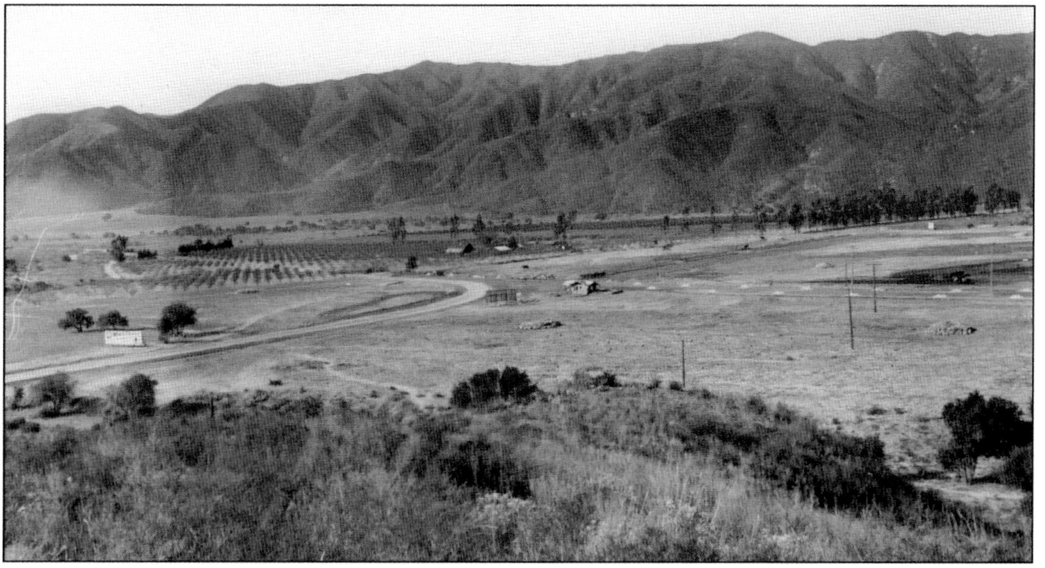

The real estate building at the corner of Verdugo Road/Boulevard and Montrose Avenue was supposedly built in 1912. This photograph shows it under construction, but the billboard mentioned on the opposite page now reads "Montrose." Is it possible the place was already named before the naming contest was announced? (Courtesy of John Newcombe.)

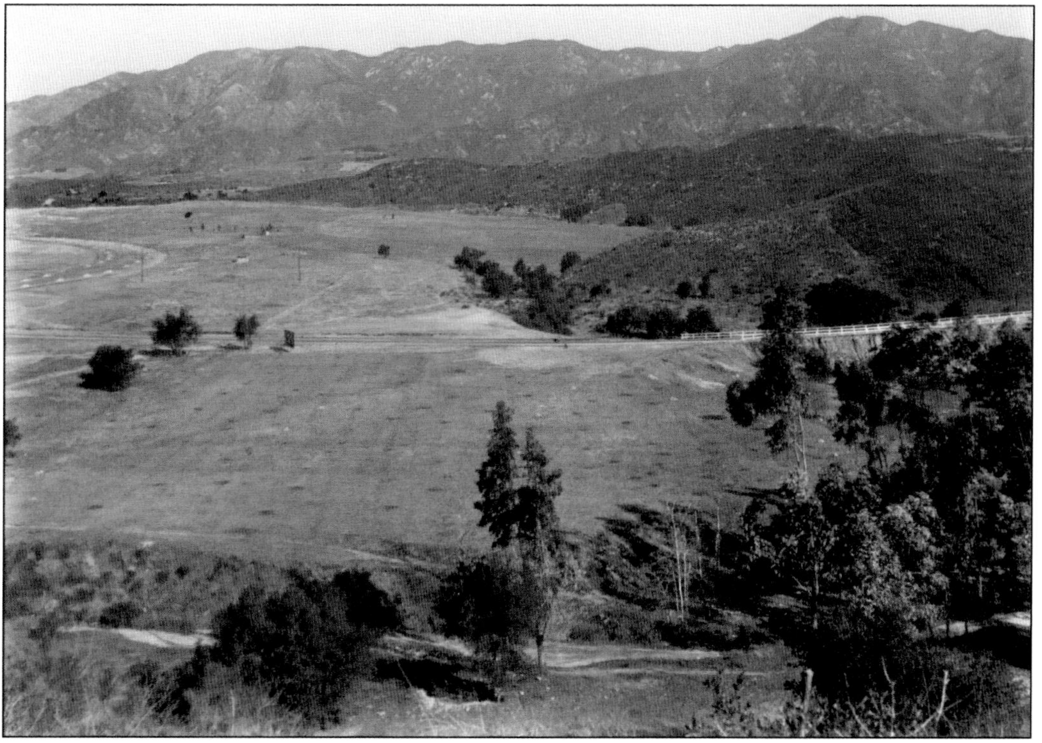

This photograph from probably early 1913 looks north along the San Rafael hills, with the distinctive guard rails where Verdugo Boulevard passes the Indian Springs canyon, on the right here. Walters had bought an additional 250 acres near the end of 1912 to add to the development, and Holmes-Walton announced that "a splendid water system with abundant water is now being installed."

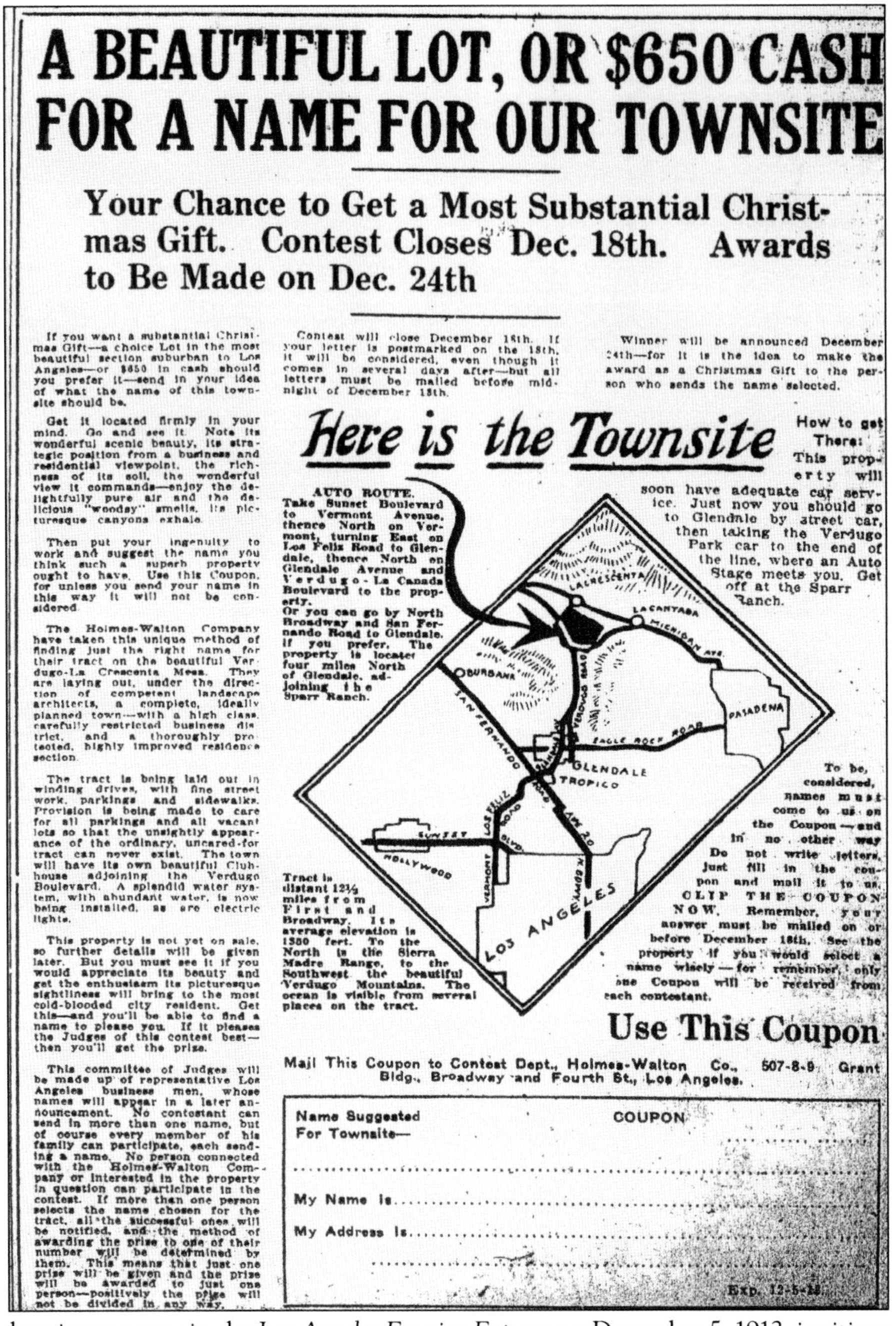

A BEAUTIFUL LOT, OR $650 CASH FOR A NAME FOR OUR TOWNSITE

Your Chance to Get a Most Substantial Christmas Gift. Contest Closes Dec. 18th. Awards to Be Made on Dec. 24th

If you want a substantial Christmas Gift—a choice Lot in the most beautiful section suburban to Los Angeles—or $650 in cash should you prefer it—send in your idea of what the name of this townsite should be.

Get it located firmly in your mind. Go and see it. Note its wonderful scenic beauty, its strategic position from a business and residential viewpoint, the richness of its soil, the wonderful view it commands—enjoy the delightfully pure air and the delicious "woodsy" smells, its picturesque canyons exhale.

Then put your ingenuity to work and suggest the name you think such a superb property ought to have. Use this Coupon, for unless you send your name in this way it will not be considered.

The Holmes-Walton Company have taken this unique method of finding just the right name for their tract on the beautiful Verdugo-La Crescenta Mesa. They are laying out, under the direction of competent landscape architects, a complete, ideally planned town—with a high class, carefully restricted business district, and a thoroughly protected, highly improved residence section.

The tract is being laid out in winding drives, with fine street work, parkings and sidewalks. Provision is being made to care for all parkings and all vacant lots so that the unsightly appearance of the ordinary, uncared-for tract can never exist. The town will have its own beautiful Clubhouse adjoining the Verdugo Boulevard. A splendid water system, with abundant water, is now being installed, as are electric lights.

This property is not yet on sale, so further details will be given later. But you must see it if you would appreciate its beauty and get the enthusiasm its picturesque sightliness will bring to the most cold-blooded city resident. Get this—and you'll be able to find a name to please you. If it pleases the Judges of this contest best—then you'll get the prize.

This committee of Judges will be made up of representative Los Angeles business men, whose names will appear in a later announcement. No contestant can send in more than one name, but of course every member of his family can participate, each sending a name. No person connected with the Holmes-Walton Company or interested in the property in question can participate in the contest. If more than one person selects the name chosen for the tract, all the successful ones will be notified, and the method of awarding the prize to one of their number will be determined by them. This means that just one prize will be given and the prize will be awarded to just one person—positively the prize will not be divided in any way.

Contest will close December 18th. If your letter is postmarked on the 18th, it will be considered, even though it comes in several days after—but all letters must be mailed before midnight of December 18th.

Winner will be announced December 24th—for it is the idea to make the award as a Christmas Gift to the person who sends the name selected.

Here is the Townsite

How to get There: This property will soon have adequate car service. Just now you should go to Glendale by street car, then taking the Verdugo Park car to the end of the line, where an Auto Stage meets you. Get off at the Sparr Ranch.

AUTO ROUTE.
Take Sunset Boulevard to Vermont Avenue, thence North on Vermont, turning East on Los Feliz Road to Glendale, thence North on Glendale Avenue and Verdugo-La Canada Boulevard to the property.
Or you can go by North Broadway and San Fernando Road to Glendale, if you prefer. The property is locatet four miles North of Glendale, adjoining the Sparr Ranch.

Tract is distant 12½ miles from First and Broadway. Its average elevation is 1350 feet. To the North is the Sierra Madre Range, to the Southwest the beautiful Verdugo Mountains. The ocean is visible from several places on the tract.

To be considered, names must come to us on the Coupon—and in no other way. Do not write letters. Just fill in the coupon and mail it to us. CLIP THE COUPON NOW. Remember, your answer must be mailed on or before December 18th. See the property if you would select a name wisely—for remember, only one Coupon will be received from each contestant.

Use This Coupon

Mail This Coupon to Contest Dept., Holmes-Walton Co., 507-8-9 Grant Bldg., Broadway and Fourth St., Los Angeles.

COUPON

Name Suggested For Townsite—

My Name Is...................

My Address Is...................

Exp. 12-5-12.

This advertisement ran in the *Los Angeles Evening Express* on December 5, 1912, inviting readers to name "our townsite." The advertisement also says "the tract is being laid out in winding drives, with fine street work, parkings and sidewalks . . . The town will have its own beautiful Clubhouse adjoining the Verdugo Boulevard." The winning name would be announced on Christmas Eve as a "Christmas Gift" for the nominee. On December 29, Holmes-Walton ran an advertisement announcing the winning name of "Montrose," which was submitted by nine people, who then had to choose one winner among themselves. Homer C. Brown of Los Angeles won and chose the $650 cash, not the "beautiful lot."

The dapper Fred Anderson was the agent for land sales in Montrose and worked out of this small, pagoda-roofed building supposedly starting in 1912, but the Holmes-Walton ads say no lots could be sold until the official opening in 1913. The building didn't last very long at this corner (Montrose Avenue and Verdugo Boulevard), but some old-timers insist it was moved to another location rather than torn down.

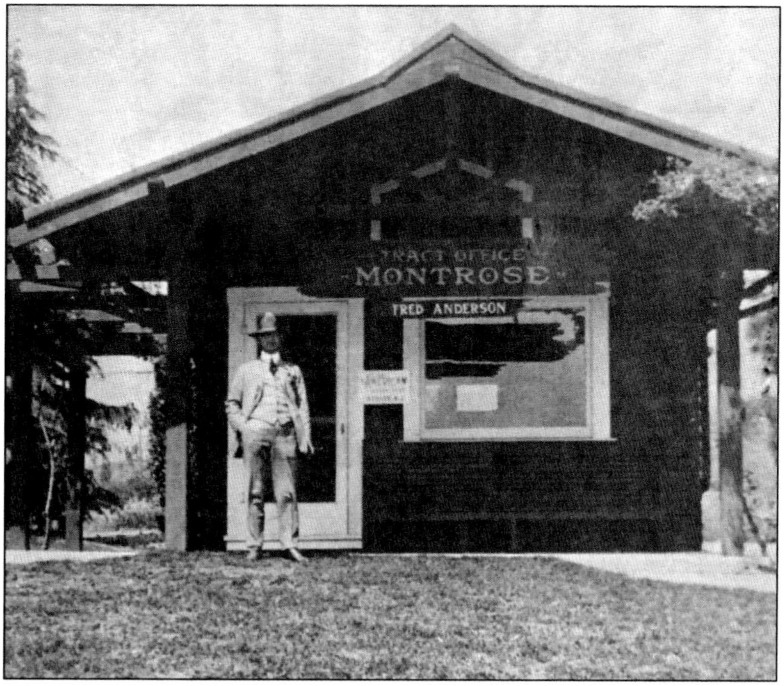

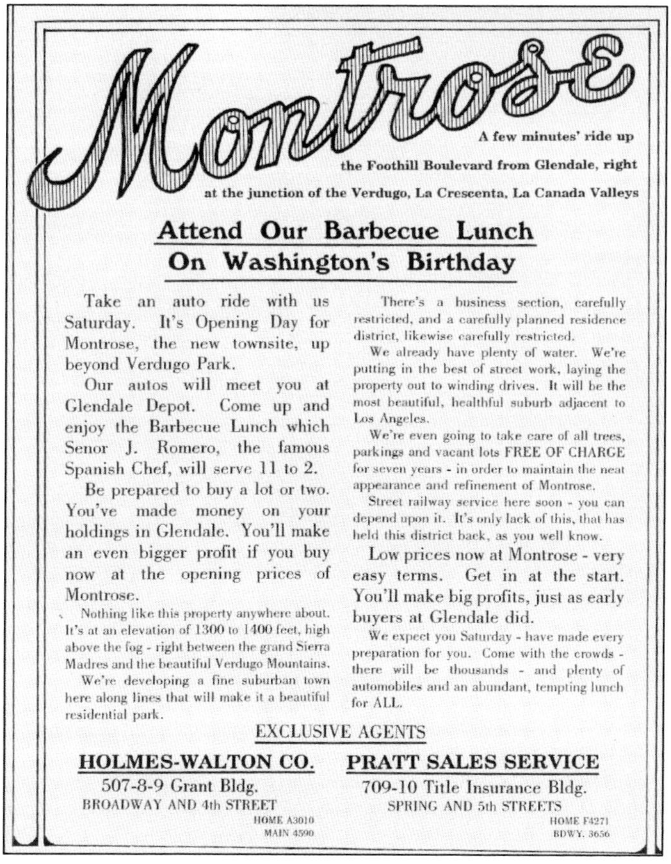

Montrose

A few minutes' ride up the Foothill Boulevard from Glendale, right at the junction of the Verdugo, La Crescenta, La Canada Valleys

Attend Our Barbecue Lunch On Washington's Birthday

Take an auto ride with us Saturday. It's Opening Day for Montrose, the new townsite, up beyond Verdugo Park.

Our autos will meet you at Glendale Depot. Come up and enjoy the Barbecue Lunch which Senor J. Romero, the famous Spanish Chef, will serve 11 to 2.

Be prepared to buy a lot or two. You've made money on your holdings in Glendale. You'll make an even bigger profit if you buy now at the opening prices of Montrose.

Nothing like this property anywhere about. It's at an elevation of 1300 to 1400 feet, high above the fog - right between the grand Sierra Madres and the beautiful Verdugo Mountains.

We're developing a fine suburban town here along lines that will make it a beautiful residential park.

There's a business section, carefully restricted, and a carefully planned residence district, likewise carefully restricted.

We already have plenty of water. We're putting in the best of street work, laying the property out to winding drives. It will be the most beautiful, healthful suburb adjacent to Los Angeles.

We're even going to take care of all trees, parkings and vacant lots FREE OF CHARGE for seven years - in order to maintain the neat appearance and refinement of Montrose.

Street railway service here soon - you can depend upon it. It's only lack of this, that has held this district back, as you well know.

Low prices now at Montrose - very easy terms. Get in at the start. You'll make big profits, just as early buyers at Glendale did.

We expect you Saturday - have made every preparation for you. Come with the crowds - there will be thousands - and plenty of automobiles and an abundant, tempting lunch for ALL.

EXCLUSIVE AGENTS

HOLMES-WALTON CO.
507-8-9 Grant Bldg.
BROADWAY AND 4th STREET
HOME A3010
MAIN 4590

PRATT SALES SERVICE
709-10 Title Insurance Bldg.
SPRING AND 5th STREETS
HOME F4271
BDWY. 3656

Holmes-Walton ran different advertisements every week leading up to the big, opening day barbecue on Washington's Birthday. One notice read, "The beauty, convenience, and novel features of Montrose are so unique that to live in this beautiful property will be like having your dreams come true." Another said, "Roads flow as naturally to this particular spot as a stream flows along the line of least resistance." (Courtesy of Chamber of Commerce.)

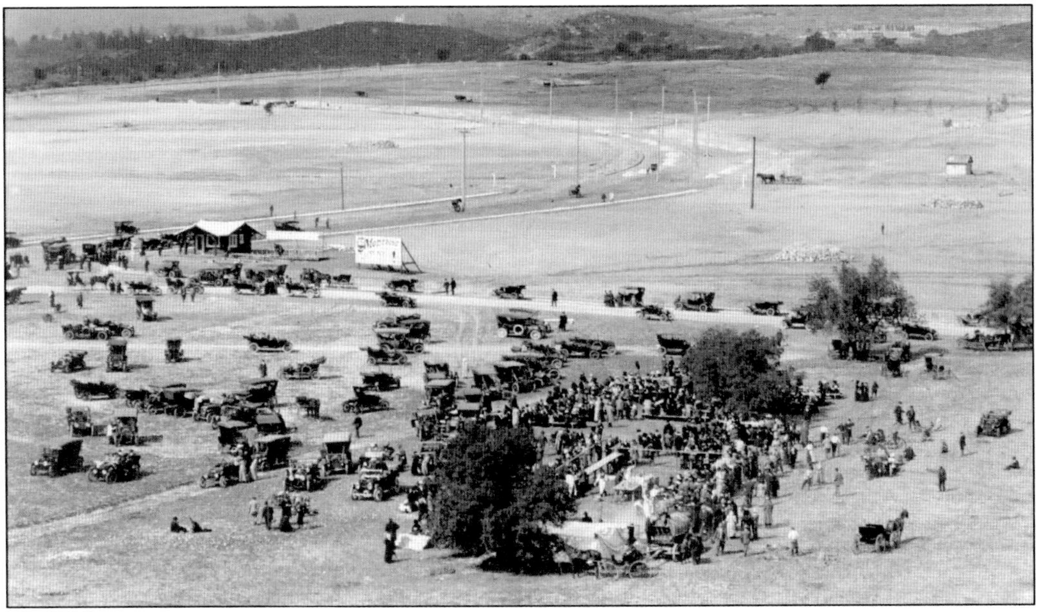

Close to 4,000 guests showed up for the free lunch catered by the "famous Spanish chef" Señor Jose Romero. They arrived by rail, buggy, and automobile. The barbecue was held in the field south and east of the Verdugo Road/Boulevard curve, roughly where Clifton Place is today. The land auction was a success, and Holmes-Walton supposedly sold more lots that day than they did for several years later. February 22 is celebrated as Montrose Founders Day. The only building then was the real estate office, but the curbs for the first block of Honolulu Avenue had been set, as visible below.

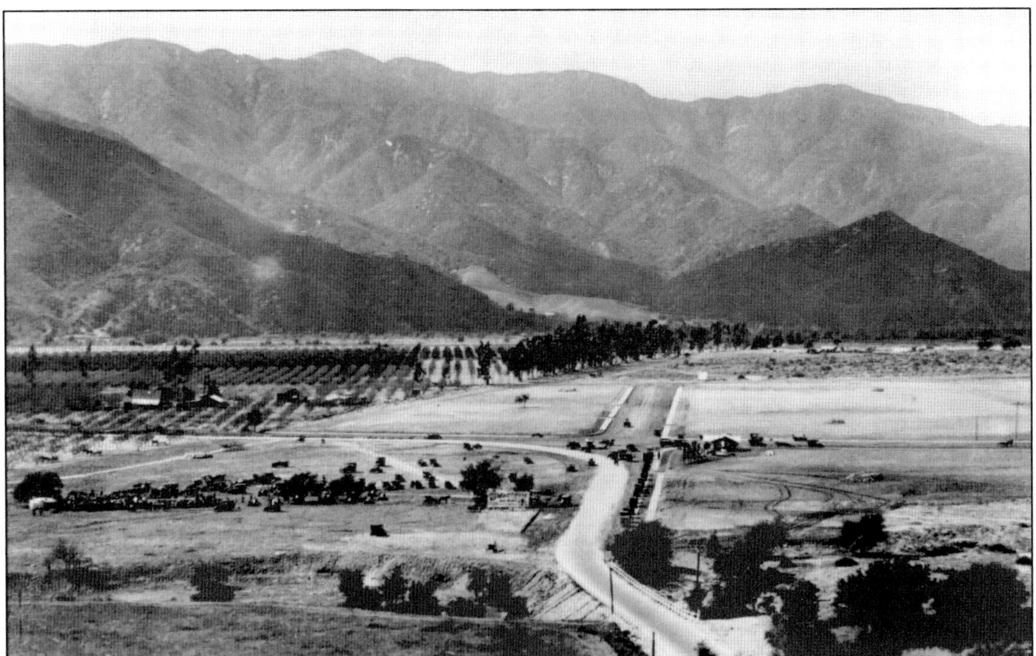

The success of the land auction was apparently not covered in the newspapers so Holmes-Walton prepared its own news coverage in a four-page souvenir booklet: "It was certainly a great day. More than 4,000 people were there . . . As the lady from Iowa said, 'This MUST be the Promised Land.'" Many people with respiratory ailments were coming to the valley because of the clean, dry air.

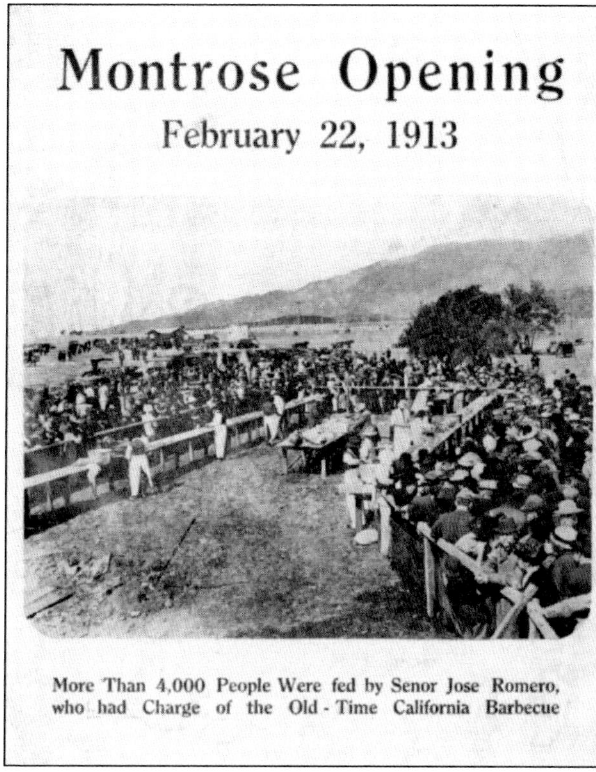

Montrose Opening

February 22, 1913

More Than 4,000 People Were fed by Senor Jose Romero, who had Charge of the Old - Time California Barbecue

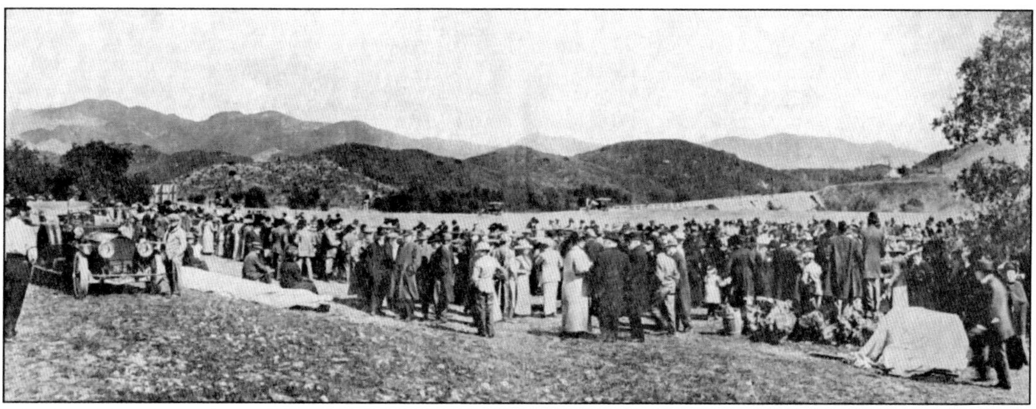

The booklet also asked and answered: "Why did they come and what impressed them after they got here? We heard it on every side and you did if you were there. They wanted to get up high, up where one unconsciously takes great deep draughts of the pure balmy air that is so exhilarating." Wait, was the air balmy or dry?

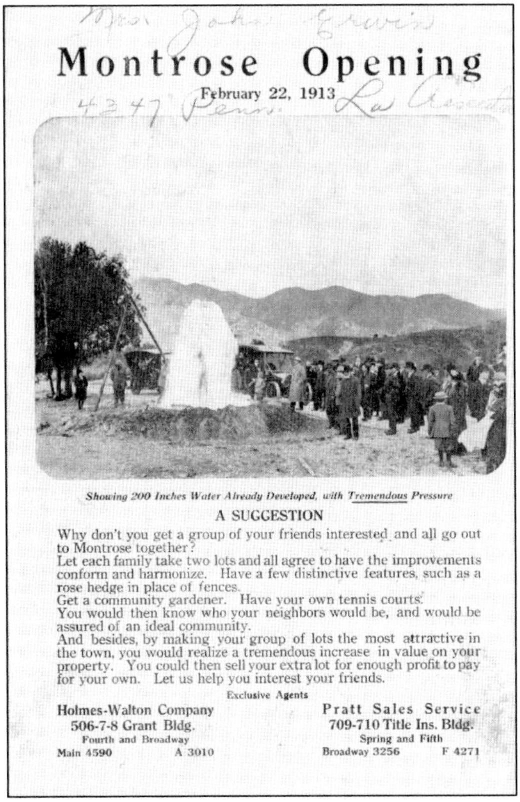

Montrose Opening

February 22, 1913

Showing 200 Inches Water Already Developed, with Tremendous Pressure

A SUGGESTION

Why don't you get a group of your friends interested and all go out to Montrose together?
Let each family take two lots and all agree to have the improvements conform and harmonize. Have a few distinctive features, such as a rose hedge in place of fences.
Get a community gardener. Have your own tennis courts.
You would then know who your neighbors would be, and would be assured of an ideal community.
And besides, by making your group of lots the most attractive in the town, you would realize a tremendous increase in value on your property. You could then sell your extra lot for enough profit to pay for your own. Let us help you interest your friends.

Exclusive Agents

Holmes-Walton Company	Pratt Sales Service
506-7-8 Grant Bldg.	709-710 Title Ins. Bldg.
Fourth and Broadway	Spring and Fifth
Main 4590 A 3010	Broadway 3256 F 4271

The back page of the brochure was to reinforce that Montrose had plenty of water, the lack of which was one of the main reasons this area had not already been settled. At the barbecue, Walton ceremoniously opened a valve to create this 200-inch-tall gusher of water to demonstrate the water pressure.

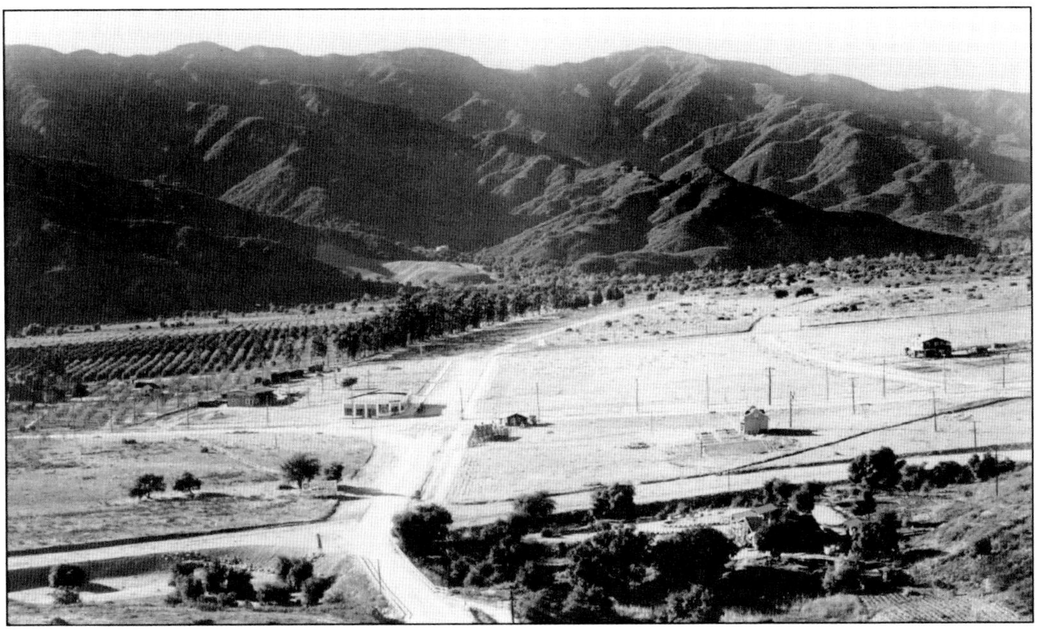

Later that year, a few more buildings went up: the trolley power station just to the northeast of the real estate building, the T.O. Potts building across the intersection from the real estate office, a lumber barn south and west of the Potts building, and a few homes. The first two of these still stand: the power house and the Potts building.

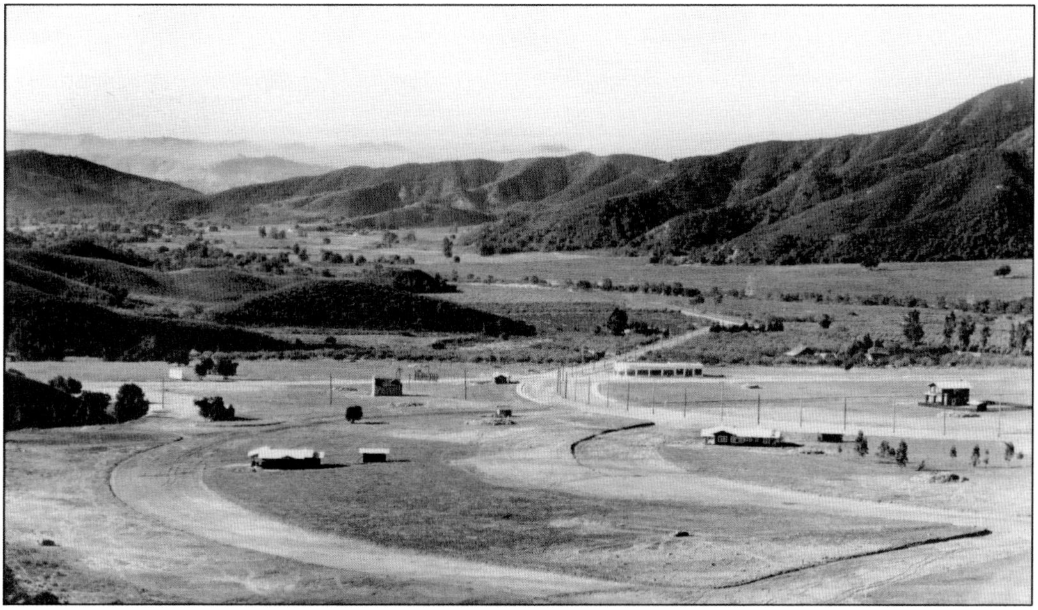

This is another photograph from the same year looking south towards Glendale. In addition to the new houses, the new curving roads of Waltonia Drive (named for Walton), Florencita Drive (named for Walters's wife), and Glenada Avenue have been graded. The house on Glenada (below the Potts Building in this photograph) was torn down in the late 2000s amidst much controversy as preservationists tried to save it.

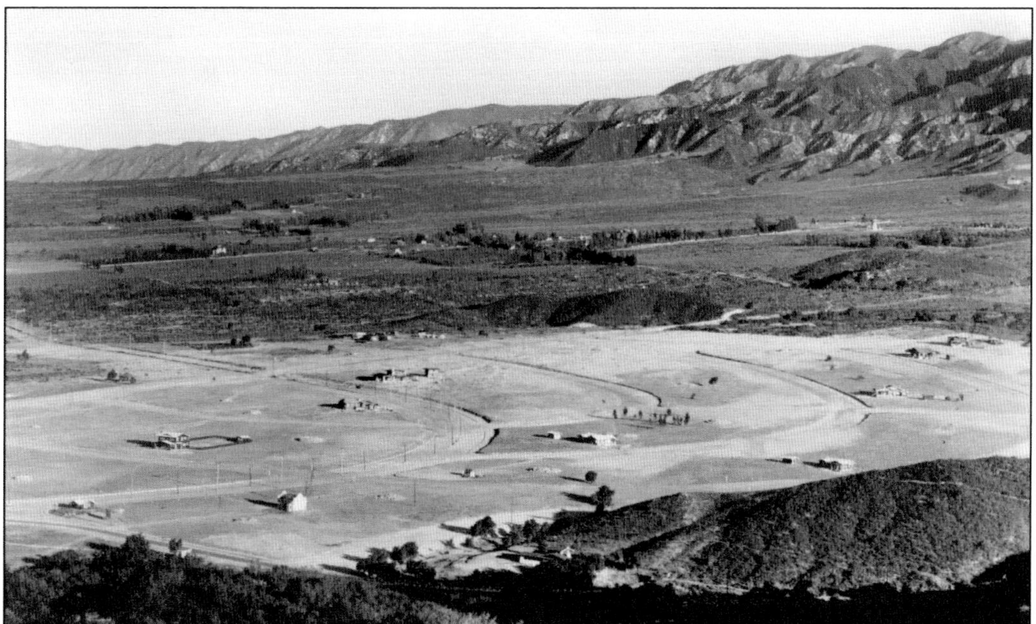

This photograph from around 1914 shows the rose starting to come into focus, with the further grading of Mira Vista Avenue, Rincon Avenue, and Del Mar Road and the construction of a few more homes. The difference between the graded Montrose and the rest of the valley is striking.

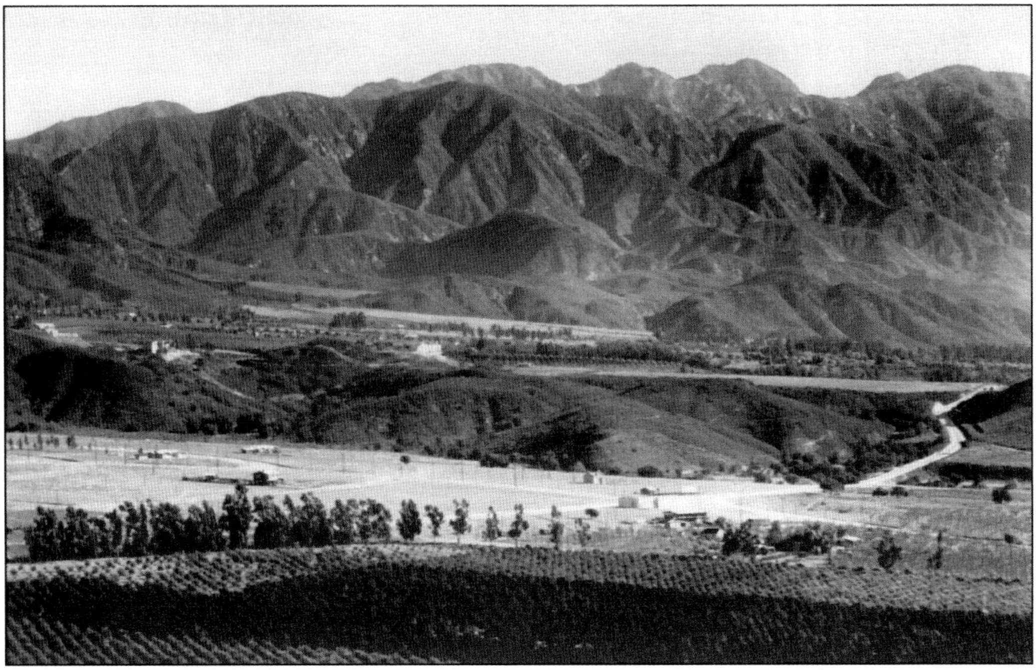

The orchards and vineyards of Sparr Heights are visible in the foreground of this photograph of Montrose from the same period. Verdugo Boulevard (lower right) curves around the Indian Springs canyon and leads to La Cañada in the distance.

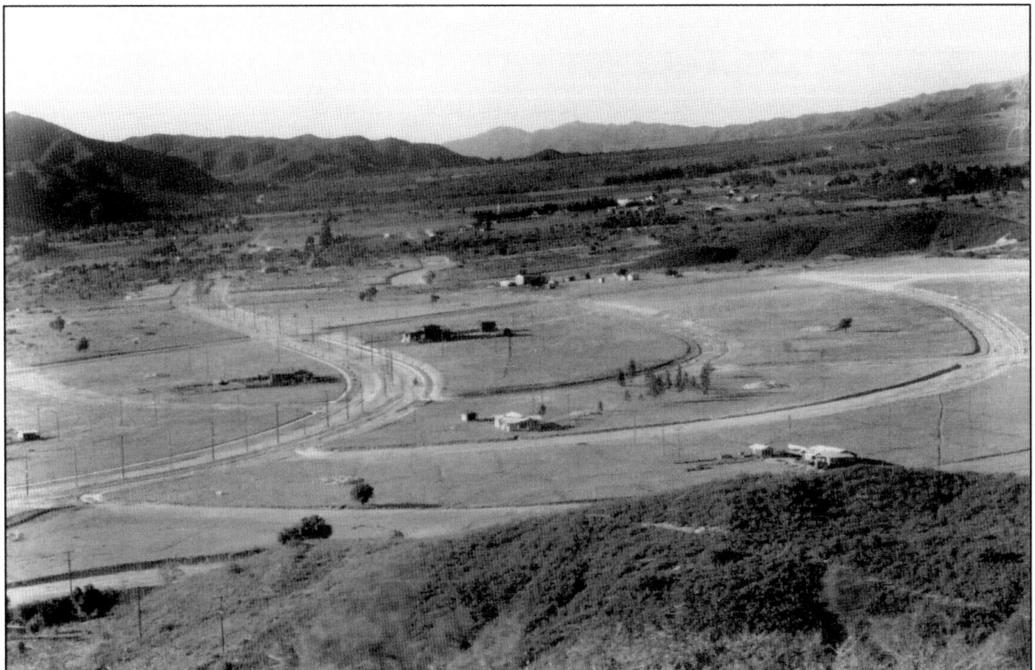

Electricity had come to the valley in 1912, but many of the first homes in Montrose had to live without it for a while, as evidenced in the previous two photographs. This photograph from around 1914 shows electric poles to the new houses.

This article from the *Los Angeles Times* that ran on July 12, 1913, read more like advertising copy straight from Walton than a news story. "One of the most attractive features of Montrose is the circular system of boulevards that gives the place a park-like effect. This boulevard system was established at heavy cost." Local historians find the line "heavy cost" hilarious since at that point, the streets had barely been graded.

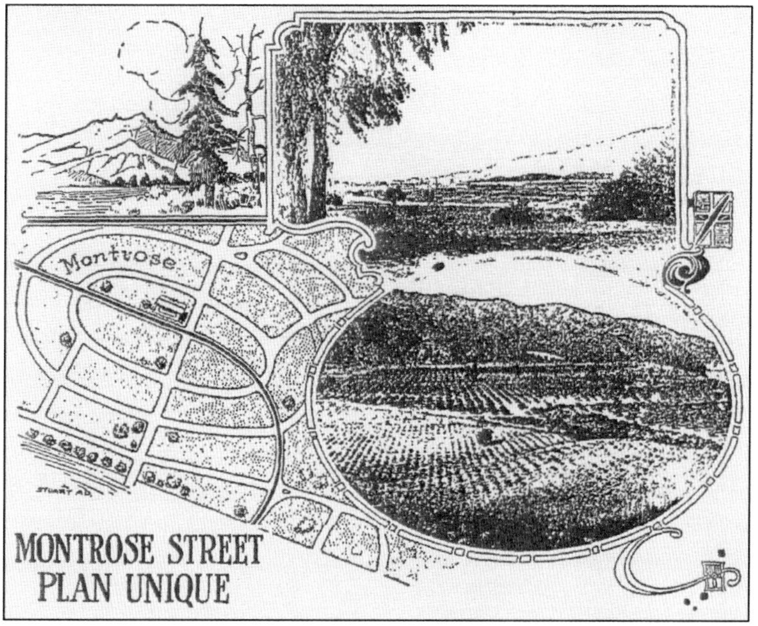

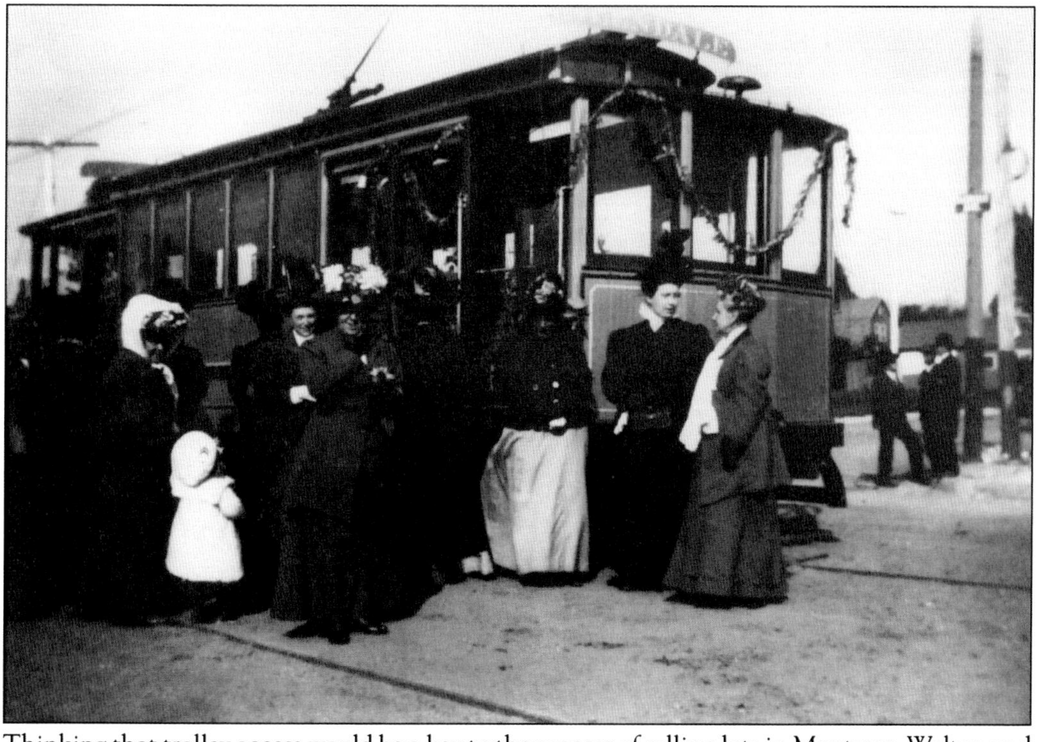

Thinking that trolley access would be a key to the success of selling lots in Montrose, Walton and Walters teamed up to buy the Glendale and Eagle Rock Railway line in 1913. They extended the line to Montrose in April 1913, using standard size ties for the narrow-gauge rails. In 1914, they renamed it the Glendale & Montrose Railway, reflecting its new destination. This photograph is of the first day's trip to Montrose on Saturday, April 26, 1913. (Courtesy of Mike Morgan.)

This map from around 1916 shows the entire Glendale & Montrose Railway line from Eagle Rock, through Glendale and up along Verdugo Road to La Crescenta Avenue in Montrose. In 1915, G&M moved one rail over a few inches to widen the tracks to standard gauge, which allowed other trolley cars to run on their tracks. In 1916 the G&M, working with Pacific Electric, began a rush-hour service offering commuters a ride from PE's Sixth and Main Street Station in Los Angeles to the end of the line in Montrose without changing cars. Unfortunately, the valley was not populated enough to warrant such service, and it was ended in 1917. (Courtesy of Orange Empire Railway Museum, ERHA-SC/Ray Younghans Collection.)

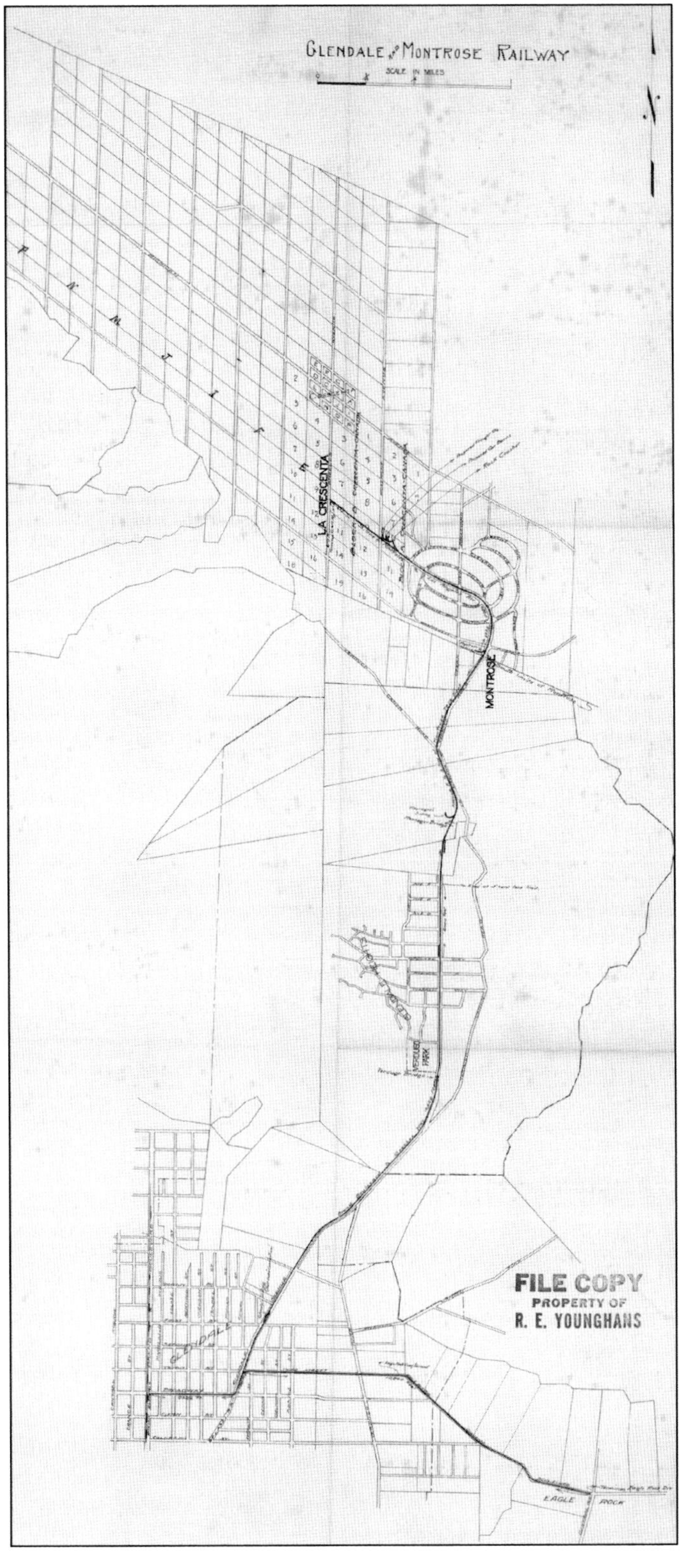

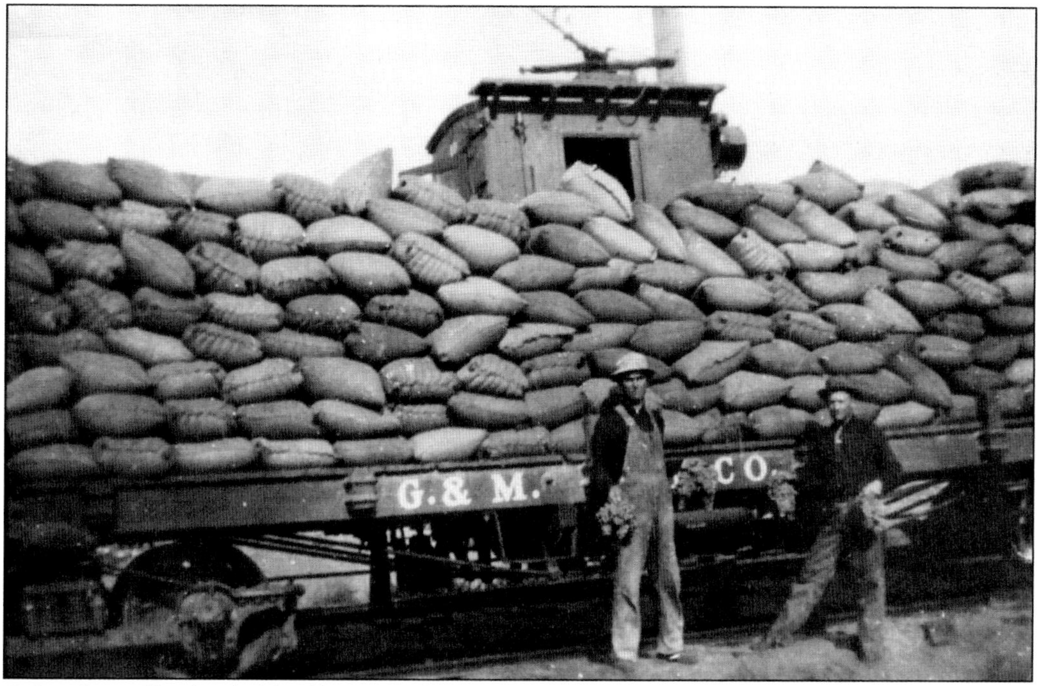

A freight trolley hauled building supplies to the burgeoning valley. Farmers would bring their grapes, olives, and other fruit to the loading dock at Montrose and La Crescenta Avenues to be hauled down to Los Angeles, so the freight car rarely made an empty trip.

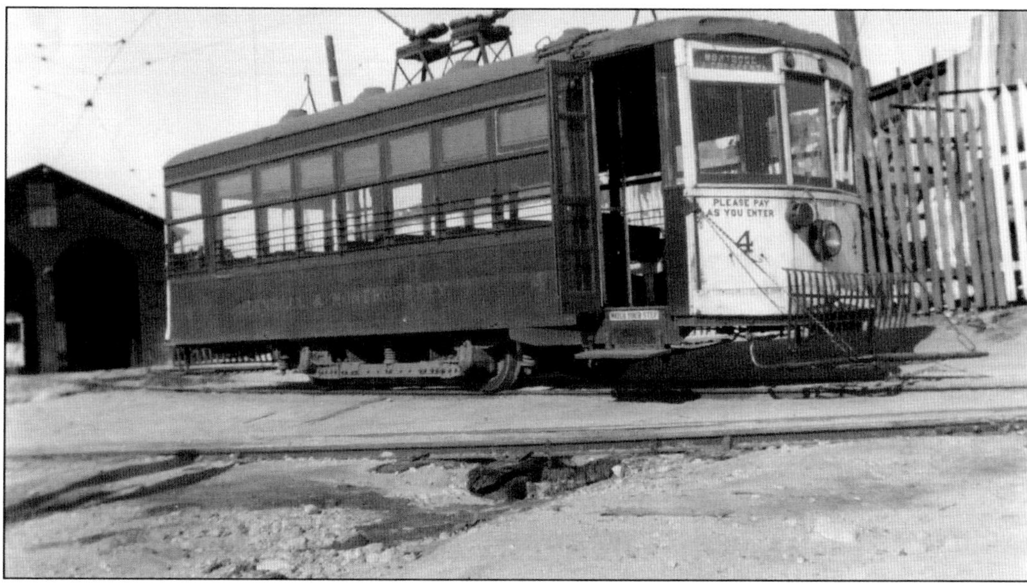

In 1920, a trolley barn (far left) was constructed for servicing the new fleet of rail cars that the G&M had purchased. In 1918, the G&M bought three single-truck Birney cars and had them painted red on the sides and front. In 1927, to differentiate from the PE, they painted the ends in white with window sashes in red. The trolley barn still stands at its original location. (Courtesy of Mike Morgan.)

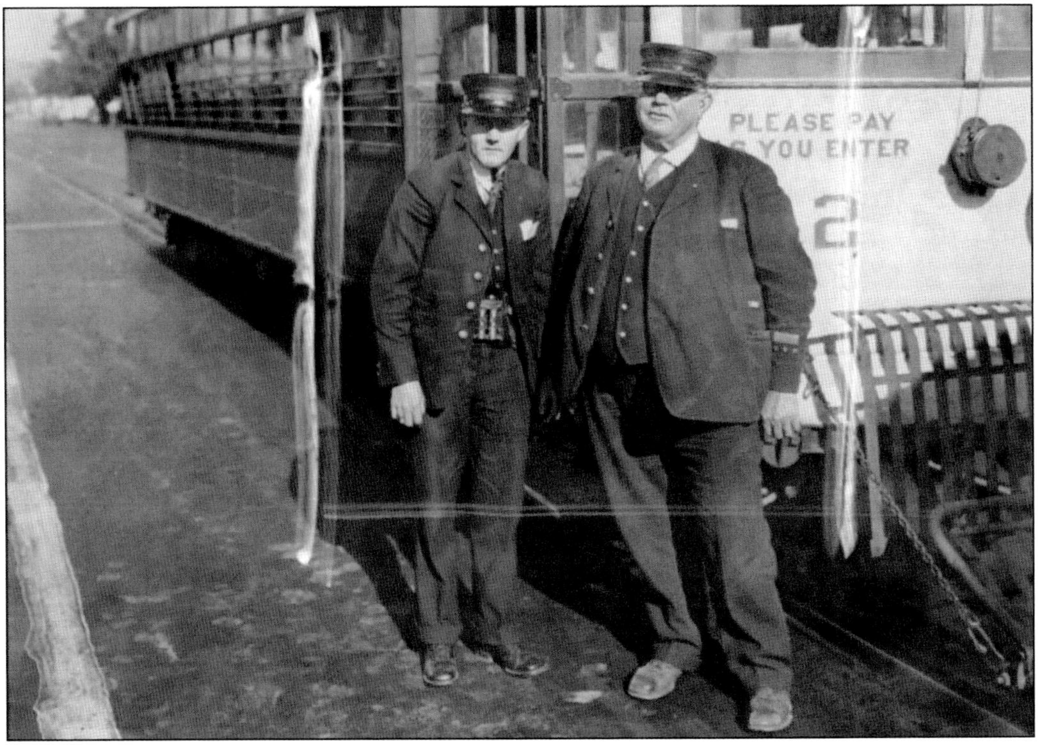

Due to competition from buses and automobiles, the G&M was already losing money by the time of the stock market crash of 1929, and the last car ran on December 31, 1930. Shown here on the final run are conductor Joseph Hingston and motorman William H. Nagel, the most senior employees of the railroad. Hingston's grandson still lives in the valley. (Courtesy of Mike Morgan.)

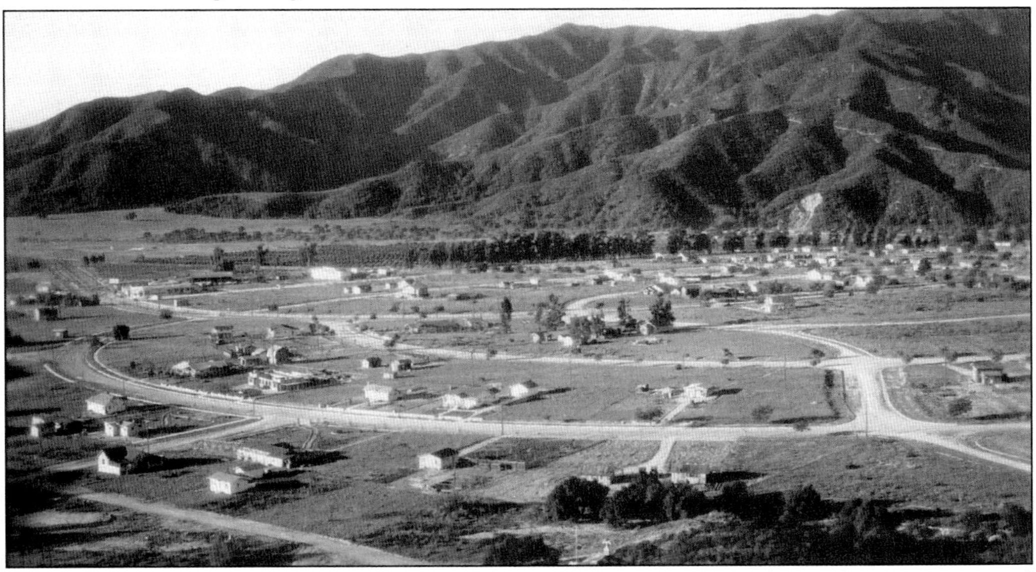

As the rose filled in at first, the pattern looked more like spokes on a wheel since homes were spread out almost evenly. Many of the homes in the foreground have been torn down and replaced with multifamily residences, but the barn on the left side–middle still stands, having been converted into an apartment. (See page 127.)

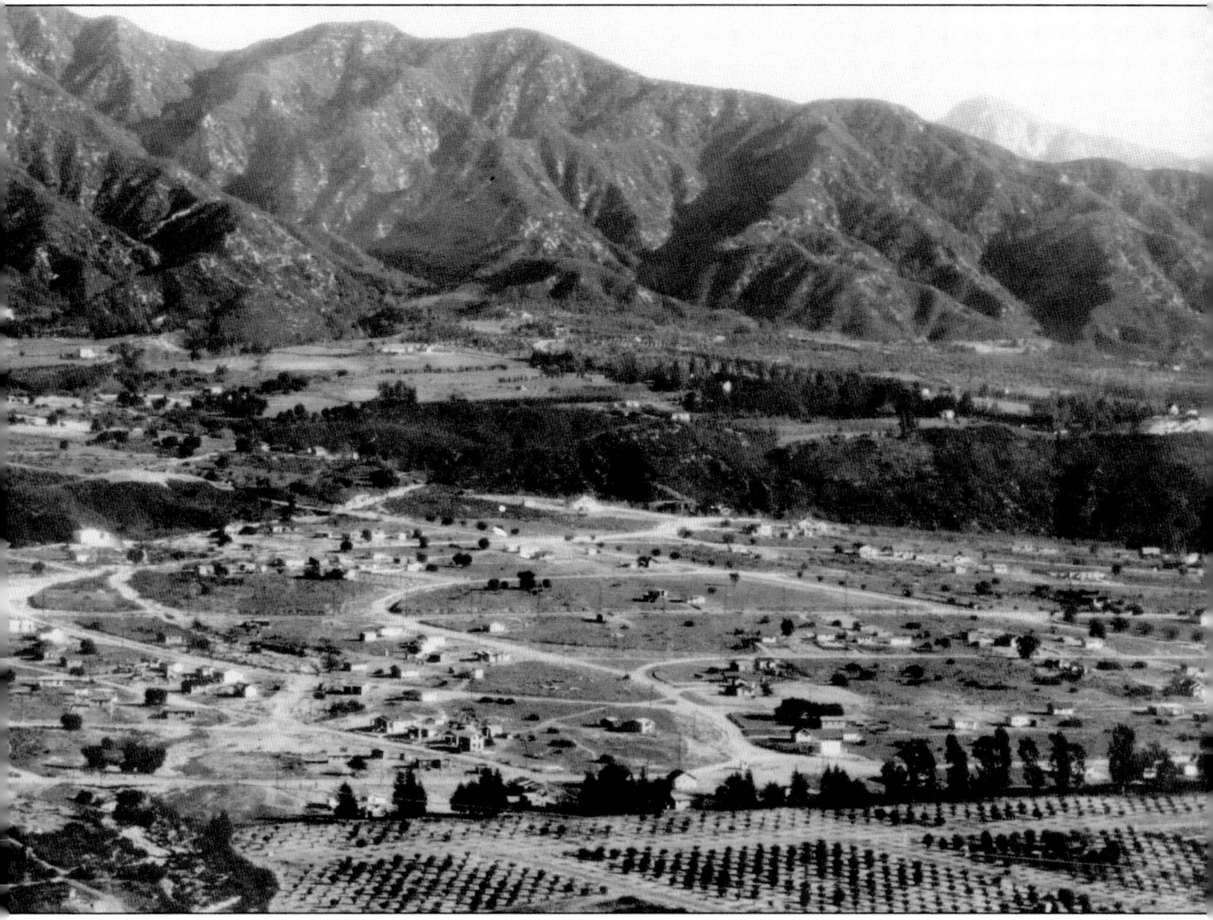

Having a freight trolley line that could deliver building supplies helped fuel the building boom of the Roaring Twenties, and Montrose was blossoming into a suburb of Los Angeles. As real estate here became more valuable, Sparr would soon rip out his orchards and vineyards (at the bottom of the photograph) and divide them into home lots.

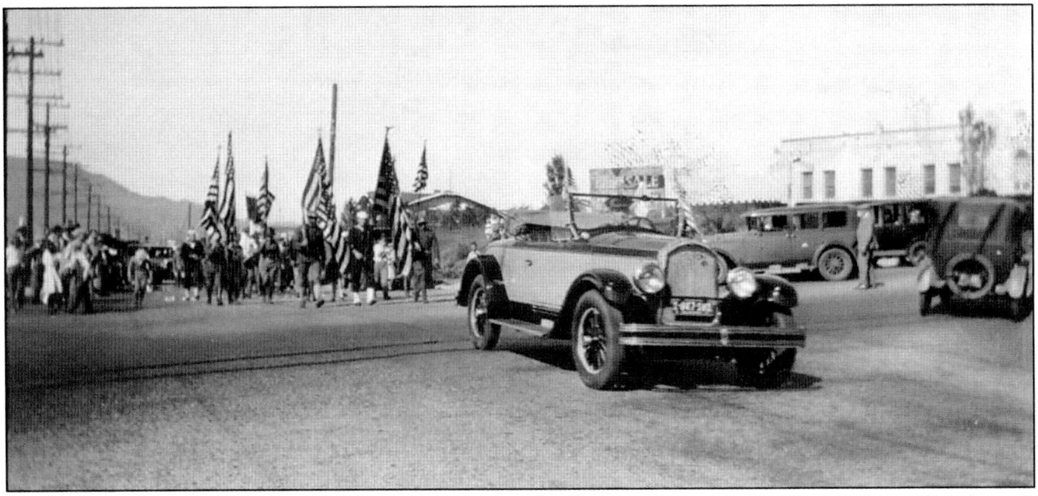

This is the intersection that was supposed to be the heart of Montrose, Ocean View Boulevard and Montrose Avenue in the late 1920s as a parade passes through. Walton had promised to build a clubhouse with "tennis courts, a putting green and croquet grounds, hand ball, a children's playground, a library, card and billiard rooms," but never did. The building to the right in the background is the telephone office, built in 1925. (Courtesy of Arthur Voltz.)

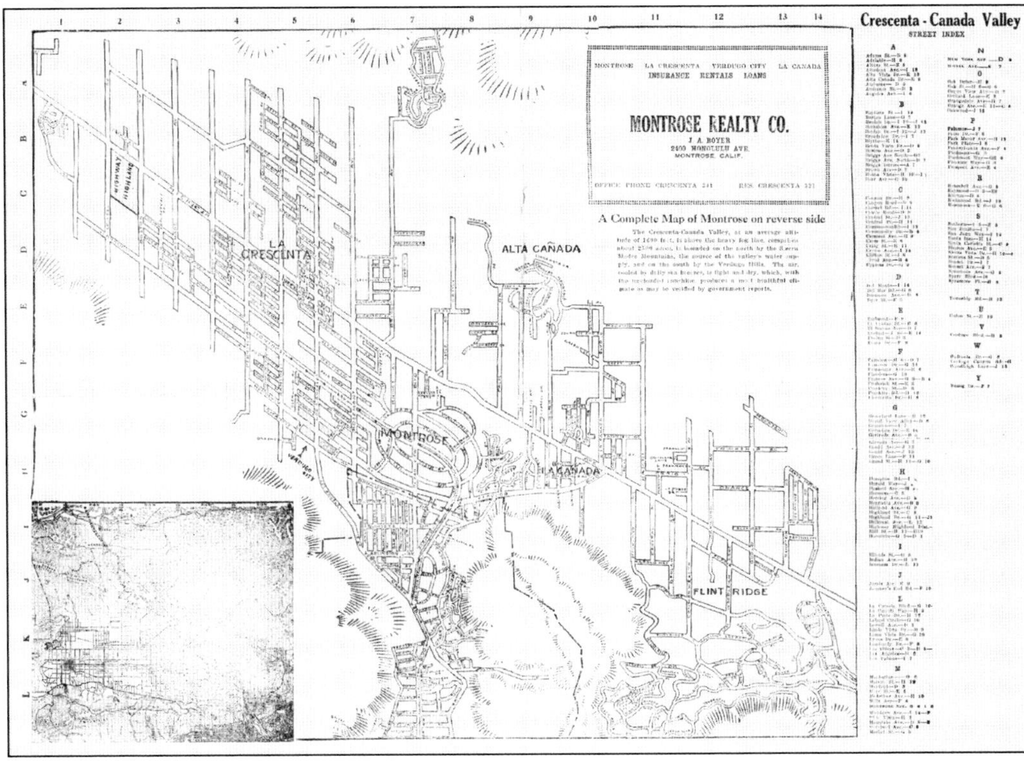

This real estate map of the Crescenta-Canada valley from the 1930s shows both the rose patterned streets of Holmes-Walton and the parallelogram blocks of Dr. Briggs. In this map, the outer loop of Florencita and Waltonia looks like a racetrack, and indeed speeding on these roads (particularly downhill) has been a problem, probably more so today than in the 1920s when automobiles were not quite as powerful.

Two

GROWTH
MONTROSE BLOSSOMS

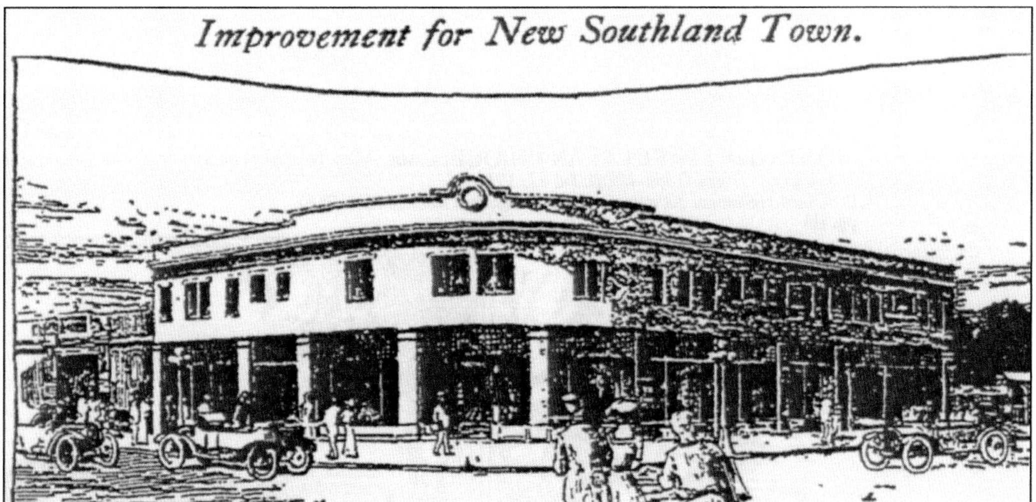

This plan for the first commercial building in Montrose was filed with Los Angeles County in June 1913 and printed in the *Los Angeles Times* on June 8. The initial concept, drawn up by the architectural firm of Walker & Vawter, called for stores on the street level and apartments on the second story. The builder was "a Los Angeles woman" who apparently decided the new community did not warrant such an elaborate building. Local historians suspect the woman was Florence Walters, but have not been able to confirm this. (This chapter is told mostly geographically rather than chronologically so readers can walk down Honolulu Avenue and see the changes. Numbers in parentheses are the Honolulu Avenue street addresses.)

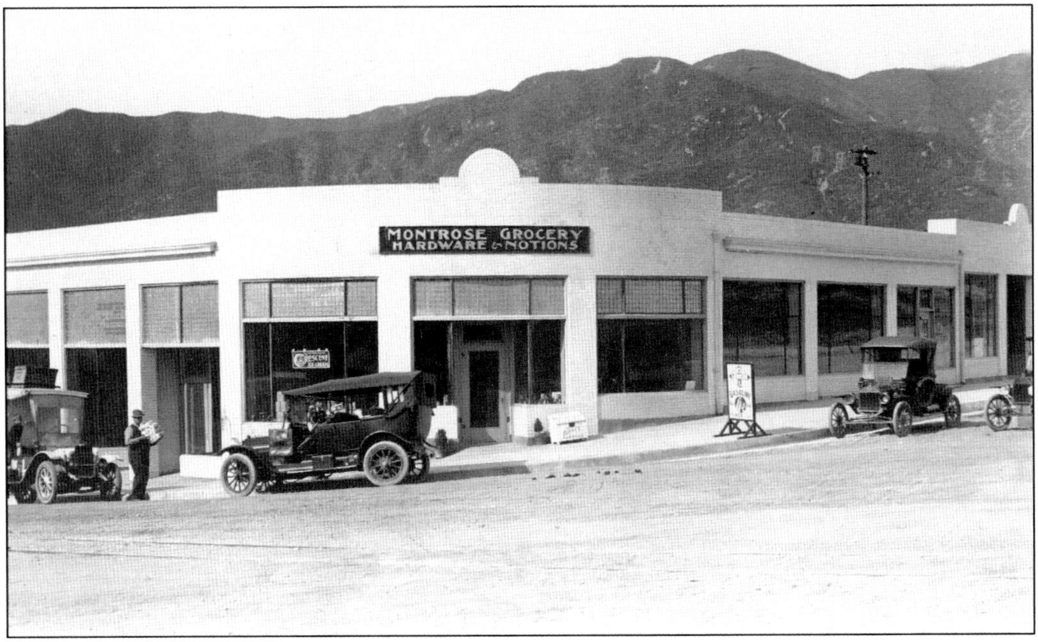

Instead, later that year, the woman built this one-story version that looked similar but without the apartments. Her name, though, is not associated with the building; that honor goes to T.O. Potts, who was the first tenant. He leased it and opened a general store, complete with a gas pump on the sidewalk, hidden by the car in this photograph. But Potts did not stay here long and opened a gas station across Verdugo Road (later called Wadey's), below.

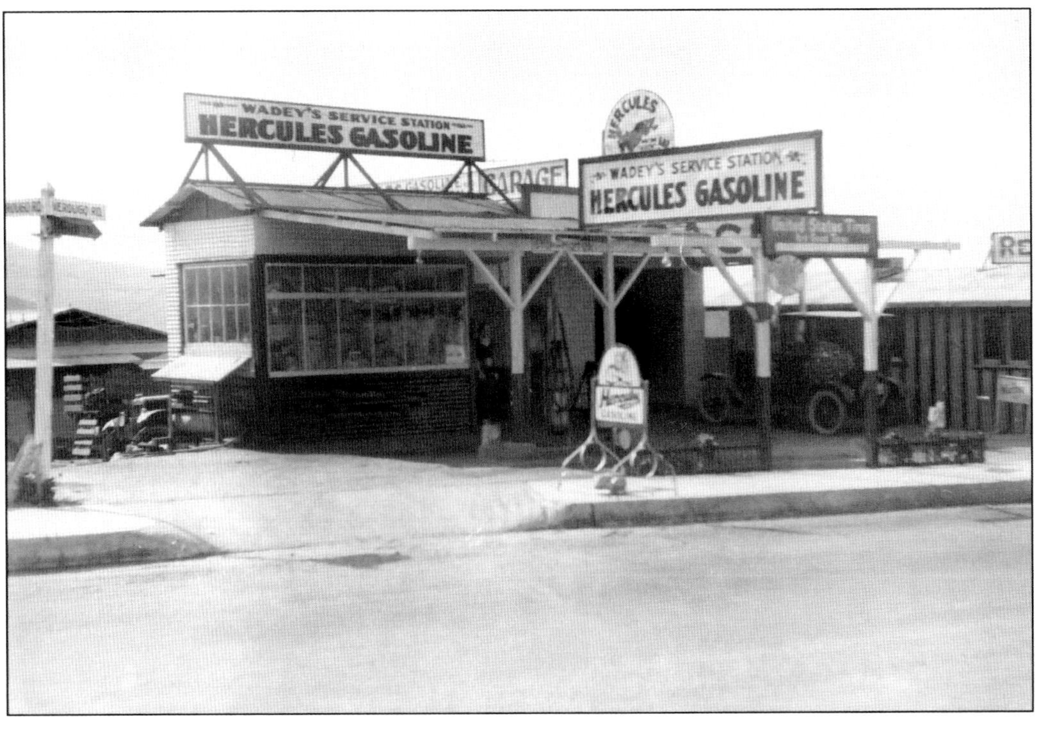

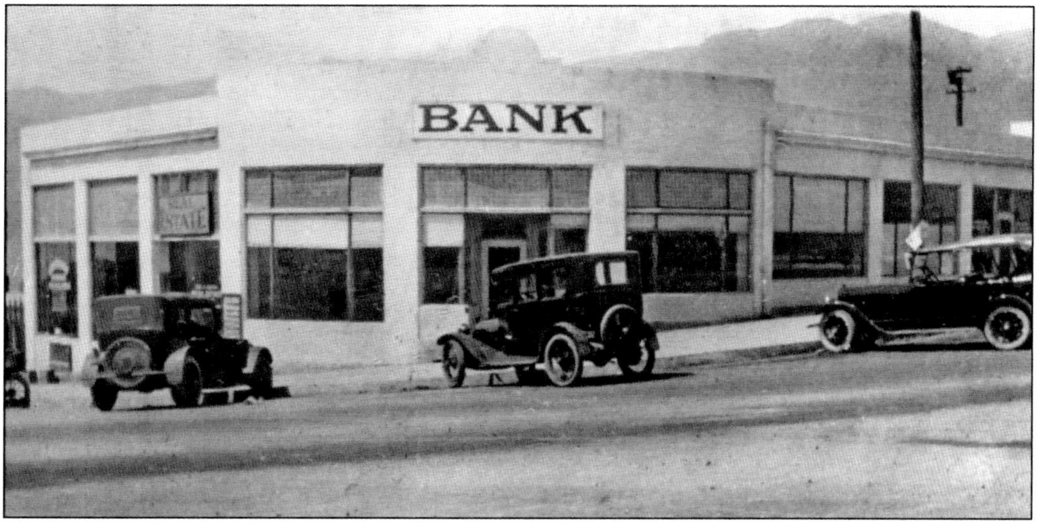

After Potts moved out, the building (2200) sat empty for several years, until 1922 when the Montrose State Bank incorporated here. However, the bank moved west before the decade was over, and the building has been occupied by a series of tenants and different kinds of businesses since then in spite of its prime location. It looks almost the same today as when it opened except the white glazed bricks have been covered with stucco and the medallion removed.

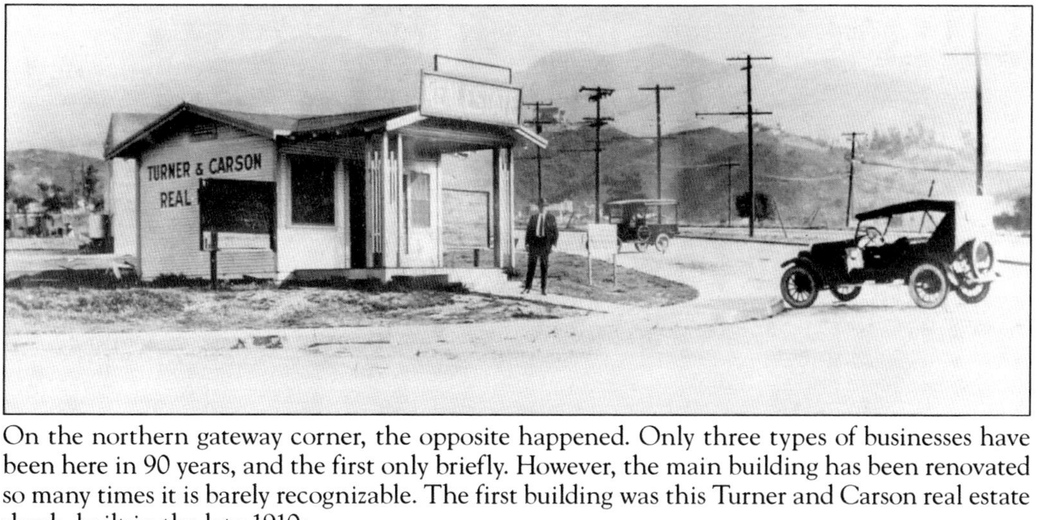

On the northern gateway corner, the opposite happened. Only three types of businesses have been here in 90 years, and the first only briefly. However, the main building has been renovated so many times it is barely recognizable. The first building was this Turner and Carson real estate shack, built in the late 1910s.

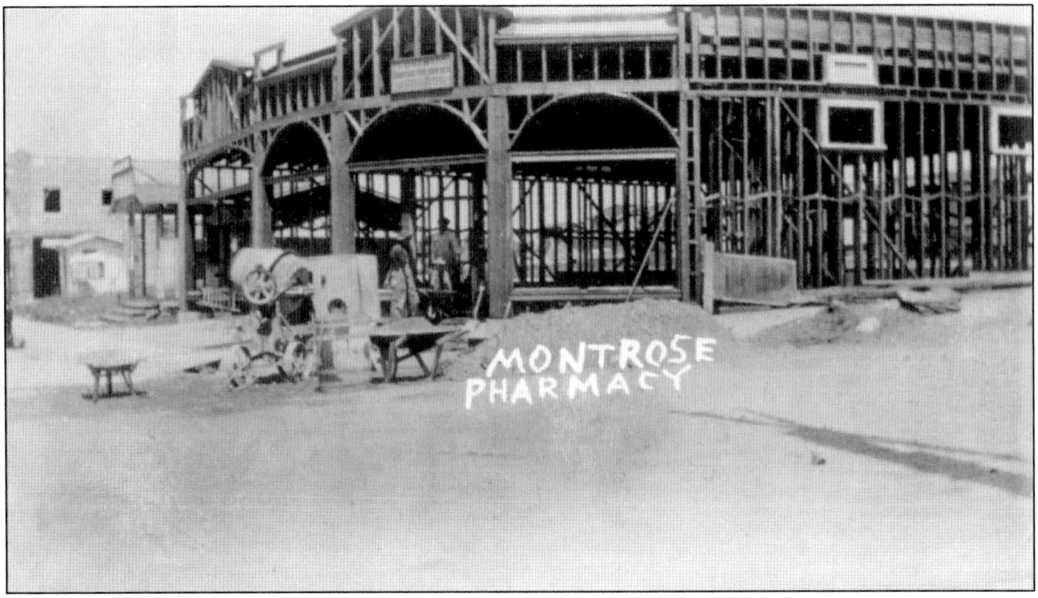

In 1923, Theodore Belanger bought the corner lot, moved the real estate shack half a block west, and started construction on what would become the Montrose Pharmacy (2201). On opening day, more than 200 patrons visited, and the day's gross was $107. To celebrate, Belanger held a dance in the building that night.

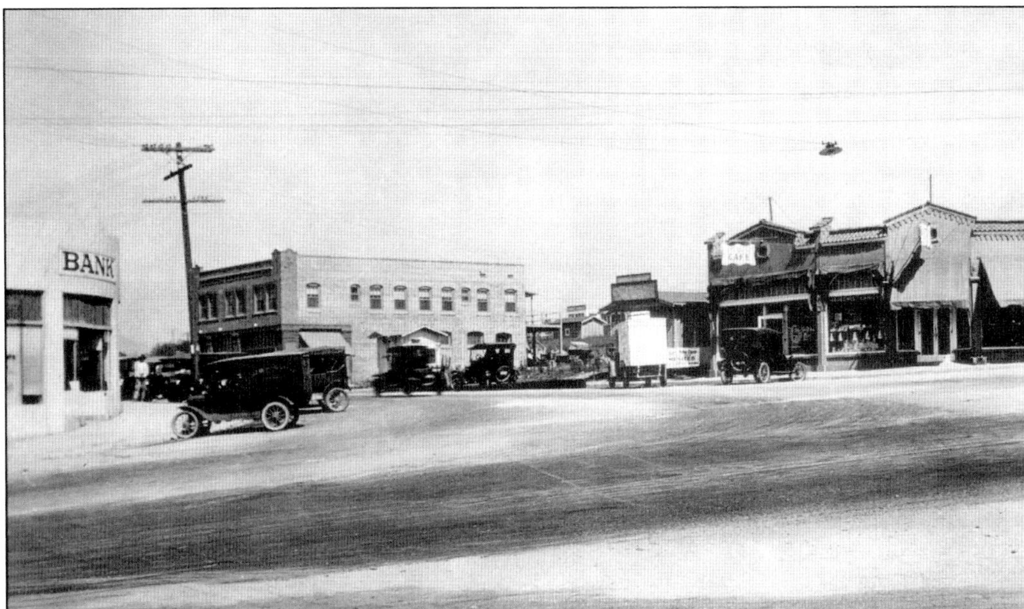

This is how the Montrose Pharmacy looked after it opened, with the relocated real estate shack to the west (behind the white truck.) C.J. Reinhard moved his family to Montrose for the climate and in 1923 built the first two-story commercial structure in Montrose, the tall building in the middle.

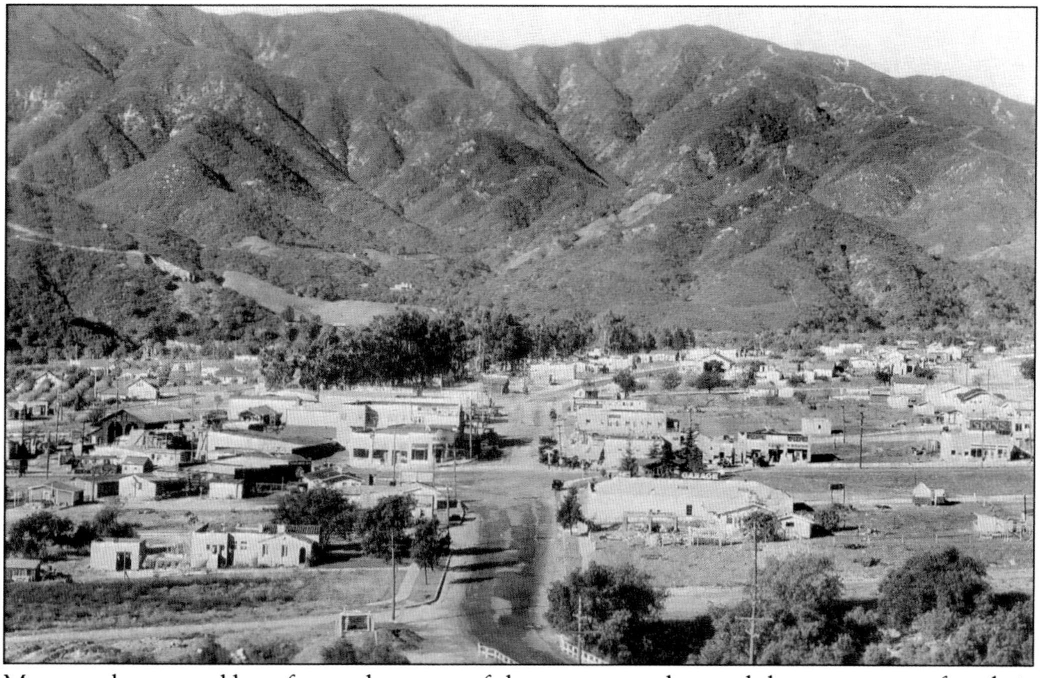

Many settlers moved here from other parts of the country and named the new streets after their home towns or states, such as New York, Pennsylvania, and Boston. Lambert A. Thompson (who had bought his land from a Verdugo descendant) named Honolulu Avenue after his childhood hometown in Hawaii. In the 1920s, houses were being built west of Ocean View Boulevard as the business district was expected to grow north instead of west.

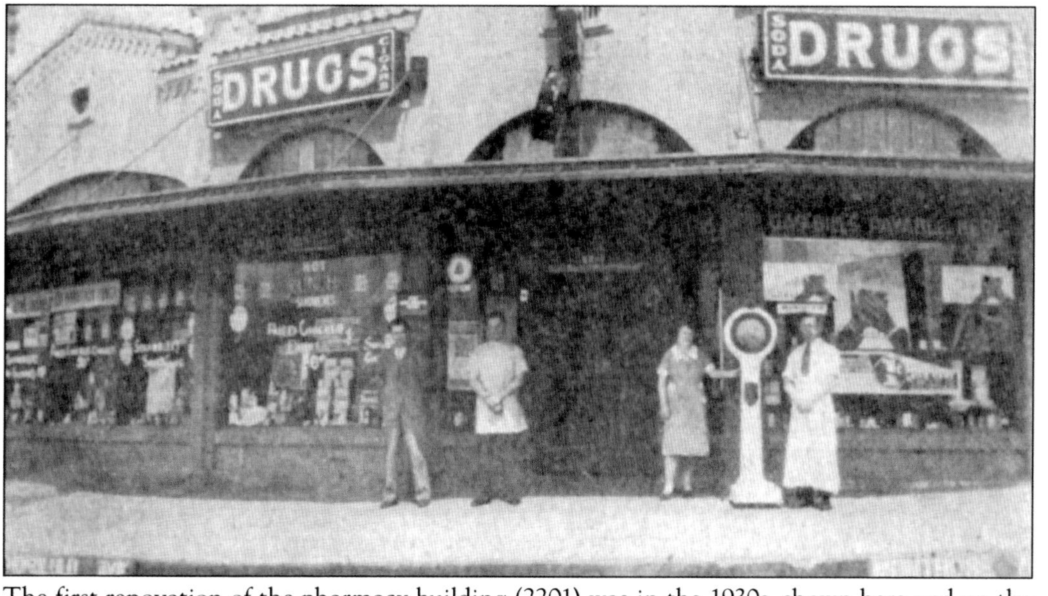

The first renovation of the pharmacy building (2201) was in the 1930s, shown here and on the cover. The brickwork and scalloped eaves were covered over with so much stucco that the building looked almost curved. The rectangular windows were replaced with large arched windows, and a horizontal awning wrapped all the way around the corner to give the merchandise, shoppers, and employees some shade.

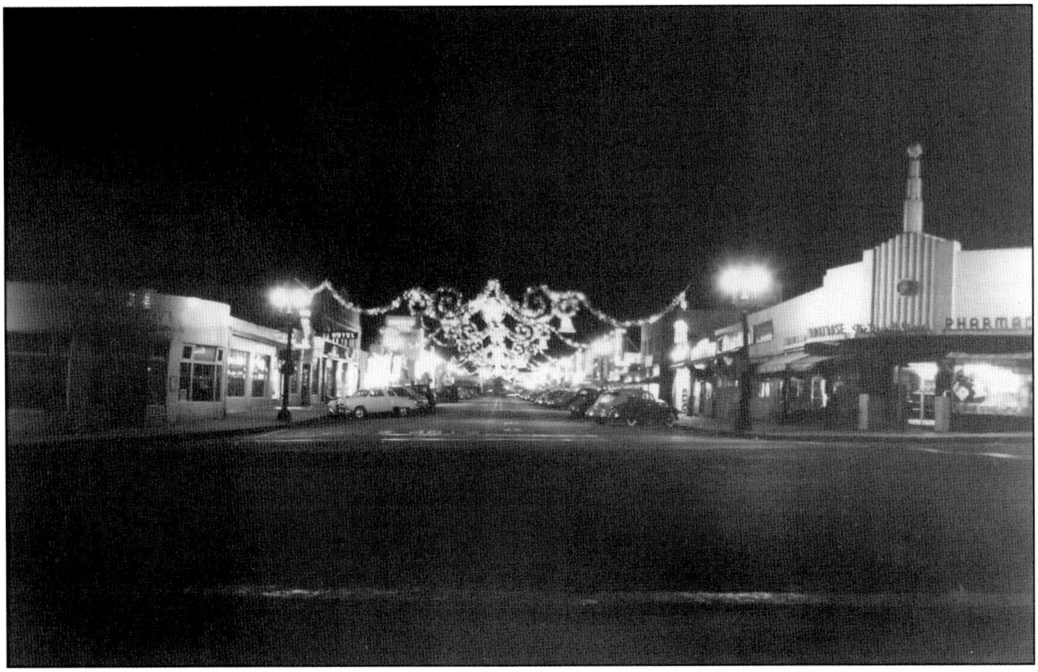

The next transformation came in the 1940s. The roofline was changed, the arched windows returned to rectangular, and the awning was replaced, made narrower, and no longer wrapped around the building. A futuristic "shield" was added to the corner above the door, topped with a neon-lit spire. Here is the gateway to Montrose decked out for the Christmas holidays probably in 1947.

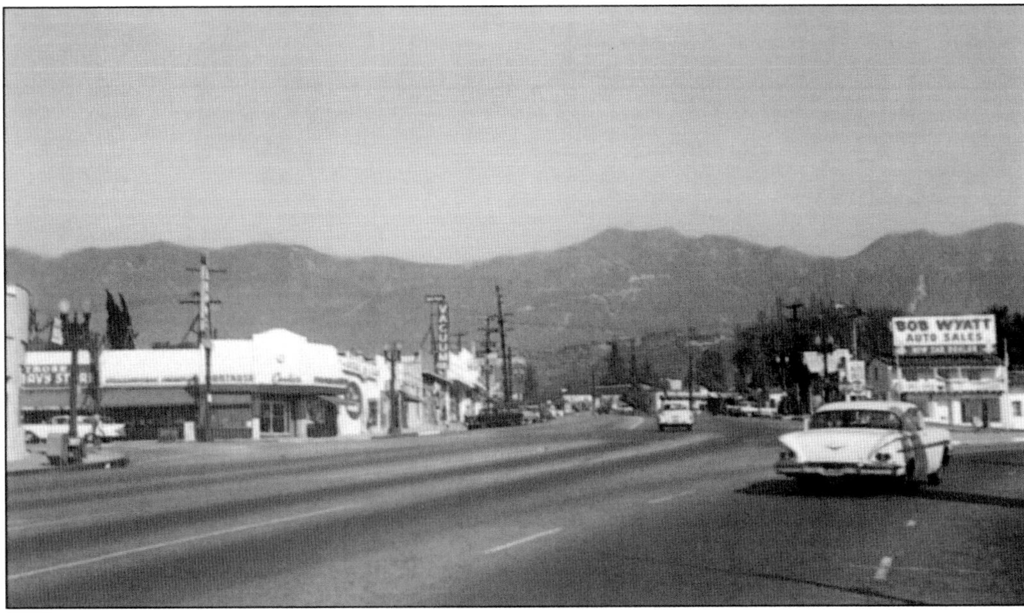

The next big change was in ownership, which meant a new name (Cooke's Montrose Pharmacy) and new signage. Joe Belanger (Theodore's son) sold the business and building in 1954 to Robert A. Cooke, who would later play a pivotal role in saving Montrose. Cooke removed the spire and added a large vertical blade sign. The vacuum store a bit north of the pharmacy was owned by movie star Rita Hayworth.

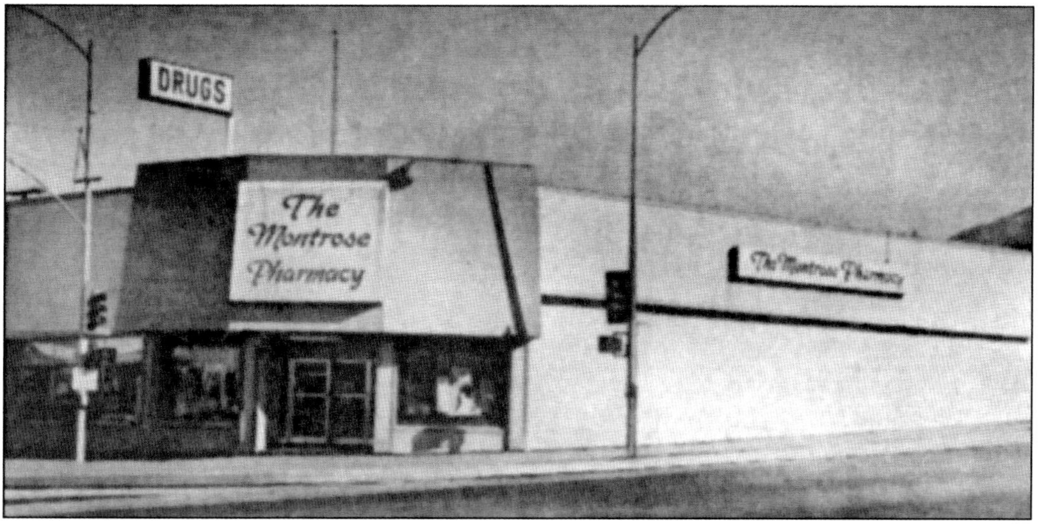

Still another renovation occurred in the 1960s when the shield was removed and replaced with three flat panels that extended from the building at the corner. The awnings were removed, and the vertical blade sign was replaced with a flag-style sign. Locals remember that parts of the pharmacy had red carpet, making it feel luxurious. This photograph was taken in 1967, just before the shopping park construction started.

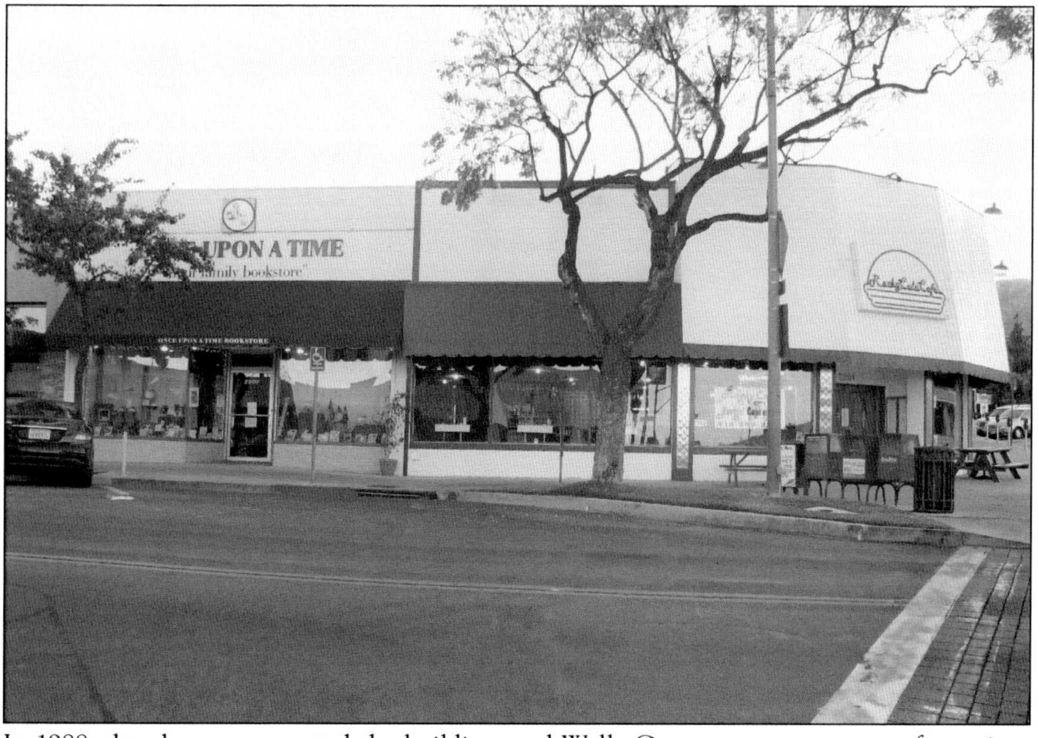

In 1988, the pharmacy vacated the building, and Wally Curry, a career manager for various restaurant chains, leased the space and opened a 1950s-style diner that he called Rocky Cola Café. He did not change the exterior much, other than painting it and removing the signs. It has been popular with locals and many celebrities, including Pres. Bill Clinton, who paid it a surprise late-night visit after speaking in Glendale.

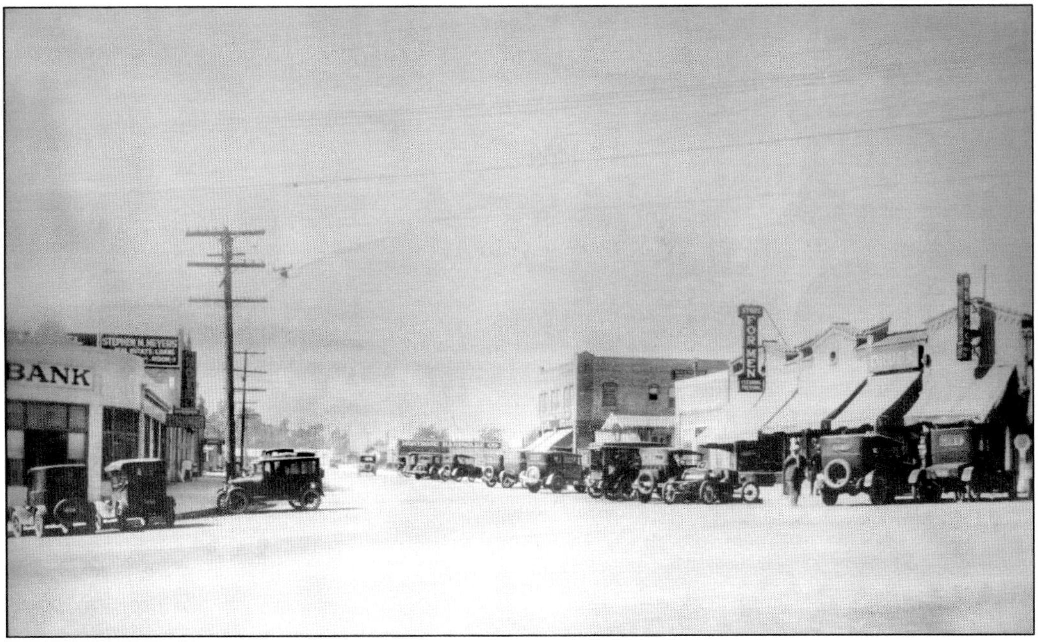

The Potts building and the pharmacy have been the gateway to Montrose ever since the latter was opened in 1923. Montrose Avenue, with its trolley line, was supposed to be the main business district, but shoppers preferred a leisurely walk along the level Honolulu Avenue to huffing and puffing up the gentle slope of Montrose Avenue.

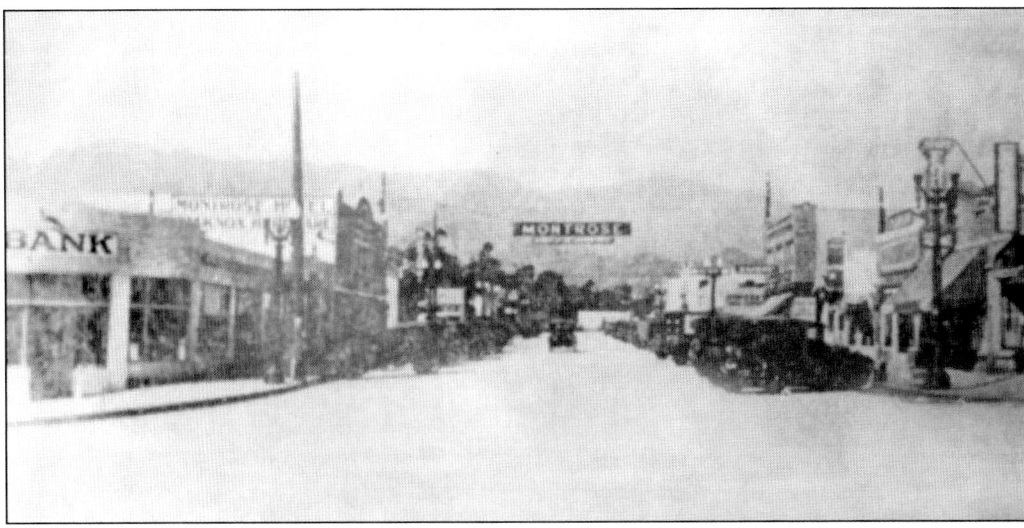

This photograph from the early 1930s shows the growth along Honolulu Avenue by then. Electric street lamps had been installed, and the electric pole that helped juice the G&M trolley was coming down since it was no longer in business. A sign cut out of half a log, with light bulbs spelling "Montrose," was strung across the street but was removed soon after, presumably because of the valley's fierce winds.

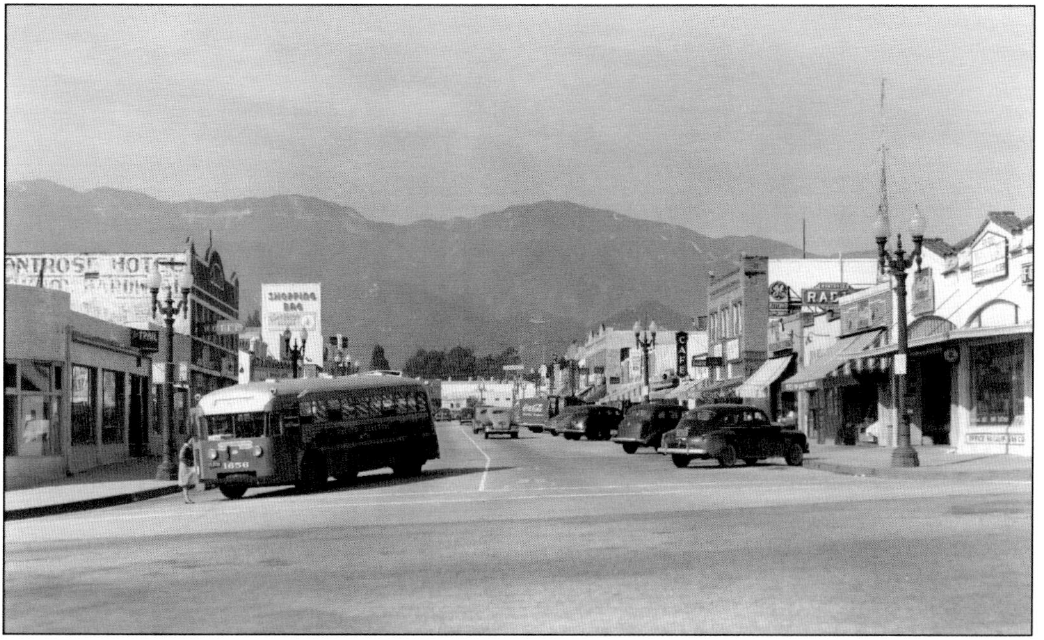

This is the gateway in 1940, and Montrose is starting to look very urban, with the Pacific Electric bus, the hotel, the movie theater, Shopping Bag, lots of bricks and concrete, and what looks like a radio station, though it is not; it is a store selling radios, and the large antenna was to make its products sound better—probably much better than the customers could get when they brought their purchases home.

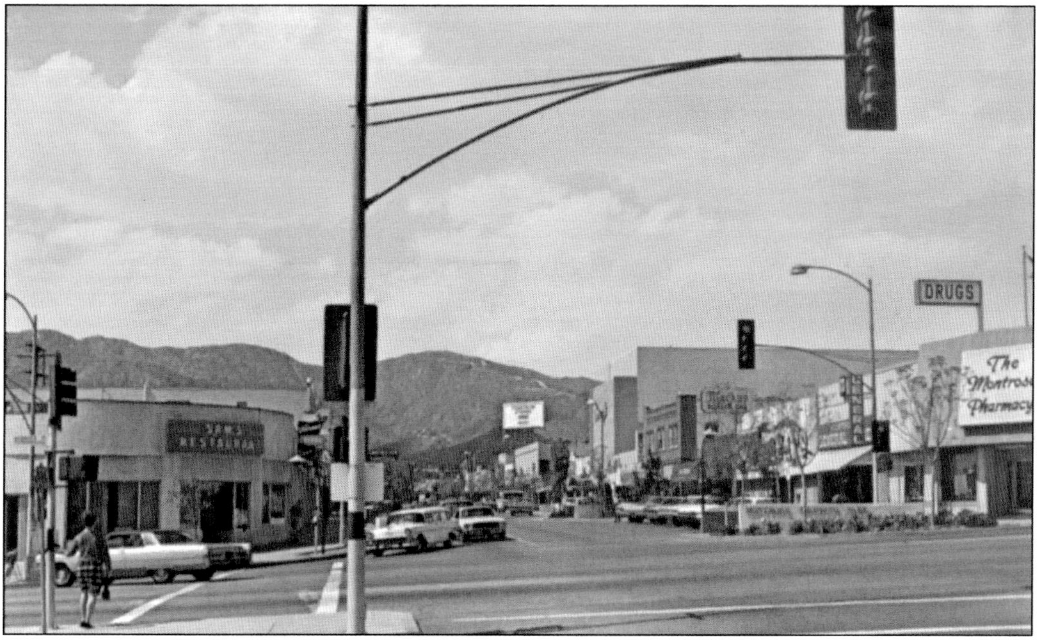

In the year after the shopping park renovation in 1967, with the trees still saplings and the billboards and large signs not yet removed, Montrose still looks just as urban as it did before. The recently constructed three-story Dorsey building dwarfs the Reinhard building, and the Montrose Shopping Park sign is so small it is barely noticeable.

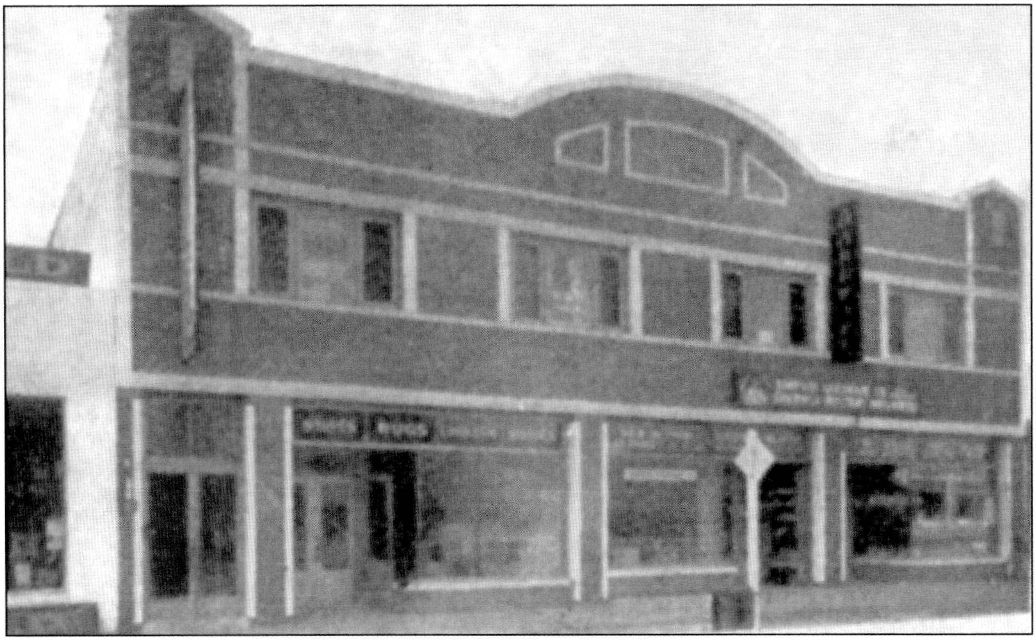

The Montrose Hotel (2218) opened around 1923, with the guest rooms on the second floor, all against the outside walls, surrounding a glass-ceilinged atrium that shed light on the lobby. The first floor was for retail shops. The hotel went out of business in the 1950s, and the second floor was used for storage until the 1971 Sylmar earthquake did so much damage that it had to be removed. (Courtesy of Tom Russell.)

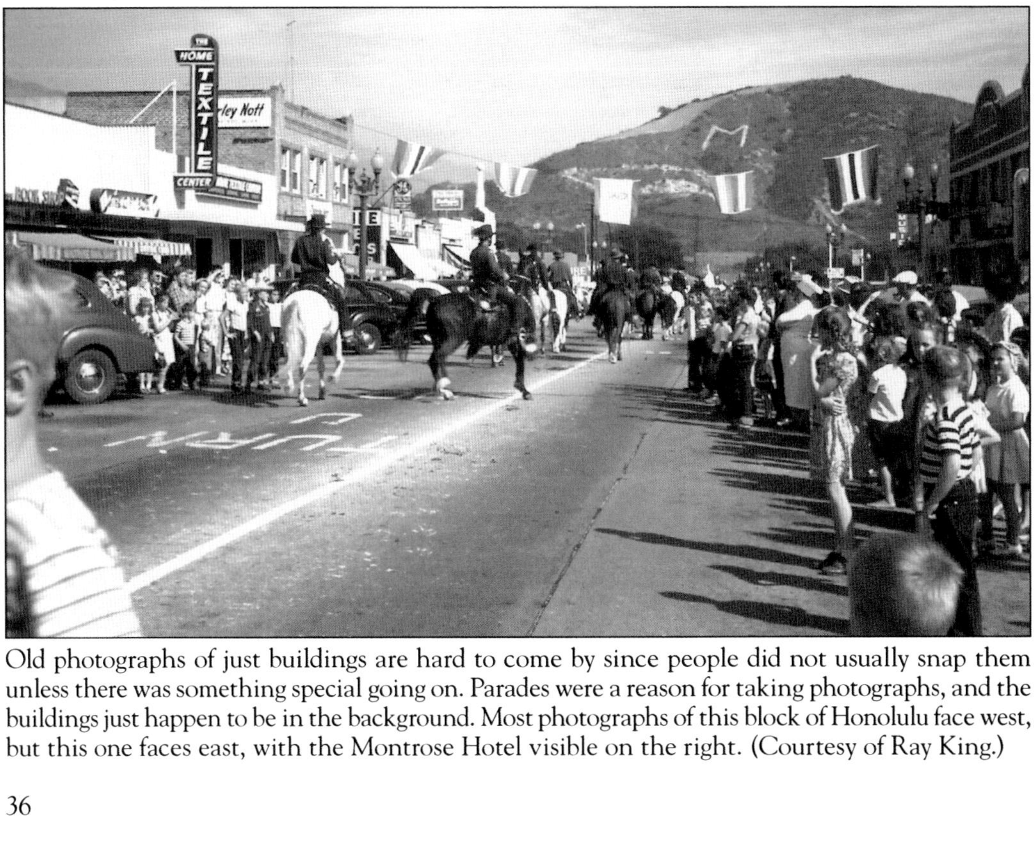

Old photographs of just buildings are hard to come by since people did not usually snap them unless there was something special going on. Parades were a reason for taking photographs, and the buildings just happen to be in the background. Most photographs of this block of Honolulu face west, but this one faces east, with the Montrose Hotel visible on the right. (Courtesy of Ray King.)

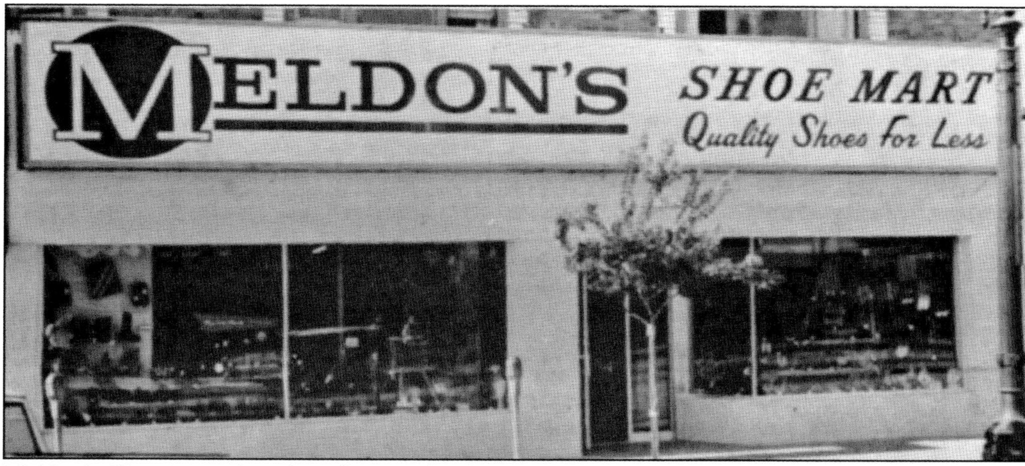

Meldon's Shoe Mart (2218) took over the first-floor space of the former hotel in 1957. Mel and his brother Don Rosenthal had opened a shoe store in Burbank in 1951 and later expanded to Montrose and Canoga Park. Don was an active member of the shopping park renovation. The Montrose store closed in the 1980s.

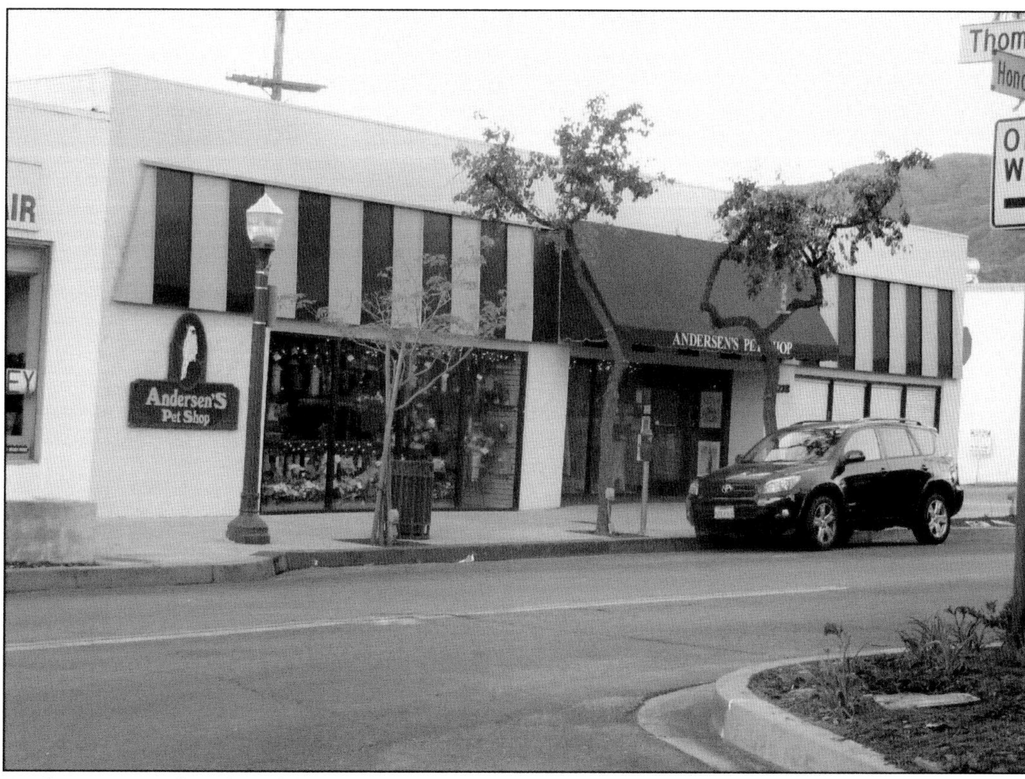

Andersen's Pet Shop (2218) has occupied the same space since 2000. In the 1930s, Andy Andersen started a feed store on Verdugo Road and had a small side enterprise selling animals. As the valley shifted from rural to suburban, his business shifted, too, dropping the feed part to focus on pets. Tom and Alyce Russell have owned it since 1978.

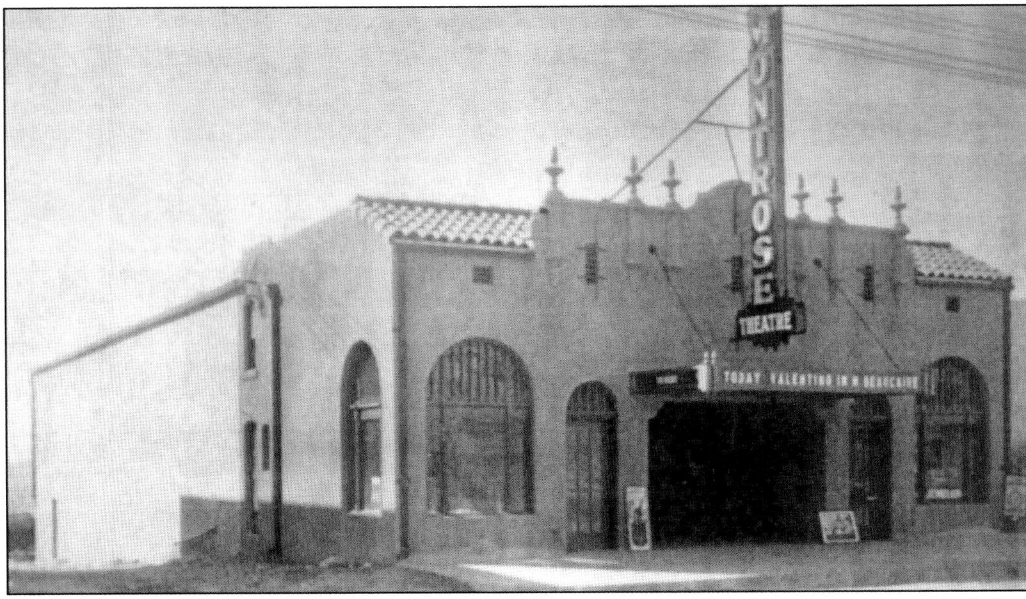

The Montrose Theater (2220) was a community project as several local businessmen pooled their resources to build it. Some of them were Theodore Belanger, H.F. Anawalt, Monte Friend, and Stephen Meyers, who owned the property (and most of that block). It opened on October 16, 1924, with a 600-seat capacity, a small stage for vaudeville acts, a movie screen, and a pipe organ to accompany silent films.

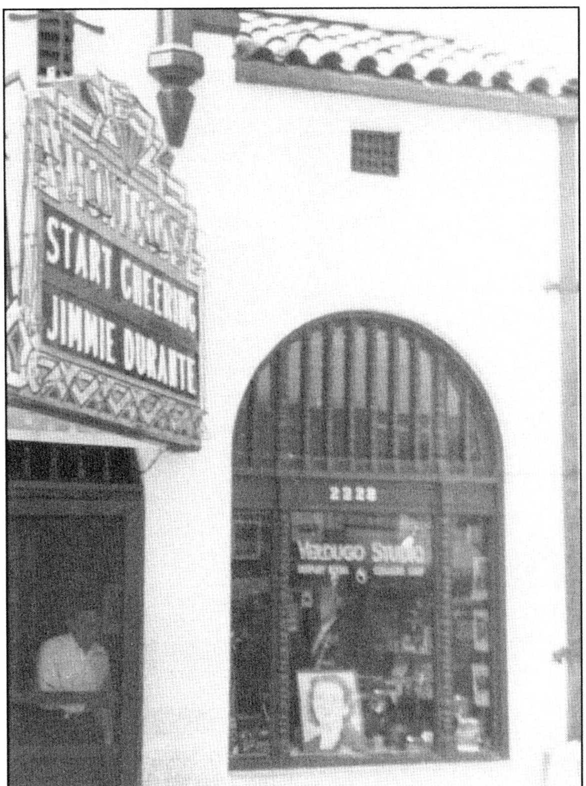

At some point in the mid- to late 1920s, a man committed suicide in the men's room, and the theater was closed for a while. Meyers's brother Bernard bought the theater in 1929 and reopened it. Bernard's daughter Phyllis recalled the theater being packed in the 1930s as customers tried to escape from the Great Depression for a few hours.

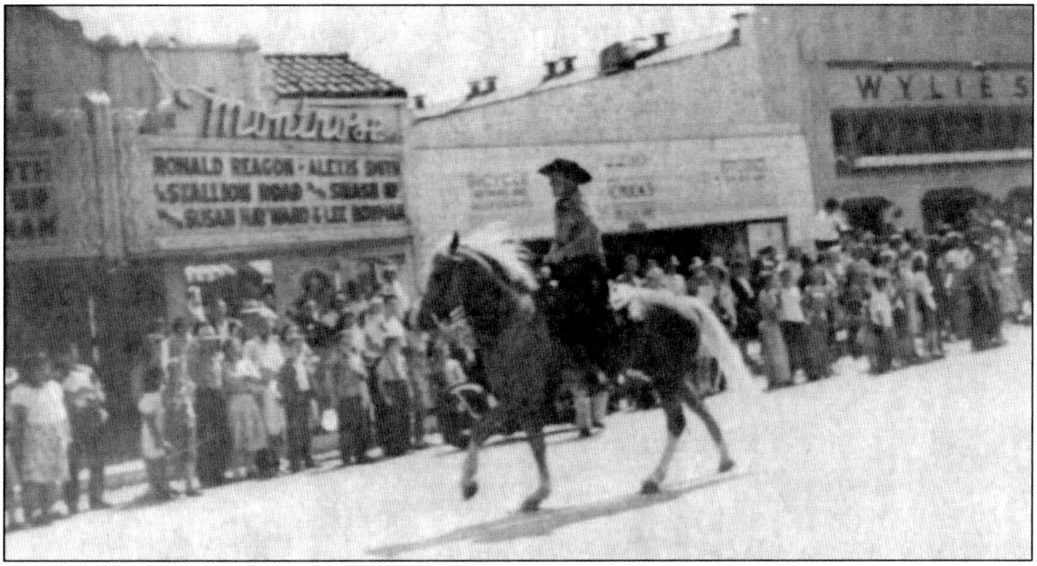

Phyllis Meyers also recalled that future Los Angeles mayor Sam Yorty worked there as a projectionist while he was going to law school. The Meyers family sold the theater in 1945 to James Edwards, and it remained in the Edwards theater chain until it burned down under suspicious circumstances in 1987. It is seen here in 1947 during a parade to promote the local rodeo.

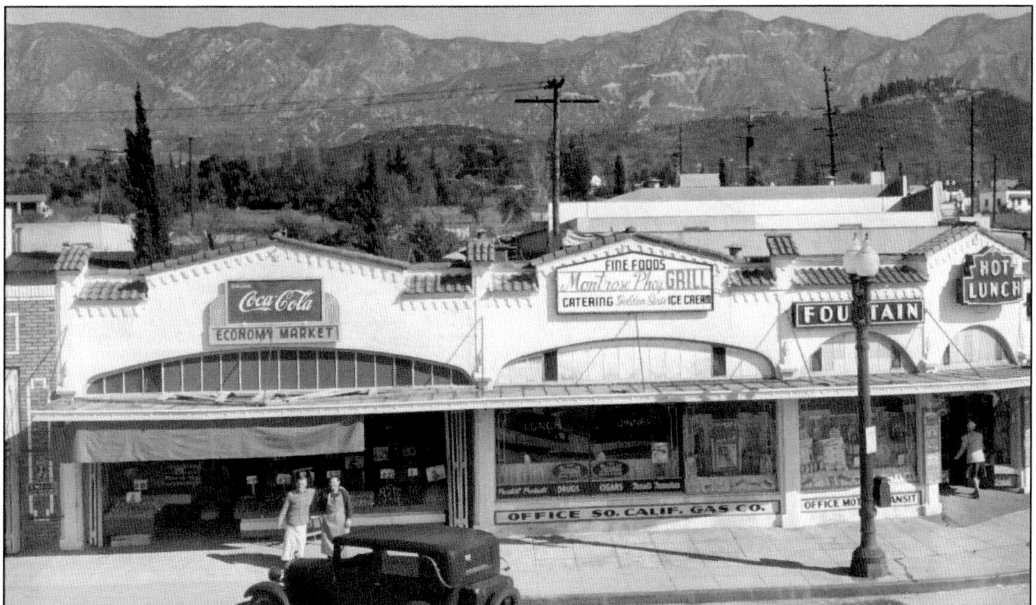

The Economy Market (2207) was in the western part of the pharmacy building. In 1938, meat cutter Pete Gelsinger moved into the space next door (2209), opened the interior wall between the two stores, and became the meat seller for the market. The Economy Market went out of business in 1950, and many different businesses have been here since, including Sy Amitin's surplus store, Timeless Treasures gift store, and currently Once Upon a Time. (Courtesy of Kathryn Halford.)

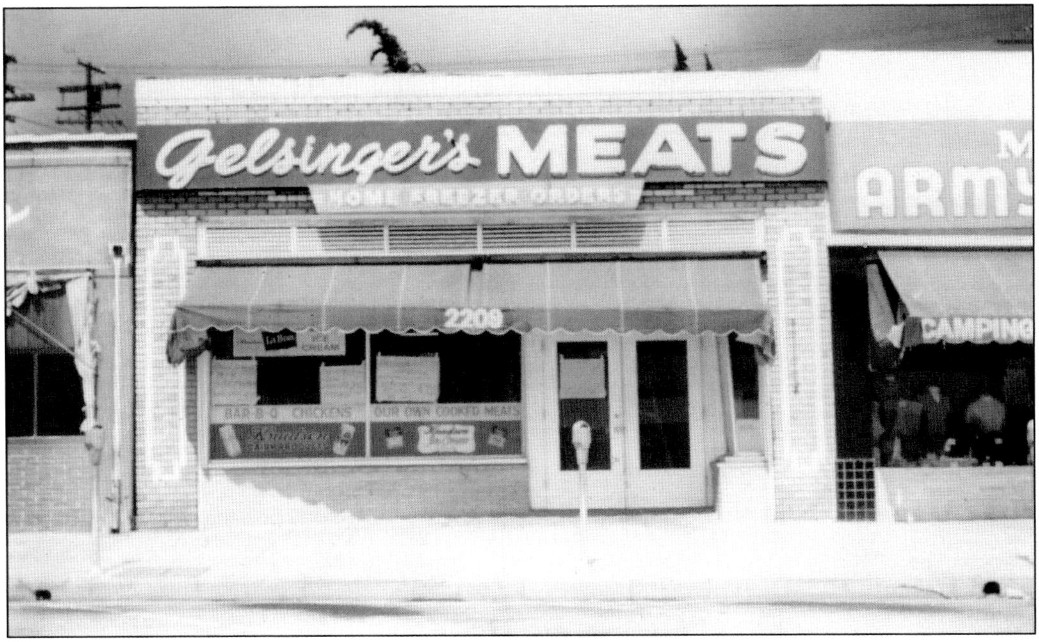

When the Economy Market closed, Gelsinger sealed up the wall between the stores, started Gelsinger's Meats Inc. in the same building (2209), and sold directly to the public. During the 1940s, Gelsinger had bought the 2209 building, and in the early 1950s, he bought the 2211 building next door. (Courtesy of Kerri Gelsinger Scott.)

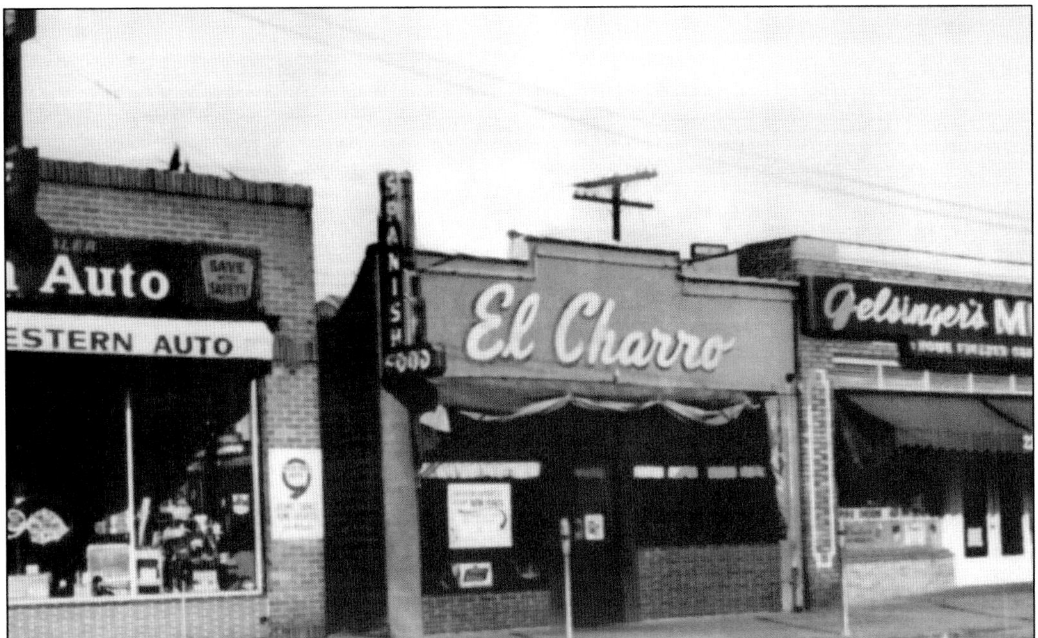

In 1955, when El Charro opened its doors in the 2211 building, it had only four tables and eight stools at the counter. John and Grace Chagolla owned it and took great pride in making all their own sauces, dressings, and other ingredients, using recipes that Grace learned as a child in Texas. El Charro grew and moved to its present site around the corner at 3741 North Verdugo in 1960.

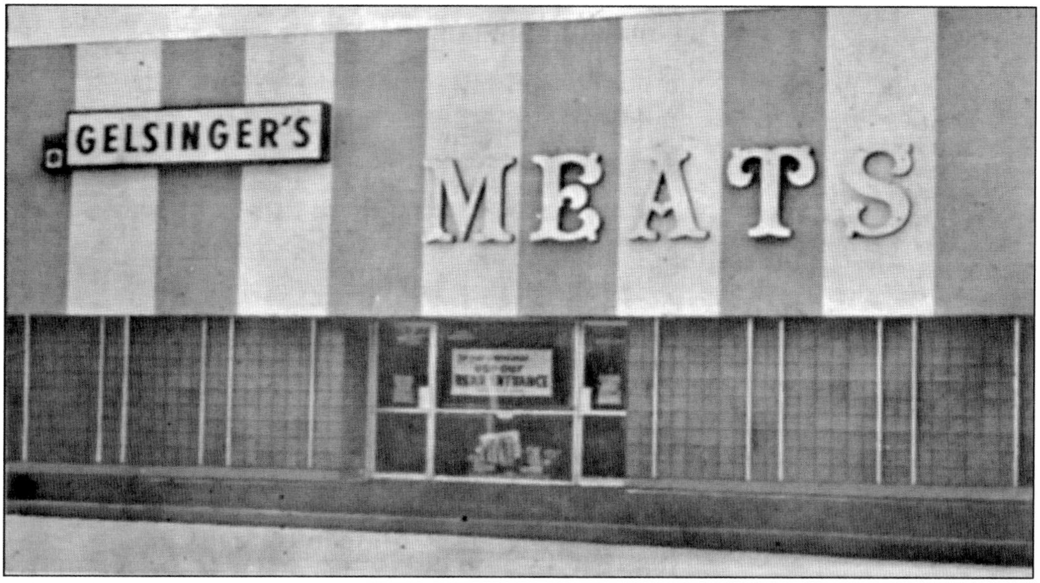

When El Charro moved out, Pete Gelsinger expanded his store into the vacated space. In order to keep his business open during construction, Gelsinger used an unusual construction technique: A shell was built around both buildings, and 2211 was torn down and replaced while keeping the existing store open. He then moved the business into 2211 and tore down and rebuilt 2209 as part of the new building.

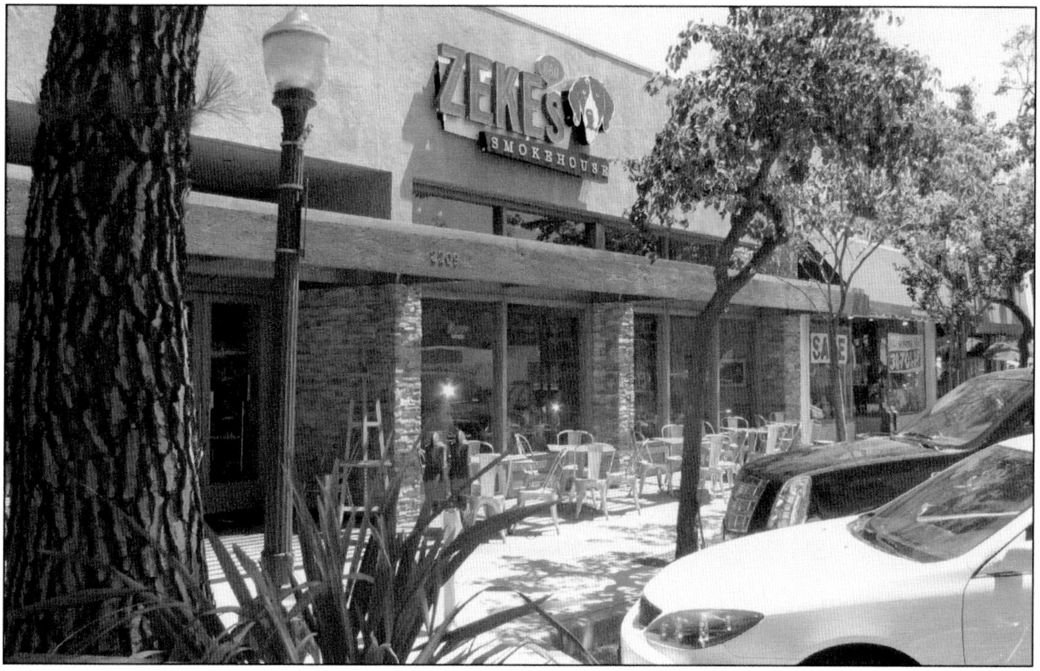

Pete Gelsinger passed the store on to his son Ron, who in turn passed it on to his kids, including son Kirk, who with his siblings expanded the business into wholesale, providing meat to restaurants around the world. As the competition from supermarkets and big box stores cut into the retail business, the Gelsingers converted the store into Zeke's Smokehouse restaurant in 2002. The company still prepares meat for its wholesale business on the property.

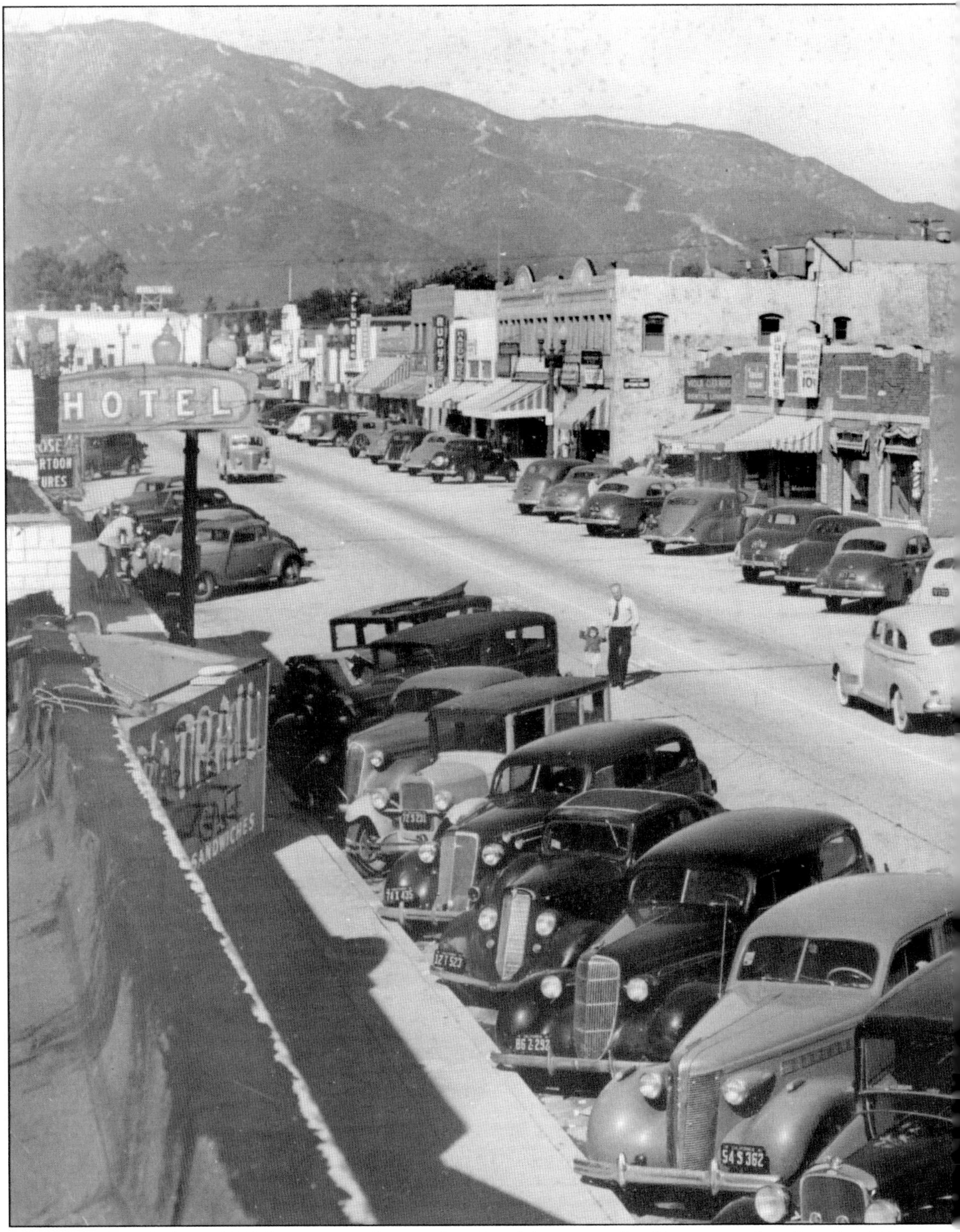

This photograph from 1941 focuses on the north side of the street, looking west showing the C.J. Reinhard building (2219) on the right, followed by a series of brick buildings farther down the street, most of which still stand. However, the 1971 Sylmar earthquake shook Montrose hard, and since then most of the brick buildings have been covered in stucco. The Reinhard building

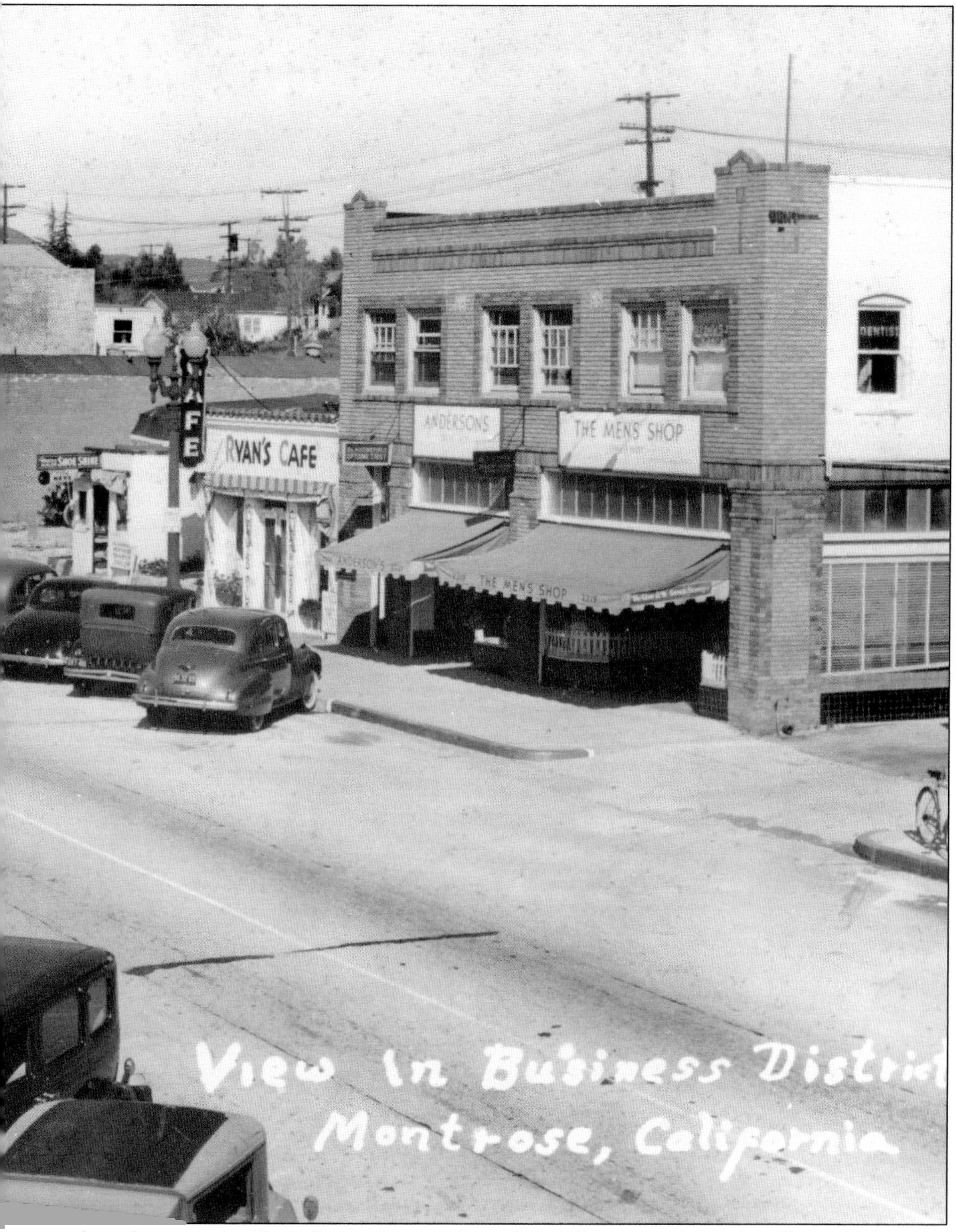

today is home to the Black Cow restaurant, but it has had many tenants in its 90 years. The most unusual one was Fairbank and Fee Pontiac which, in the 1930s, turned the first floor into a car showroom. Baby Boomers remember the record store Here, There, and After being here, there, and no longer by the 1980s.

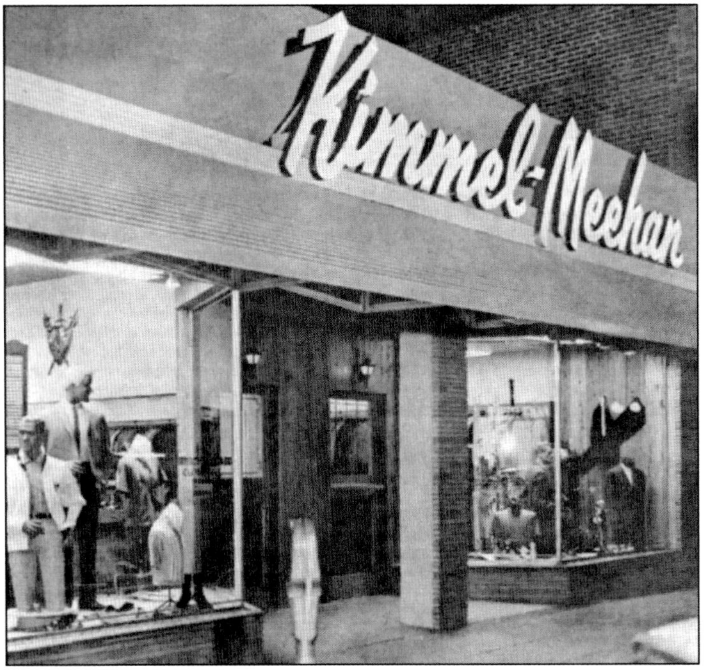

Kimmel-Meehan Clothiers (2227) was started in 1955 by Gale A. Kimmel and Howard T. Meehan, and their motto was "the store for the man who wears his clothes with distinction." They moved into this location in 1957. Jim Larson, who had worked at the store from almost the start, bought it in 1972. It went out of business in 2009.

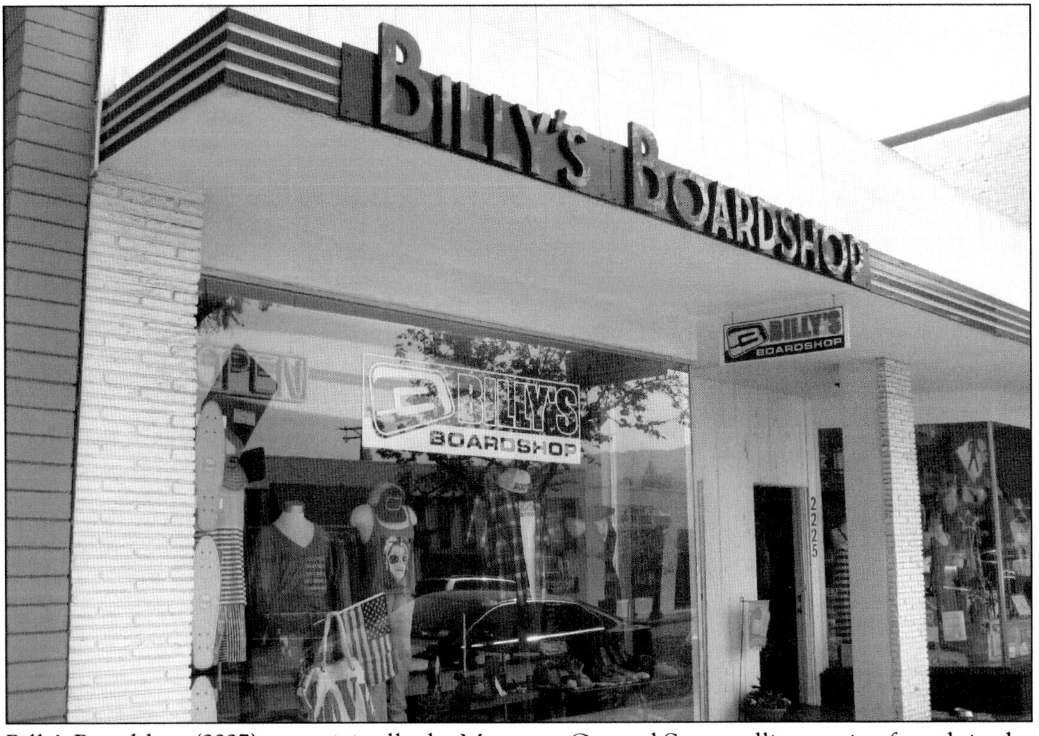

Billy's Boardshop (2227) was originally the Montrose General Store, selling a mix of goods in the former Shopping Bag space in 1976. Shifting the focus to skis and snowboards, owner Alan Amitin (Sy's son) changed the name to Billy's Ski and Sport and in 1998 moved out of the shopping park. Longtime employee Tim Shepard bought it from Amitin in 2006 and changed the name again, moving into this space in 2009.

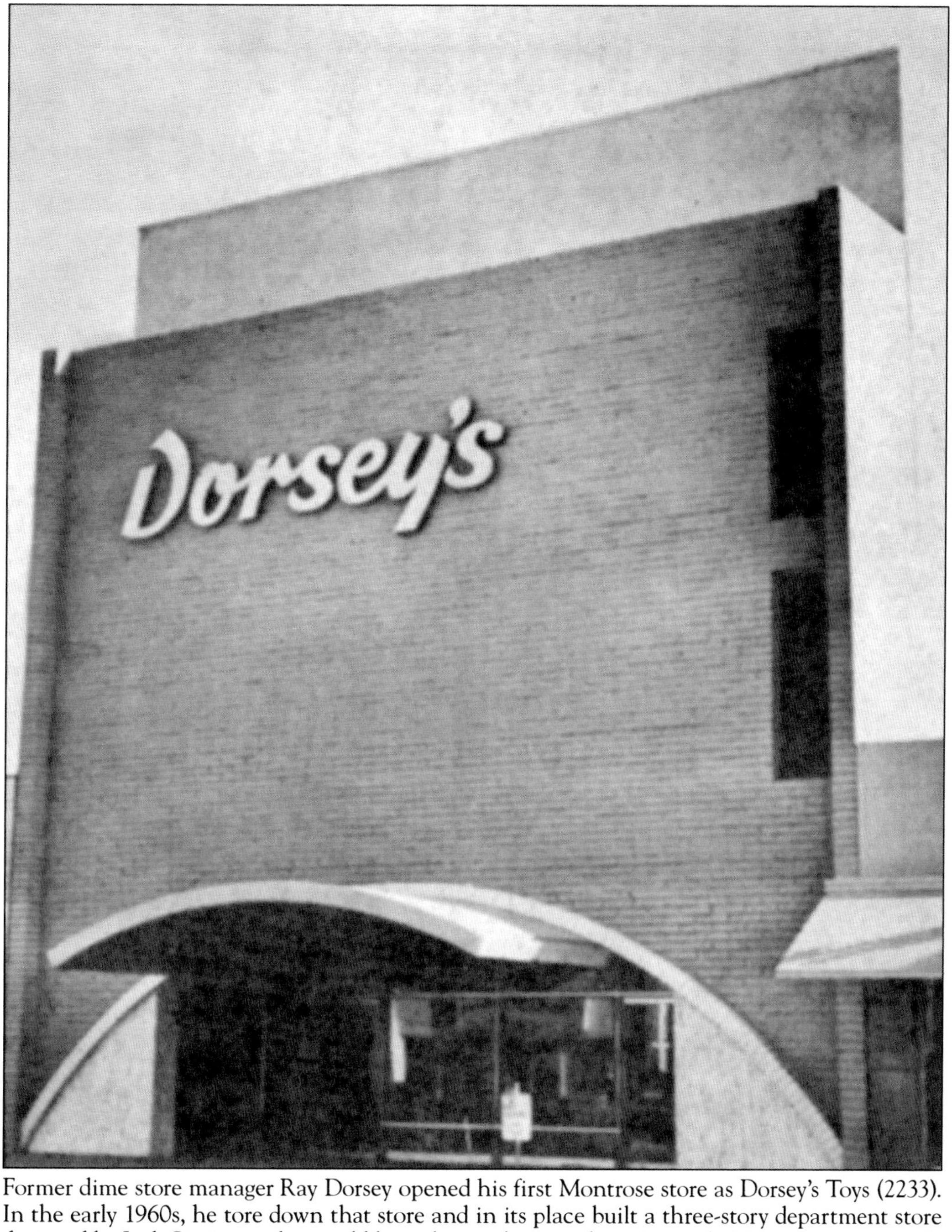

Former dime store manager Ray Dorsey opened his first Montrose store as Dorsey's Toys (2233). In the early 1960s, he tore down that store and in its place built a three-story department store designed by Jack Simison, who would later design the new shopping park. Dorsey was extremely proud of his modern-looking building, the only three-story building in the shopping park, with 20,000 square feet of office and retail space. After Dorsey's closed in the mid-1980s, the building sat empty for many years. A remodel in the 1990s added windows to the front upper stories and removed the curved awning, but it still has had difficulty keeping tenants. For a while, the owner tried unsuccessfully to turn the second floor into a "shopping mall" with half a dozen or so small stores. Since about 2005, the second story has been used for offices.

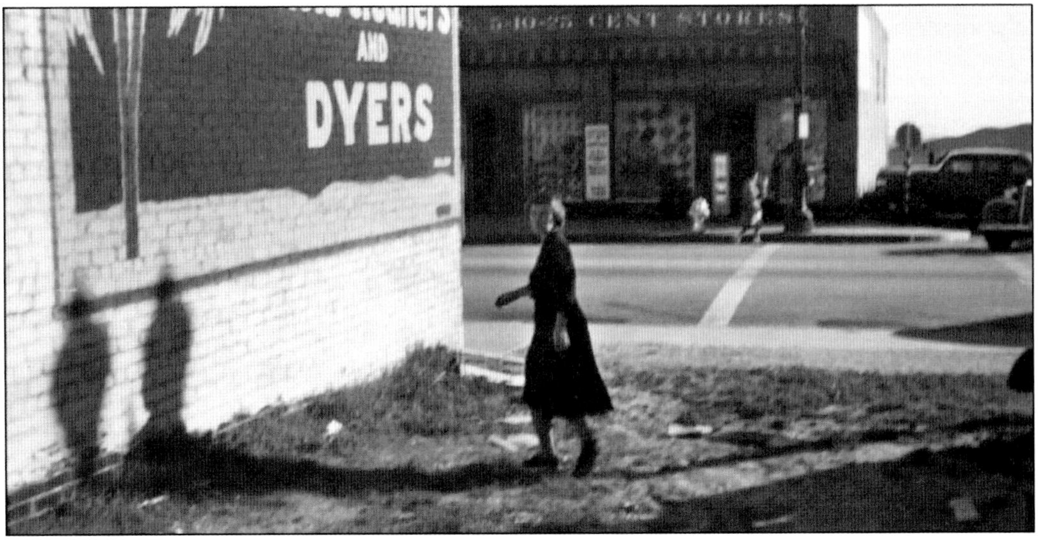

This moody photograph looks south from an empty lot towards the southeast corner of Honolulu Avenue and Market Street around 1940. The store across the way very much resembles the P.B. Carrell's 5-10-25¢ store that later opened on the north side of the street (at 2271), but this location was not listed in the company history in 1967.

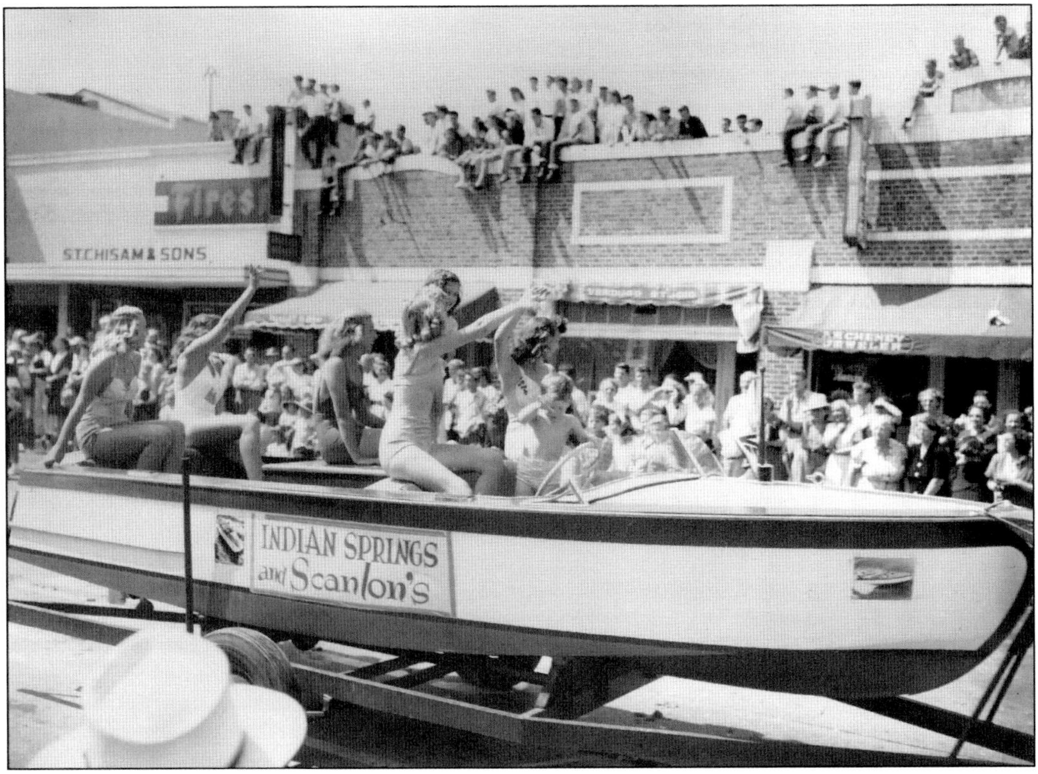

This is most likely a Western Days parade in the late 1940s. This Indian Springs entry gives new meaning to the word "float" as it passes the wide, one-story brick building on the north side at the 2241 section of the block. Tenants of that building have included the Montrose Camera Shop, Caroline's, and more recently, Collector's World. (Courtesy of Pat Robinson.)

The Montrose Camera Shop originally opened in the 2300 block in 1946 but moved to this location (2243) in 1948. The husband and wife team of Frank and Menetta Pritchett started the business, but he passed away in the early 1960s and Menetta continued to run it with the help of two longtime employees.

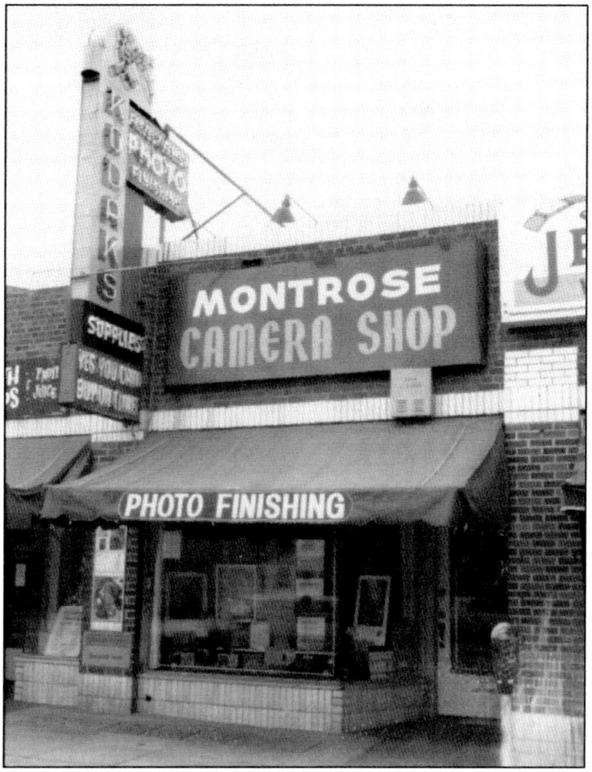

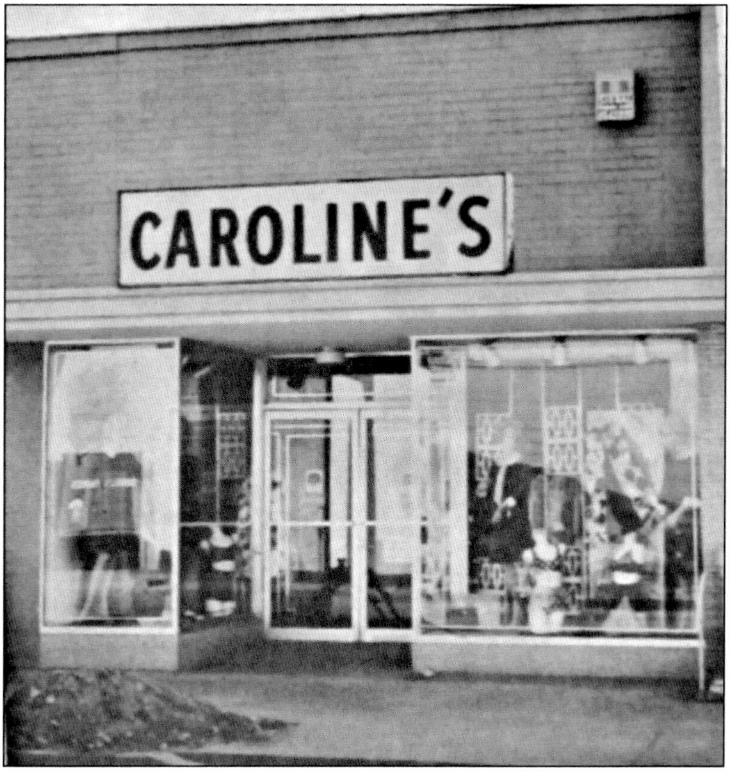

Immigrant George Lubow moved from Poland to New York in 1949 and within days opened his first store. In 1955, he moved to Southern California and opened a women's clothing store in Monrovia, another in South Pasadena in 1957, and finally Caroline's of Montrose (2247) in 1959. Caroline's specialized in what Lubow called "California apparel," and it clearly had appeal since Caroline's was in business here for almost 40 years.

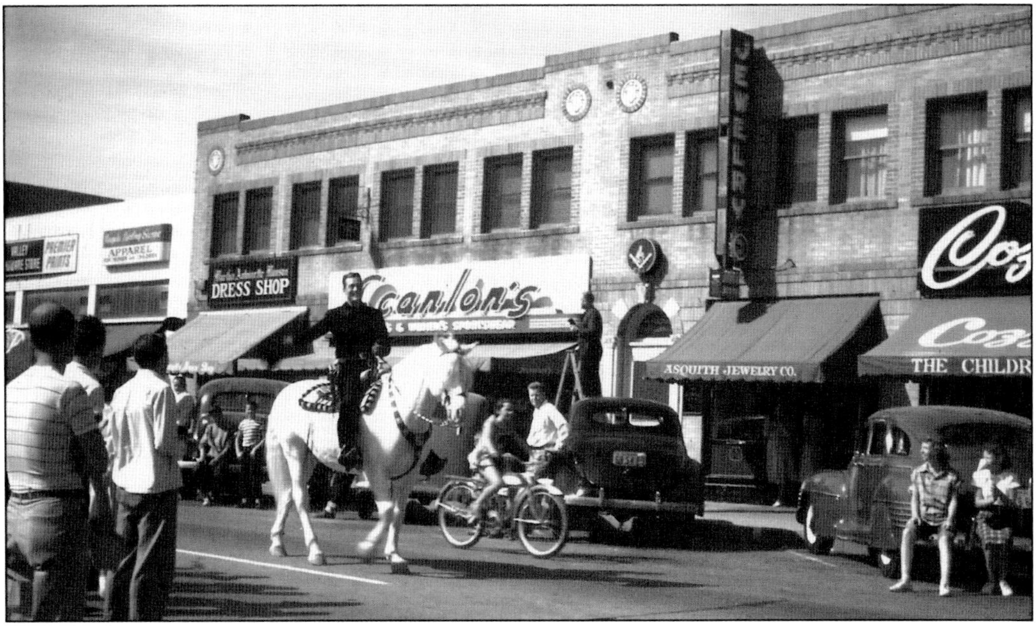

The Western Days rodeo took place at the nearby Onandarka Ranch and was promoted with a Montrose parade. The man on the horse is Charles Starrett, best known as "The Durango Kid" in a series of Western films. In the 2255 building behind him are Cozzette's and Scanlon's. The building was a Masonic lodge for a while; note the sign above the door. (Courtesy of Ray King.)

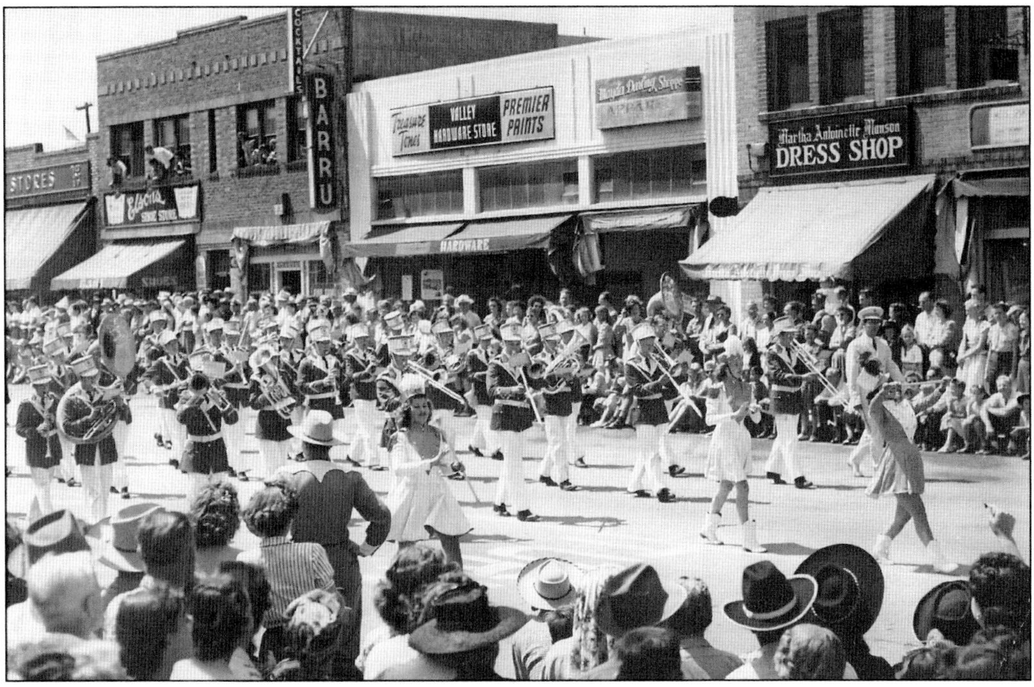

This photograph, from probably the late 1940s, overlaps with the above photograph but shows the buildings to the west. Scanlon's is on the far right (with a different style sign.) The Marie Antoinette Dress Shop (2259, next to Scanlon's) was Faye Snow's first women's apparel store in Montrose and would later be named Faye's. Farther down are the Barru and Elson's Shoes.

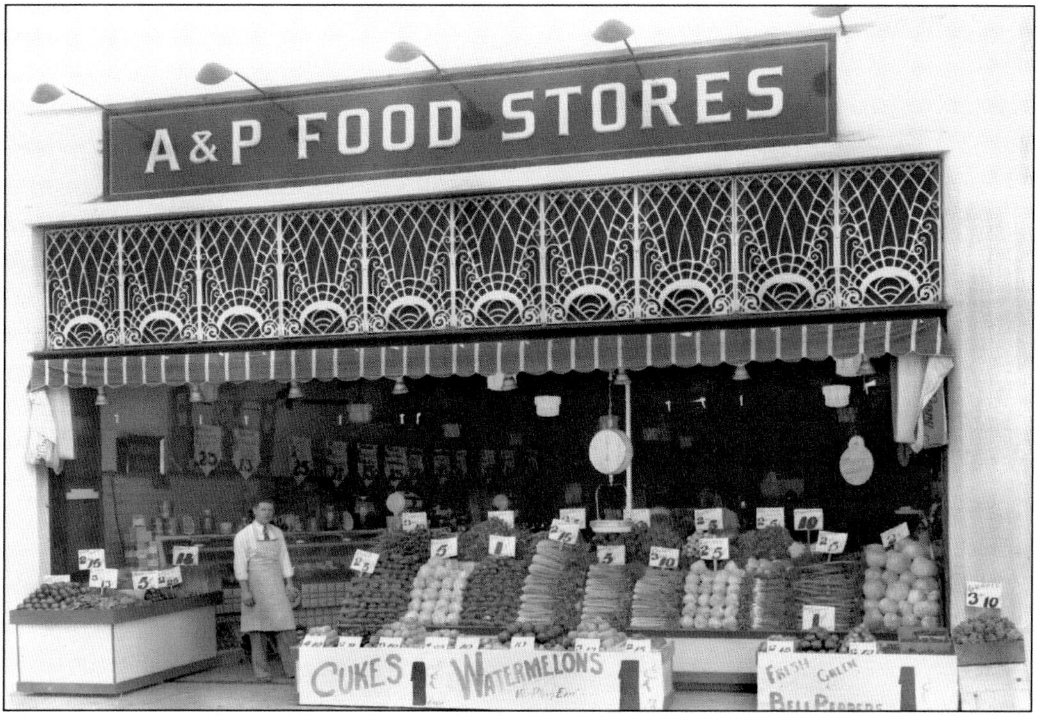

The paint store in the middle of the parade photograph had been home to an A&P Food Store (2261–2263). Without reliable refrigeration in the 1920s and 1930s, people had to shop for food almost daily, and Montrose had many markets to accommodate them. The vertical concrete ridges on either side of the opening are still visible today on the sides of Blue Fish.

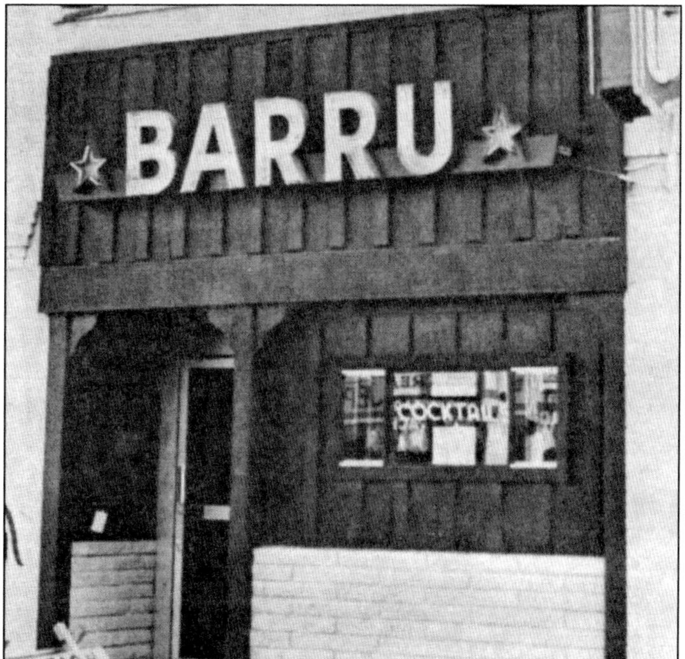

The Barru (2265) was established in the late 1930s. In 1946, Pete Marguglio bought it but kept it pretty much the same. Old-timers remember Hollywood movie star (and La Cañada resident) Dennis Morgan bending his elbow here regularly. In about 2002, the new owner remodeled it and renamed it The Barru Martini Bar but sold it only a few years later. It is currently known as The Fat Dog.

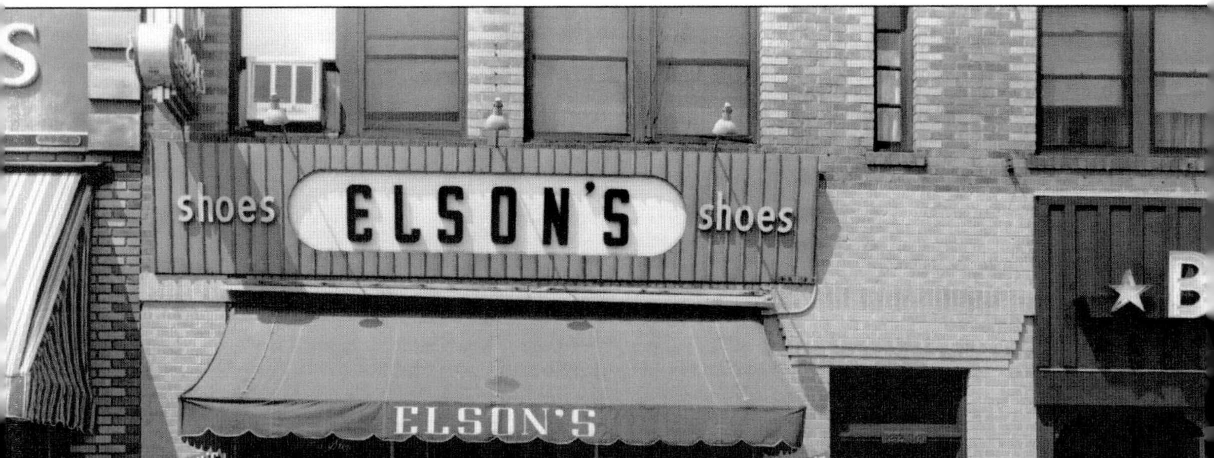

Elson's Shoes (2267) was another longtime business in Montrose. Locals recall that the owner, Irv Elson, would greet people by their shoe sizes—even when walking about town: "Hello, 9 1/2 wide." The Paper Rabbit moved into this location in 1981 and kept the original display windows and entryway, but the current owner gutted the entire storefront in 2012.

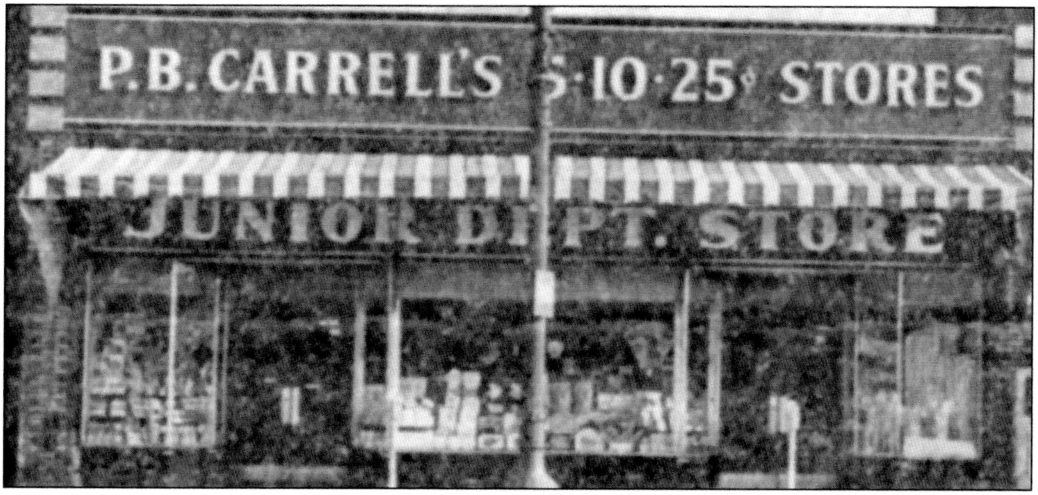

Since 1932, there had been a "variety store" at 2271 Honolulu (next to Elson's Shoes). At one point it was a Ben Franklin 5&10. P.B. Carrell was a La Cañada resident who founded a small chain of "junior department stores," and in 1949, he convinced the owner to switch his store to P.B. Carrell's 5-10-25¢ stores. This photograph is from 1953.

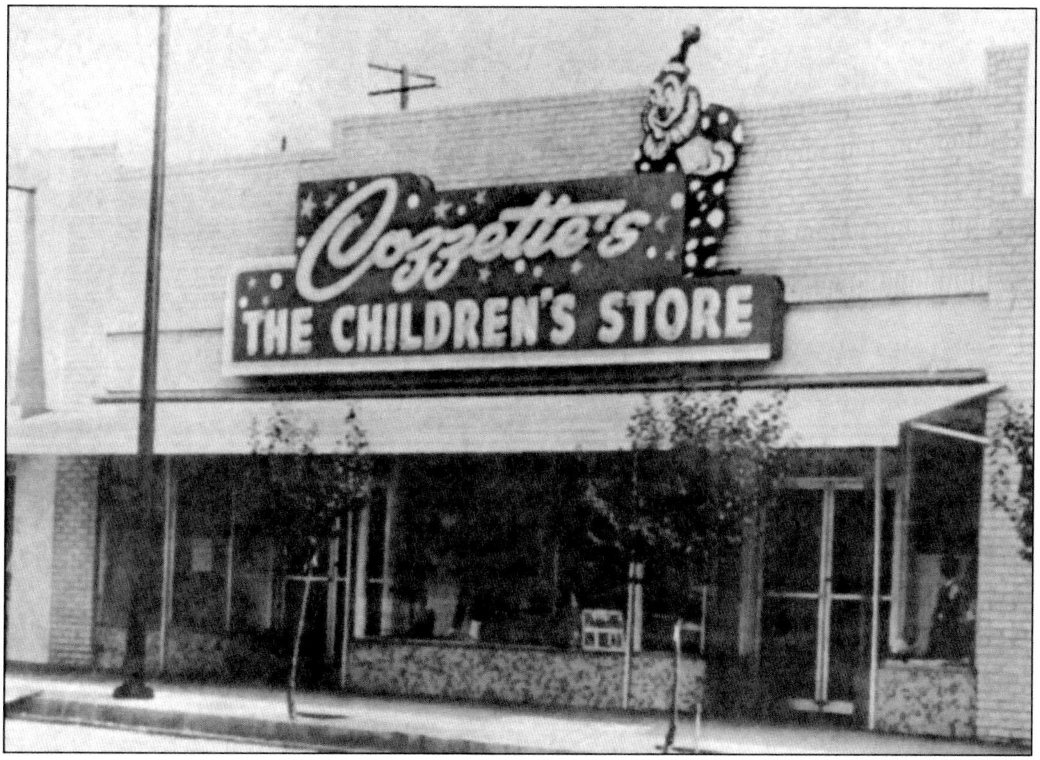

Sensing a need for a children's store in Montrose, Cozzette Gray opened Cozzette's Baby Store in 1941. She moved three times, settling in at 2271 for the longest tenure and changing the name to Cozzette's—The Children's Store. The Baby Boom kept Cozzette's in business through the 1950s and 1960s. For a brief time, Cozete's moved into the vacated Shopping Bag building but finally closed shop around 1975.

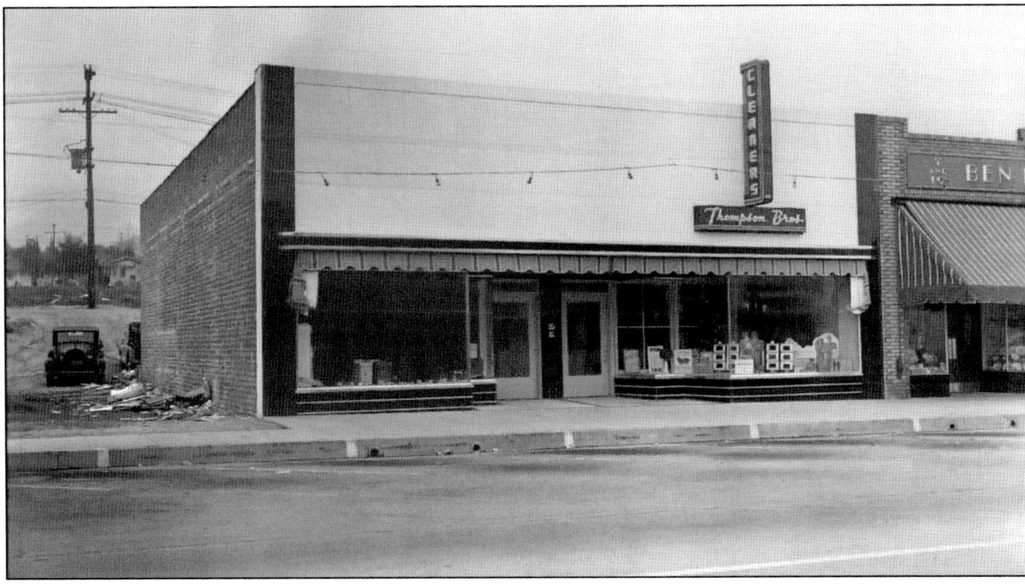

Thompson Bros. Cleaners (2275) is one of the oldest Montrose businesses. W.E., H.G., and J.P. Thompson started it in 1929 at this location but eventually moved to a building behind the Reinhard building on Thompson Court (which was named after them.) On the roof, the Thompsons had a steam whistle that blew every day at noon; they moved it to the new building, but the family took it with them when they sold the cleaners.

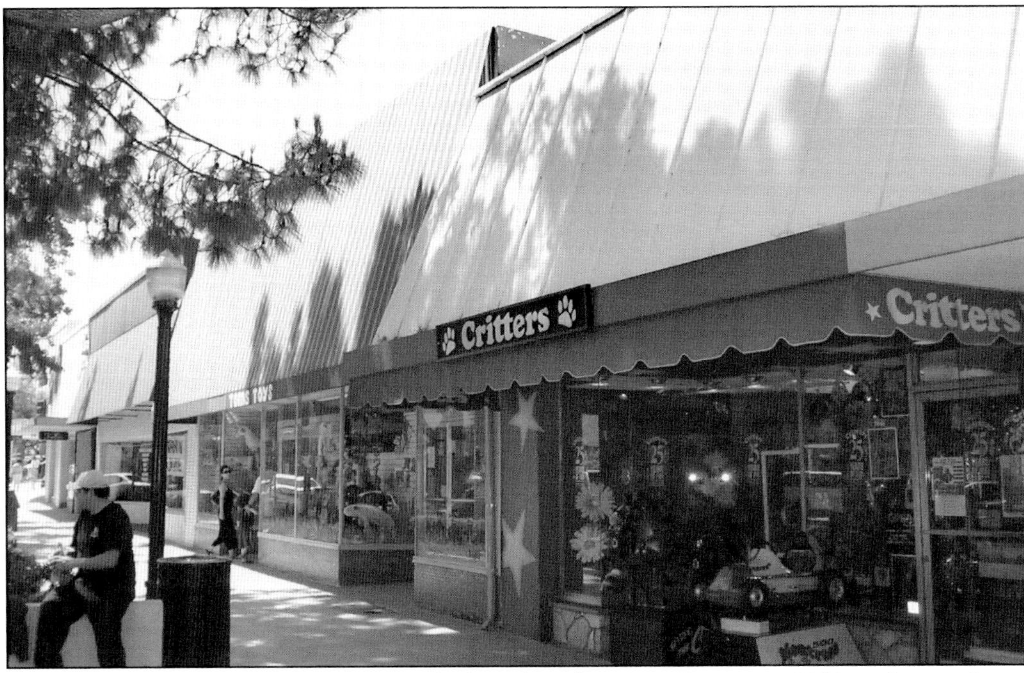

Bob Lambrecht started the Critters gift shop (2277) in San Dimas in 1979 and moved it to Montrose in 1982. John Plenowski joined him a few years later, and the two were actively involved in the shopping park until they sold the store in 2006 and moved across the country. Almost every child who has visited Montrose in the last 30 years has ridden one of the coin-operated rides in front of the store.

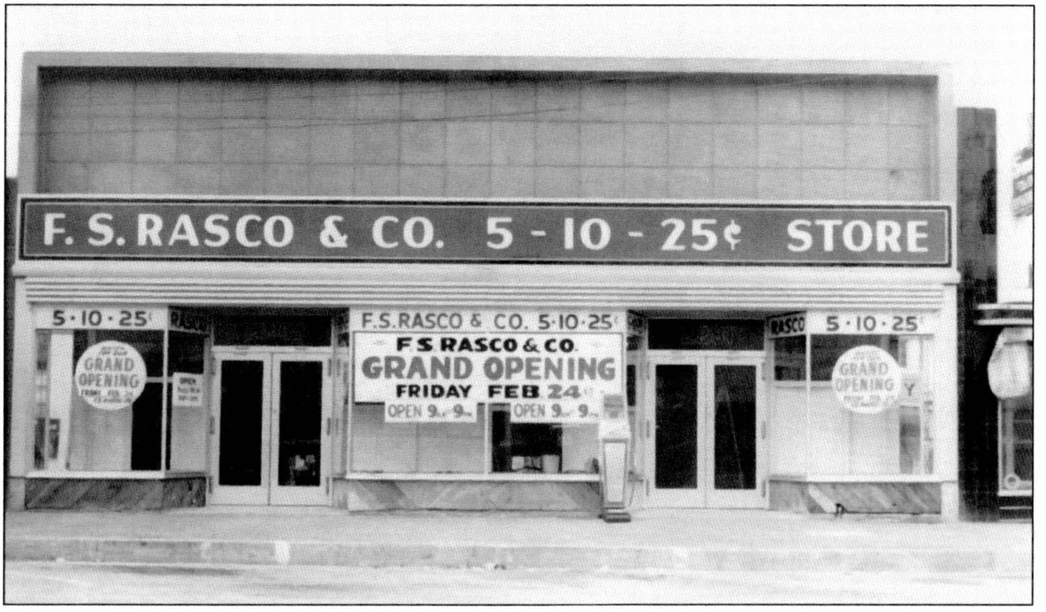

The Rasco 5-10-25¢ store (2281) was the first tenant in this building, which was constructed in the late 1940s on the last empty lot on the north side of Honolulu Avenue between Verdugo and Ocean View Boulevard. (The empty lot is partly visible in the Thompson Brothers photograph on the opposite page.) Ray Dorsey was an early manager here and later started his own store (see page 45.) Tom's Toys is currently here.

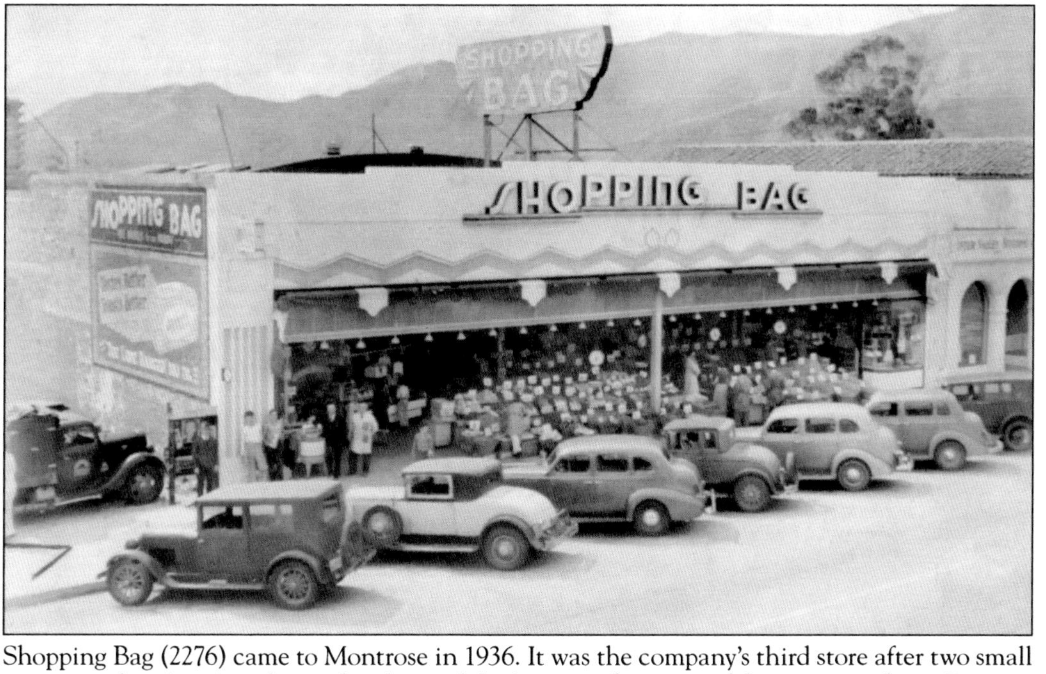

Shopping Bag (2276) came to Montrose in 1936. It was the company's third store after two small stores in urban Los Angeles, and it changed the business direction of this growing chain. Because the valley was filled with health-seekers who had come here for a better climate, they preferred many of the healthier options that Shopping Bag offered. As a result, the chain started to focus on quality over price.

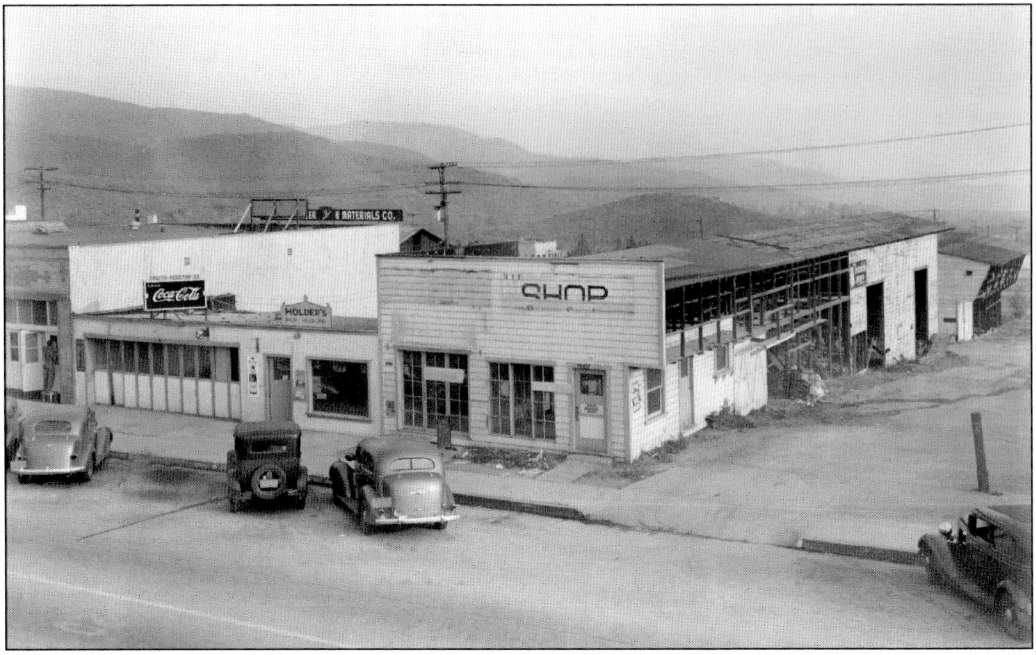

These long lumber sheds (2260) were built in the early 1920s and helped supply materials for the building boom of that decade. The Great Depression, though, put these suppliers out of business. This photograph is from around 1940 when these buildings were about to be demolished to make way for several new stores in that block.

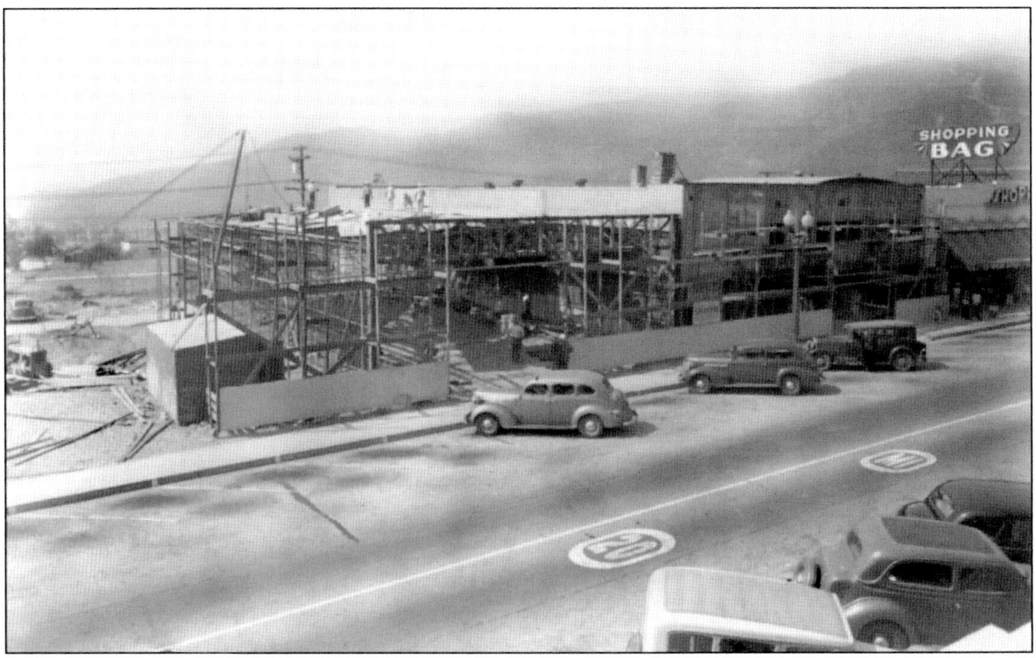

Next to the Shopping Bag store, in 1940, the J.C. Penney store (2270) and annex (2262–2266) were built on the south side of Honolulu Avenue. The Penney store actually opened to the public before the annex was finished. There is a mid-1950s photograph of these buildings in the background on page 108.

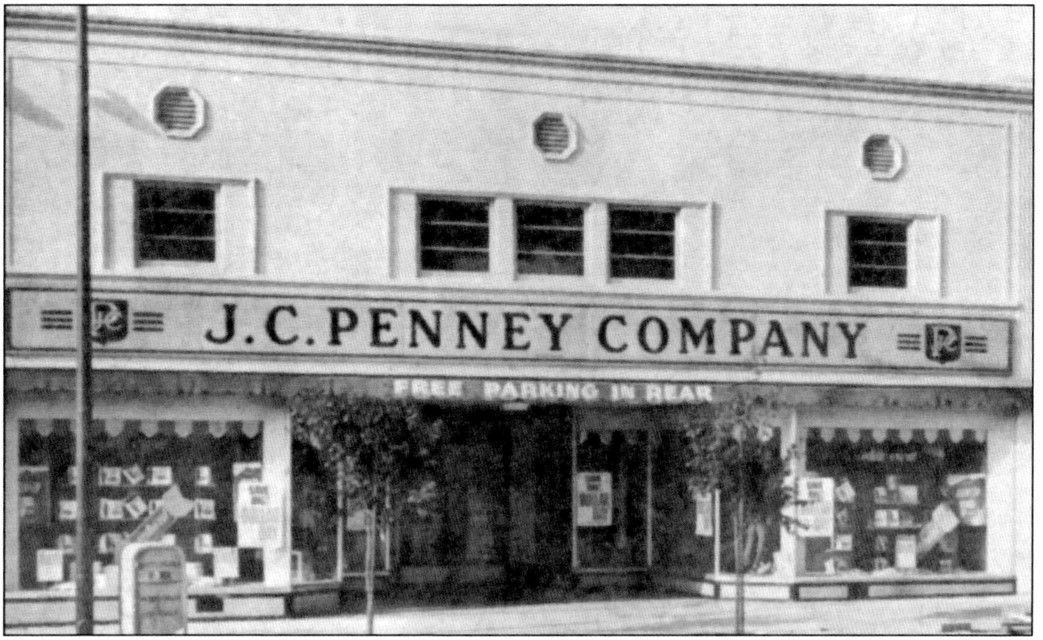

The J.C. Penney store was immediately popular in spite of the fact that it only carried a fraction of the goods that larger Penney stores carried, but shoppers could buy anything else through the Penney catalog. Locals were extremely disappointed when this store closed around 1980. The building has hosted a number of different types of stores since then and was even turned into a mini-mall for a short time.

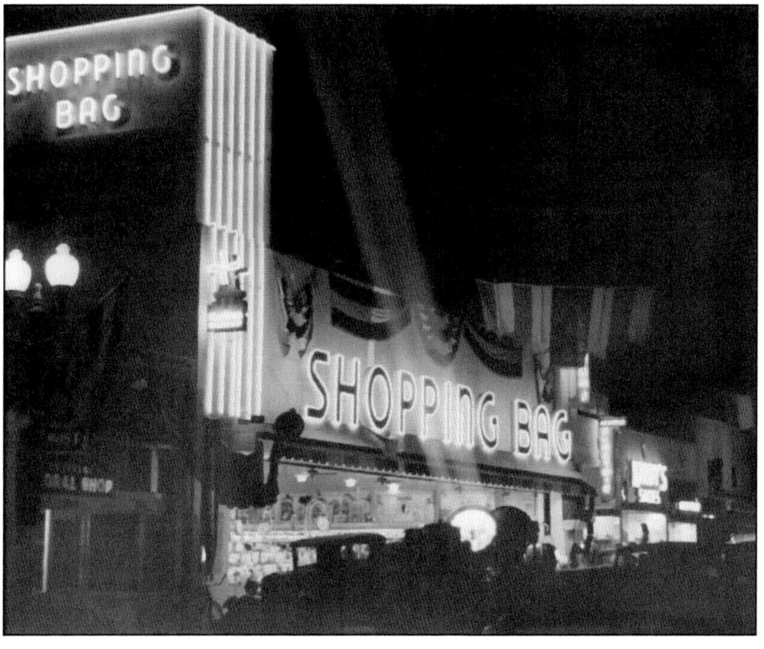

The success of the Montrose Shopping Bag store encouraged the company to expand. It built a new store at 2256 just east of the Penney annex and celebrated opening night in style in 1940. There were two other Shopping Bag stores in the valley, and the chain expanded to about 25 stores before being acquired by Vons. The Montrose store closed in the early 1970s.

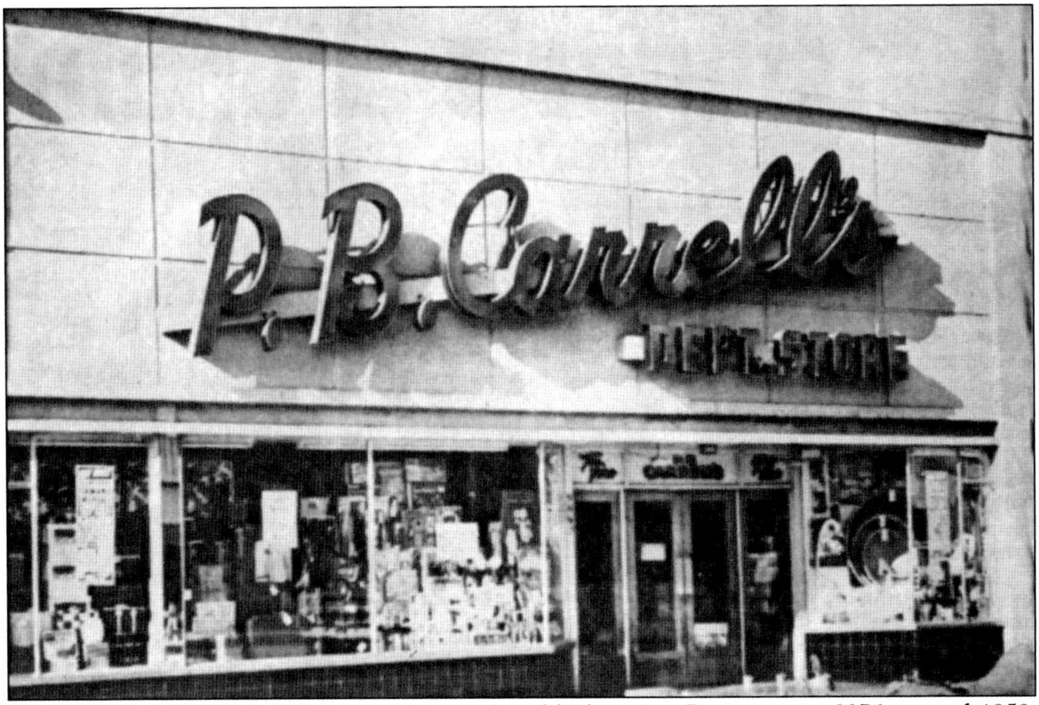

The P.B. Carrell's Dept. Store moved into the old Shopping Bag space at 2276 around 1959. For Montrose Baby Boomers, P.B. Carrell's brings back fond memories of first Barbie Dolls and Hot Wheels. Locals remember the toy section being in the basement. It went out of business in the 1970s. In the 1990s, the building was refaced with a stone facade and is currently home to two restaurants.

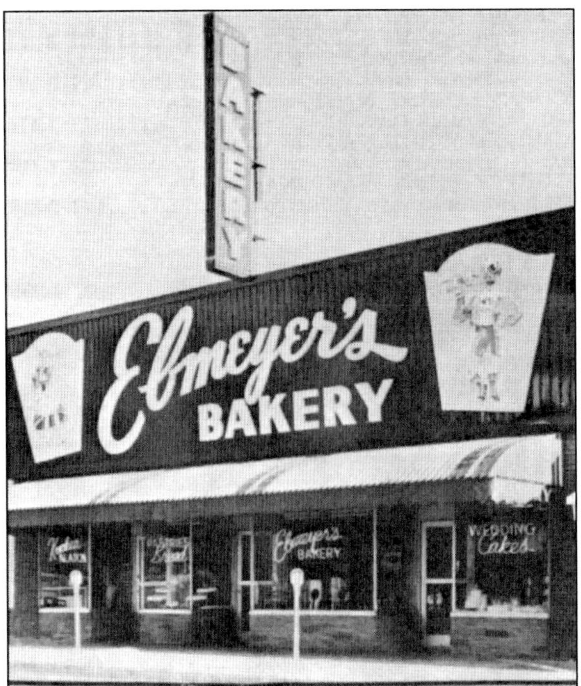

The Ebmeyer family, from Herford, Germany, had been in the baking business for more than three centuries when sixth-generation Hugo Ebmeyer opened Ebmeyer's Bakery (2287) in 1943 with a small store. He added a coffee shop, "Kuchen Klatch," in 1957 and a second story in the mid-1960s. Ebmeyer's was a longtime favorite of Montrosians, but closed in the 1970s when the next generation of Ebmeyers moved to the Apple Valley.

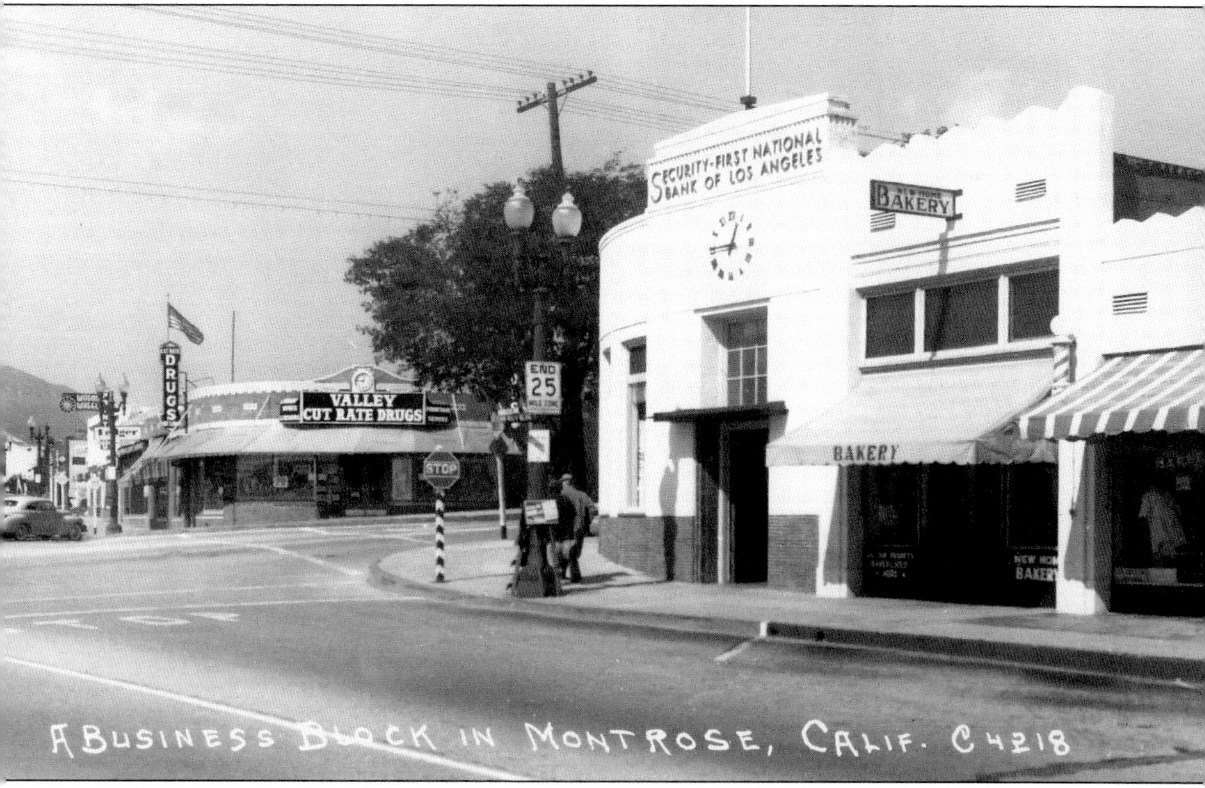

Security First National Bank (2340) was a descendant of the Montrose State Bank (the first bank in Montrose) and the owner of this building at the northeastern corner at Honolulu Avenue and Ocean View Boulevard since the late 1920s. The small bakery to the right of the bank is the space that Hugo Ebmeyer first moved into, which would have been shortly after this photograph was taken. Security First National was acquired by Bank of America, and Faye Snow bought the building, converted it to retail space, and opened Faye's Intimate Apparel there in 1959. (Courtesy of Mark Havlik.)

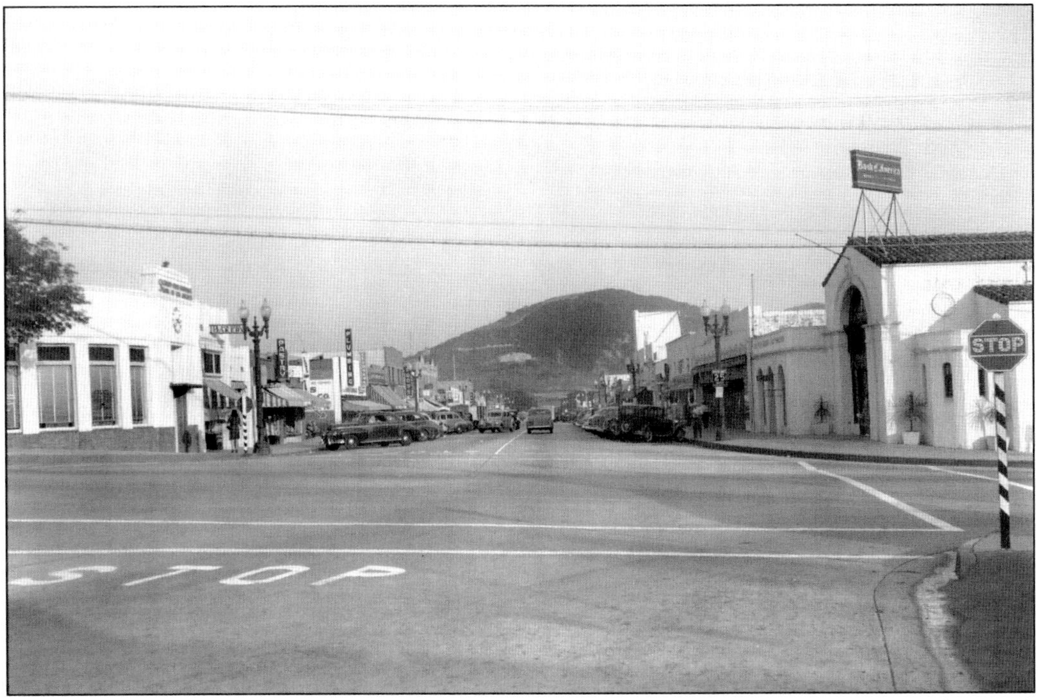

This view looks east on Honolulu Avenue at Ocean View Boulevard in about 1940. The Bank of America came to Montrose in 1936 and moved into the Crescenta-Cañada Bank building, leaving it pretty much intact. Next to the bank is the boarded-up former Shopping Bag, with the new one visible a few doors down. On the north side of the street is the vacant lot that would become Rasco.

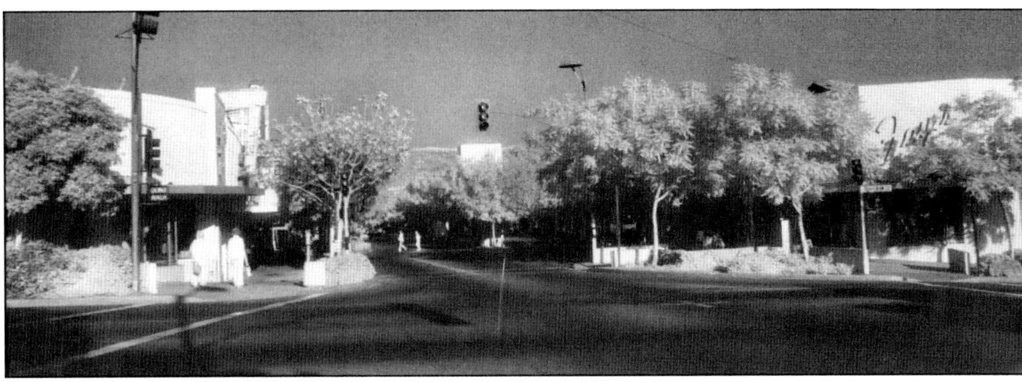

This is the same intersection in the late 1970s, ten years or so after the planting of the trees for the shopping park. The large canopy of the not-yet-tall trees and a few too many shrubs made the shopping park look almost like a forest in this dramatic photograph. The trees grew taller and some of the shrubs were replaced with grass, giving Honolulu Avenue the desired park-like effect. (Courtesy of Chris Humphrey.)

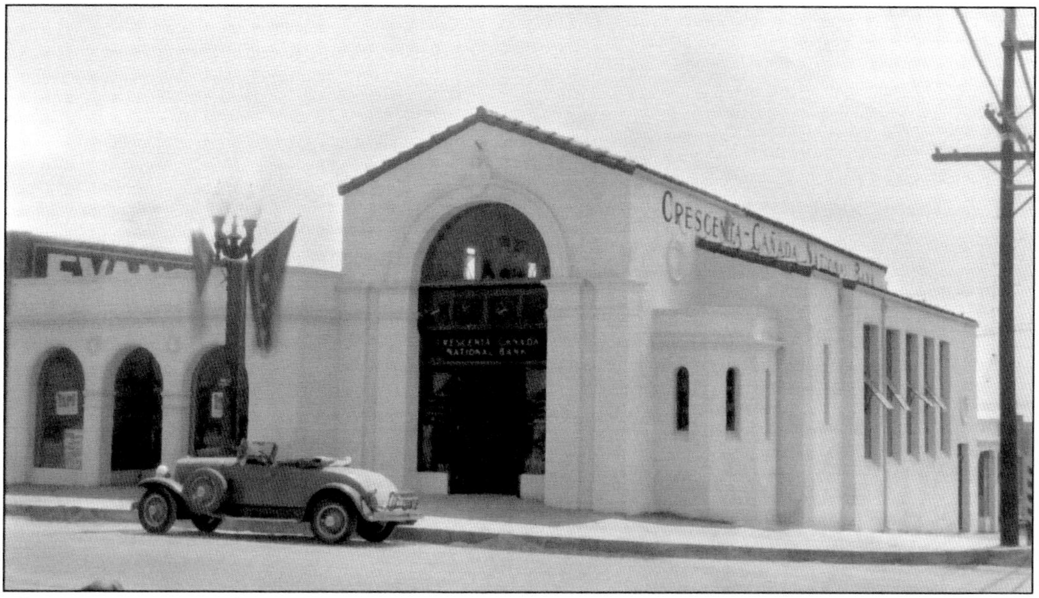

The Crescenta-Cañada Bank was built in 1929 at the southeast corner of Honolulu Avenue and Ocean View Boulevard. This beautiful two-story structure featured a magnificent arched window with elaborate wrought-iron fencing. Inside, the lobby was open-beamed, and the dark-stained beams were hand-painted with blue and red designs (see page 123). High windows on the east provided morning light, and the bank of windows on the west offered a view of the Verdugo Mountains.

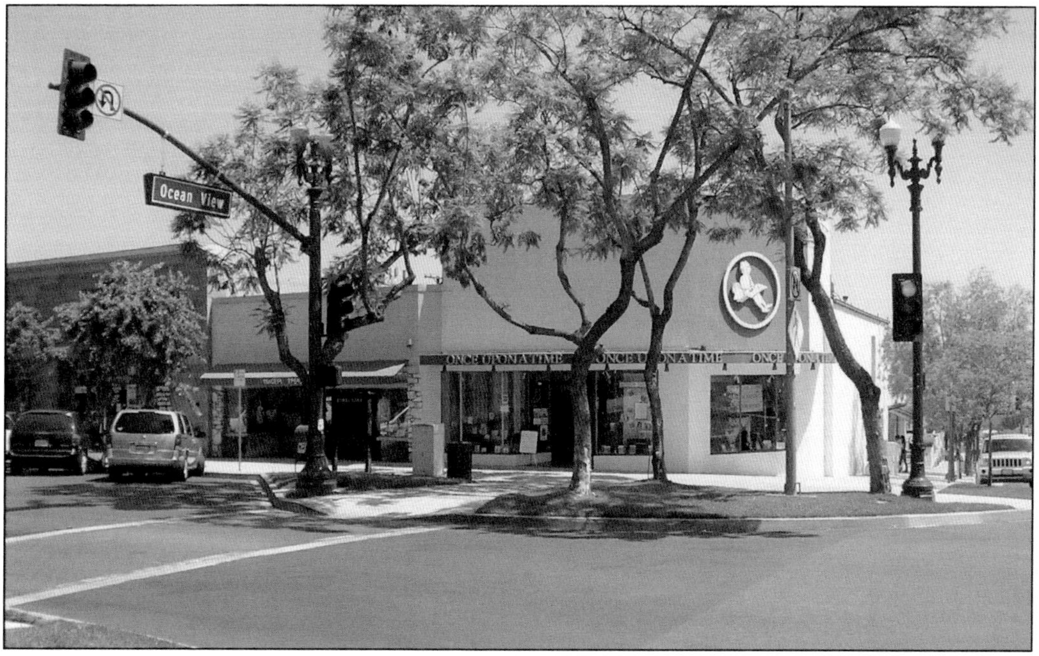

In 1953, Bank of America moved out, and Faye Snow bought the building. She had the ceiling dropped (covering up the hand-painted beams), removed the arched window, and built a new facade with display windows to make it more retail-friendly. After Faye's death in 1980, Once Upon a Time moved in and became something of a landmark (shown here in 2006) until it moved down the street in 2007.

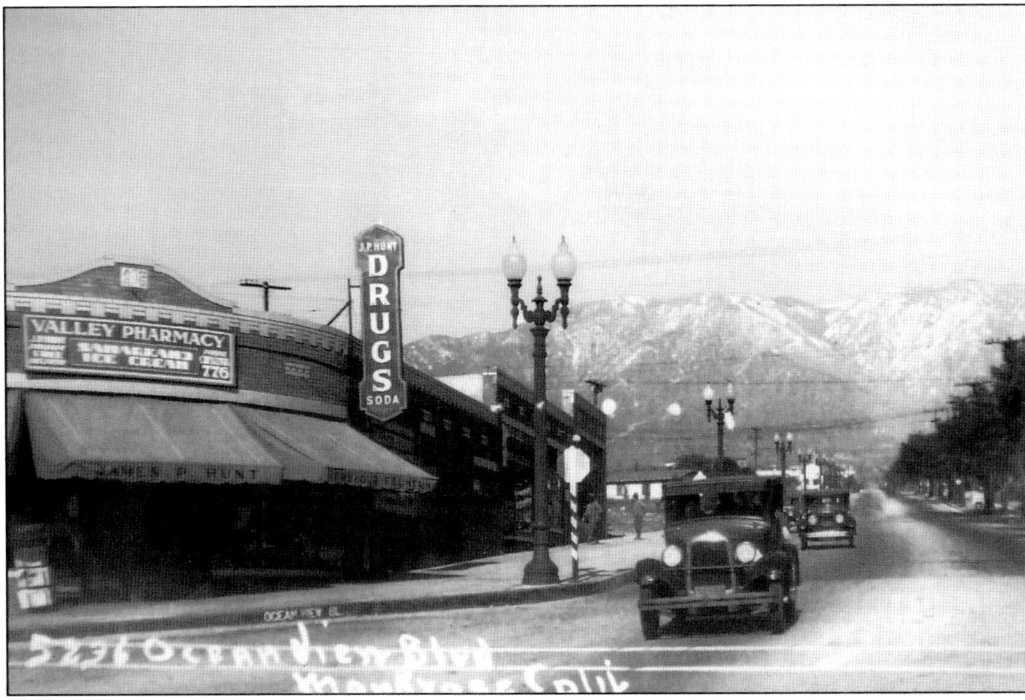

This is looking north on Ocean View Boulevard. The Valley Pharmacy (shown in the early 1930s) was built on the northwest corner of Ocean View Boulevard and Honolulu Avenue in 1926. What is most striking about this view is that the west side of Ocean View Boulevard is lined with street lamps while the east side is lined with trees.

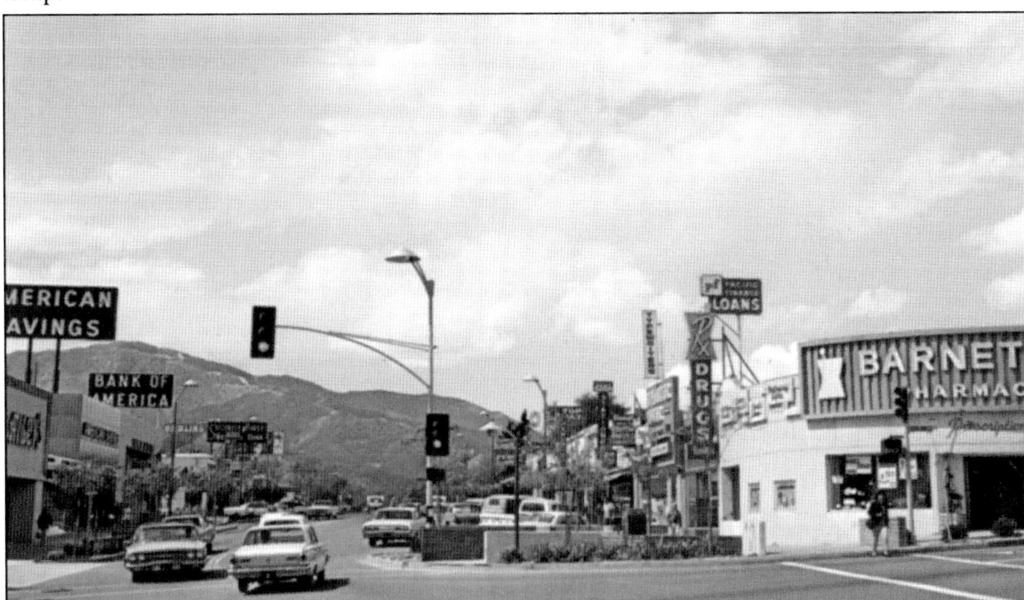

Brothers R.J. and Durwood Barnett opened Barnett's Pharmacy at this location in 1965. It was a family affair for them, as Durwood was the pharmacist, brother R.J. ran the business, and their mother ran the cosmetics department. Barnett's closed in the mid-1970s, and the space became a nondescript podiatrist's office for many years until a yogurt shop opened there in 2008.

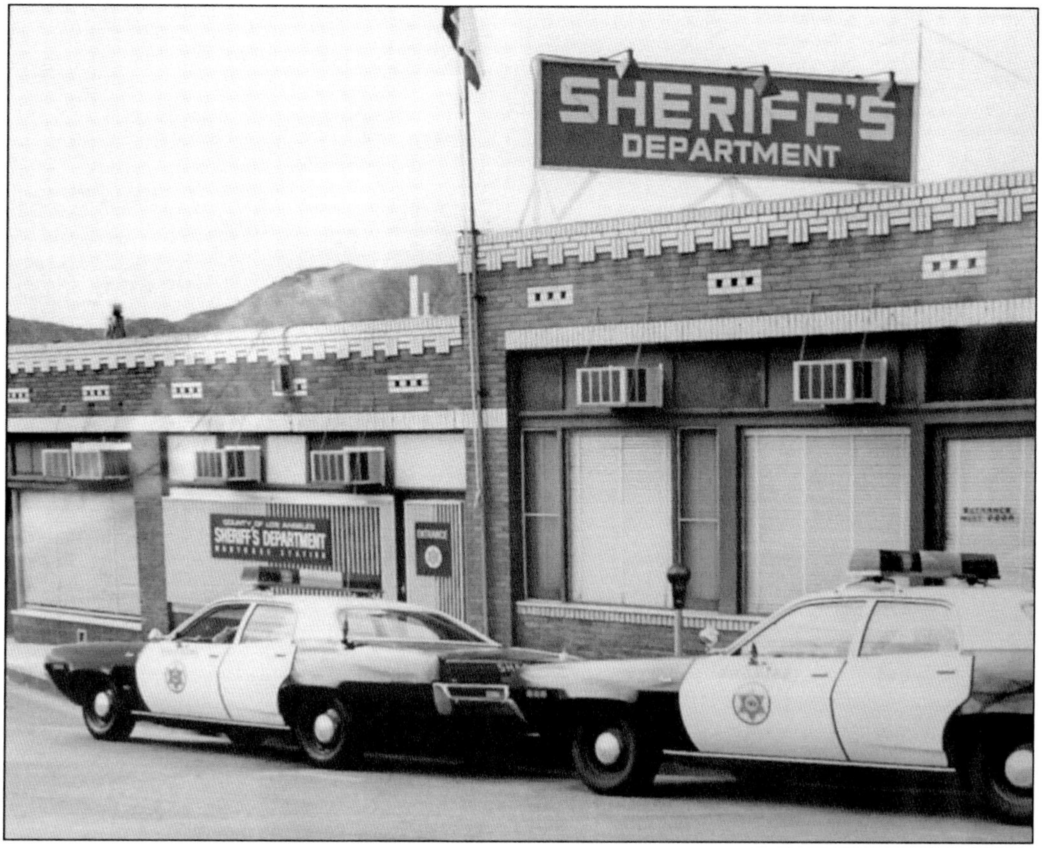

This split-level single-story brick building on Ocean View Boulevard just north of the pharmacy was built in the 1920s to house the Los Angeles County Sheriff's Department. For 50 years, the law in La Crescenta was enforced by officers working out of this building. After the department moved to new quarters in 1973, the former jail cells have been used for fitting rooms, storage, and dog grooming by the various businesses that have since occupied the space.

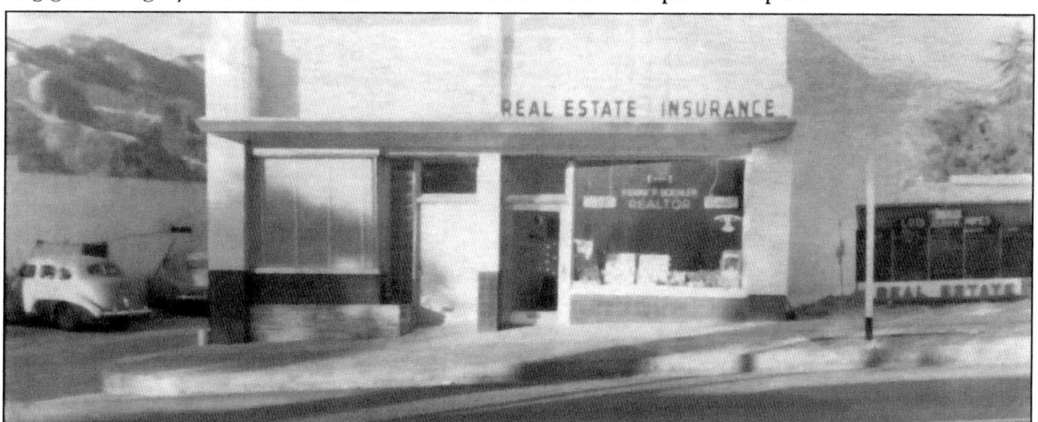

During construction of this building at 3819 Ocean View Boulevard (across the alley from the sheriff's department), the owner, Ernest Carlander, placed a time capsule in the cornerstone. As far as local historians know, it is still there. Perhaps when it is finally dug up the contents will reveal the truth about what really inspired the name "Montrose."

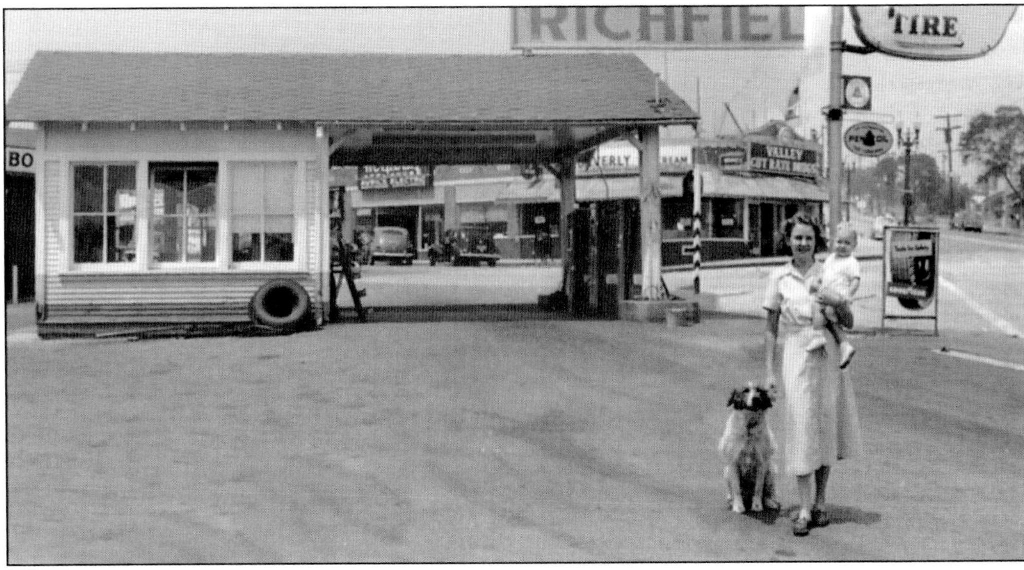

For more than 50 years, the southwest corner of Ocean View Boulevard and Honolulu Avenue (where Coffee Bean is today) was occupied by a gas station. The station was built in 1923 and owned and operated by Bill Nizsche. Bill Bowman ran it from 1950 to 1960 as a Richfield station. It later became an Arco and closed in the 1970s. Shown here are Bowman's wife and dog in 1950. (Courtesy of Bill Bowman.)

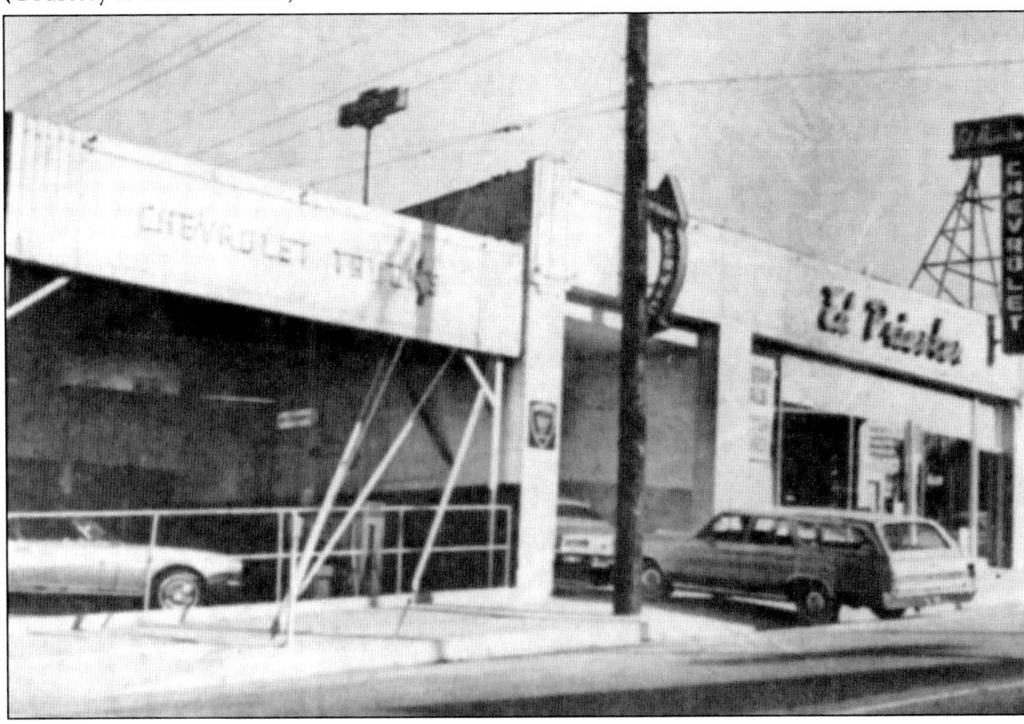

Ed Priester established his Chevrolet dealership at 3701 Ocean View Boulevard, half a block south of Honolulu Avenue in 1930. He had a showroom and full-service shops and later expanded to include a used car lot across Ocean View Boulevard, and another up on Foothill Boulevard. In the 1980s, Priester moved to Verdugo Boulevard in La Cañada, where the movie theater is today.

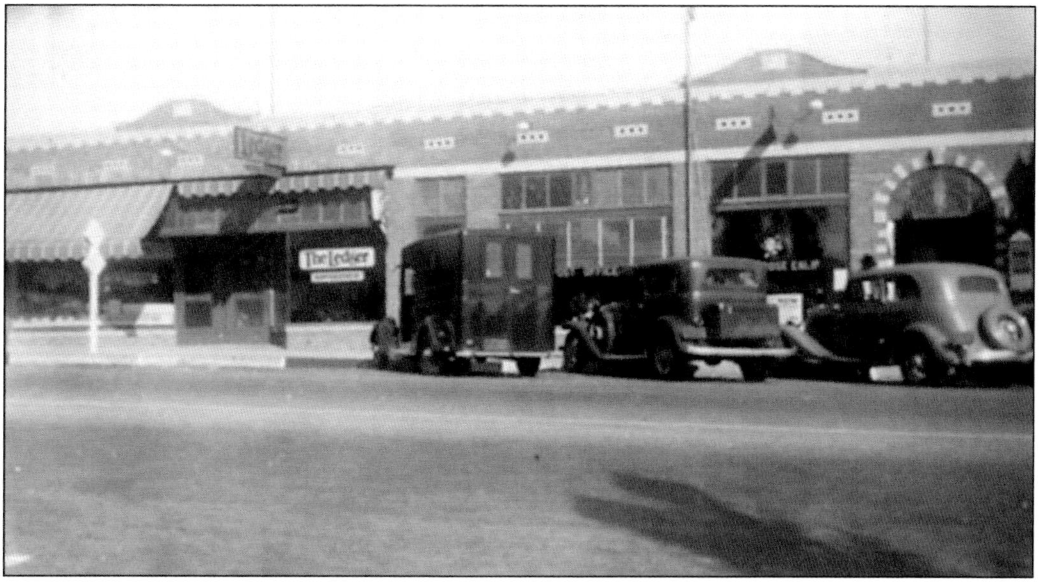

After a time in the Potts Building, the *Crescenta Valley Ledger* moved to this storefront (2307) in the 1930s. The bicycle in the window was a prize in a contest for newspaper delivery boys. The store on the left (2309) would later be home to Once Upon a Time for a while, and to the right was the original Montrose Post Office.

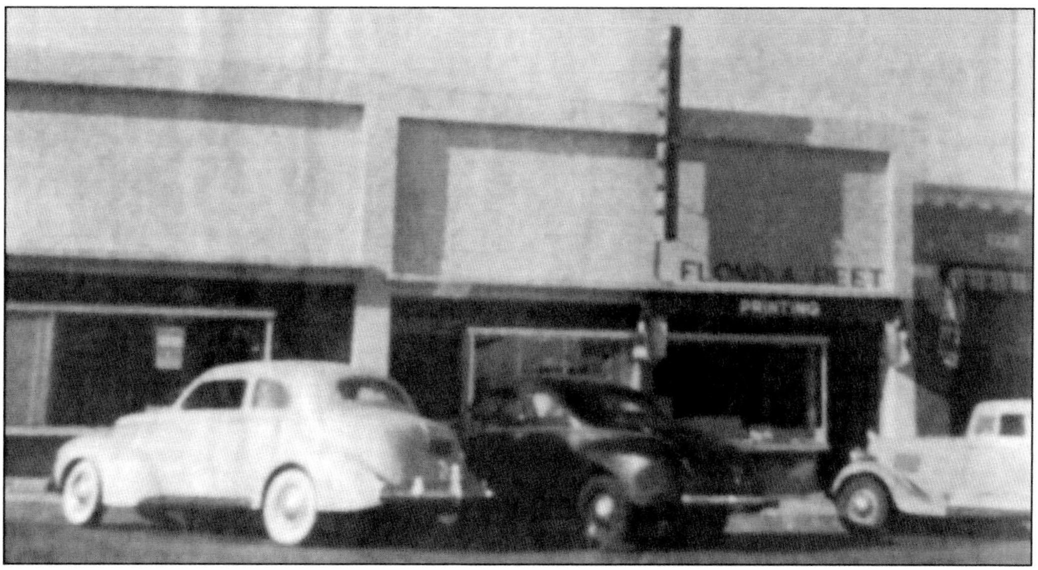

Floyd A. Peet, a former Iowa newsman, established a printing business in Montrose in 1930. During World War II, Peet and his daughter Anita Peet Geyer added stationery and office supplies to the expanding business. They were active members of the community, and Peet Stationers (2311) was a mainstay from 1941 until around 1999. In her will, Geyer bequeathed a large sum of money to both the chamber of commerce and the shopping park (see page 111).

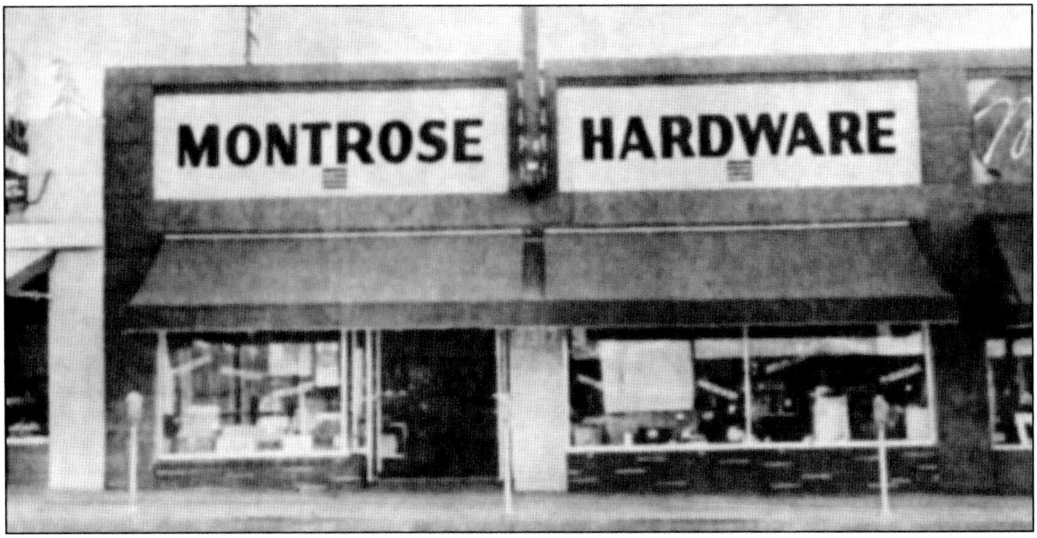

Montrose Hardware (2317) was opened in 1949 by Bill Gardner, who in the 1960s was on the committee that visited Grand Junction and played a role in the transformation of the shopping park. Gardner sold the business in 1972 to Glen Reed, who had lost his Verdugo City store when the Sylmar earthquake destroyed the building. Montrose Hardware sold its last nail in the mid-1980s.

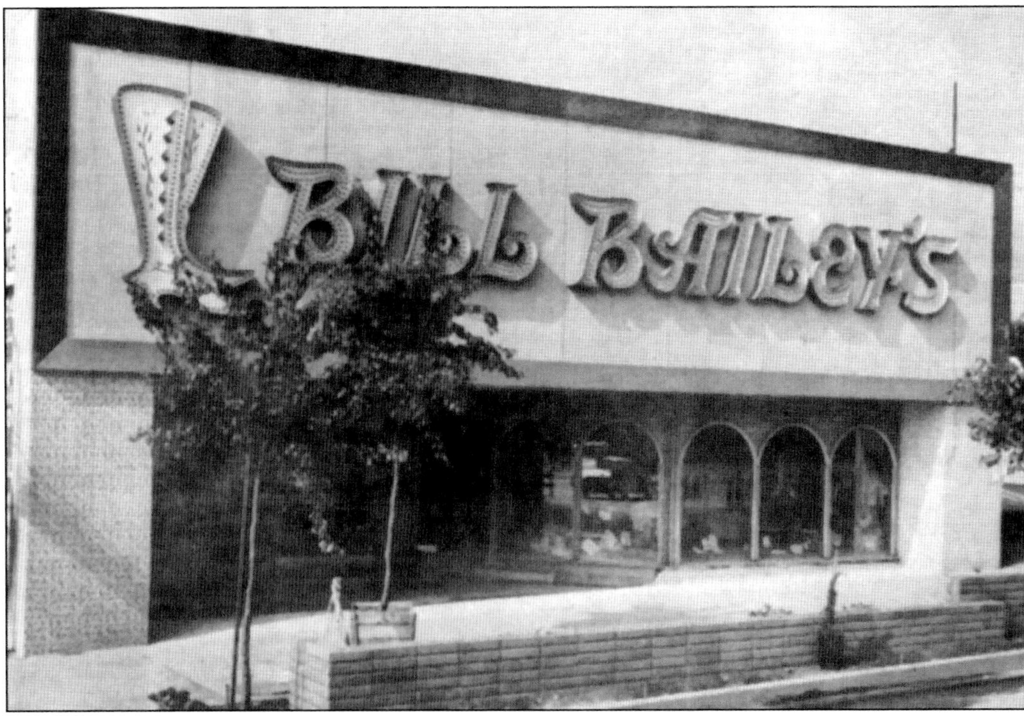

There were two merchants in the area with the name Bill Bailey. One owned the Trade Rite Market in Verdugo City and was a long time civic leader. The other was a women's shoe salesman who had two stores on Honolulu Avenue, the second (shown here) at 2306. Longtime residents remember the shoe on the sign blinking on and off all night. The building was torn down to create a parking lot.

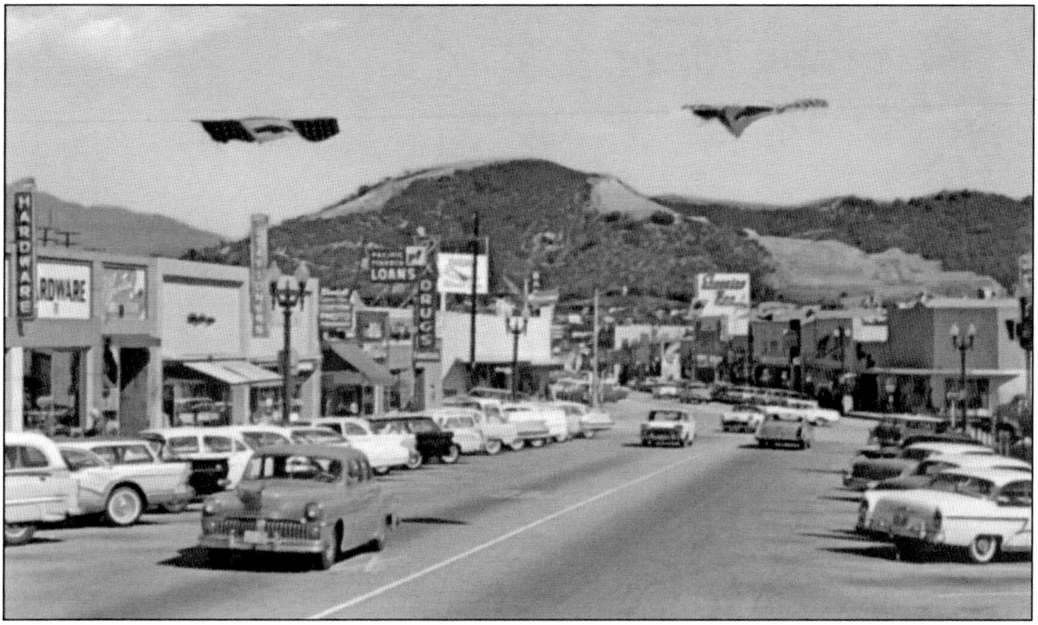

This is the 2300 block of Honolulu Avenue looking east in about 1960, with Montrose Hardware, Peet Stationers, and the other Bill Bailey shoe store visible on the left. The corner pharmacy has already been stuccoed over. Farther down Honolulu Avenue, Shopping Bag has added a west-facing wall to its tower sign. The visual noise from all the signs is striking. (Courtesy of John Newcombe.)

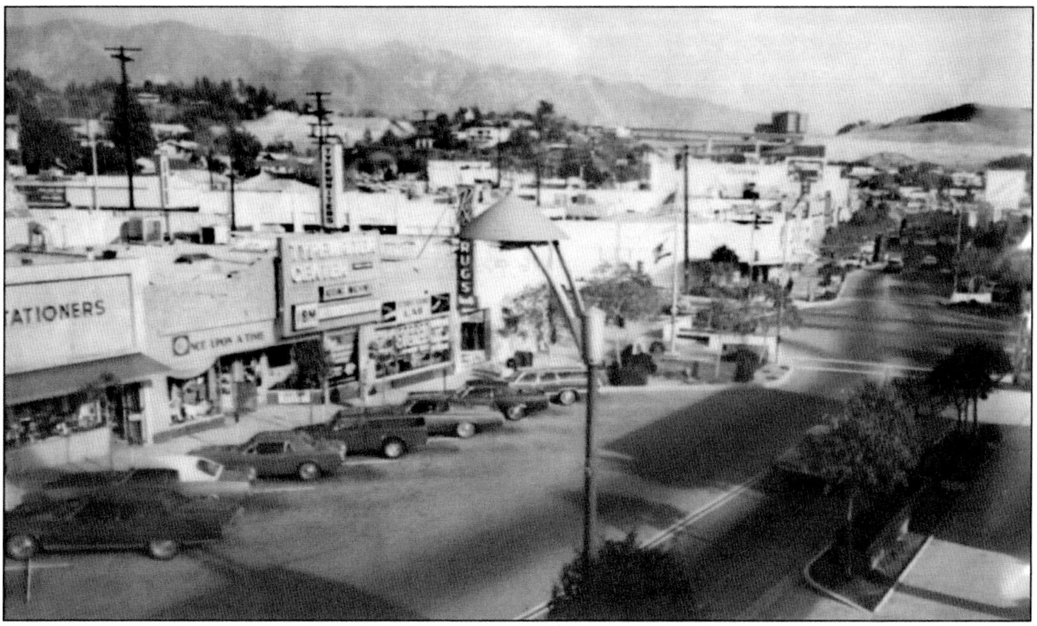

This is a higher-angle view of the same block about 10 years later, after the 1967 renovation of the Montrose Shopping Park. Besides the obvious changes of the trees and the sunhat street lights, some stores have moved: Once Upon a Time is on the left at 2309 and, down Honolulu Avenue, Cozette's has moved into the Shopping Bag building. The 2 and 210 Freeways are under construction in the distance. (Courtesy of Chamber of Commerce.)

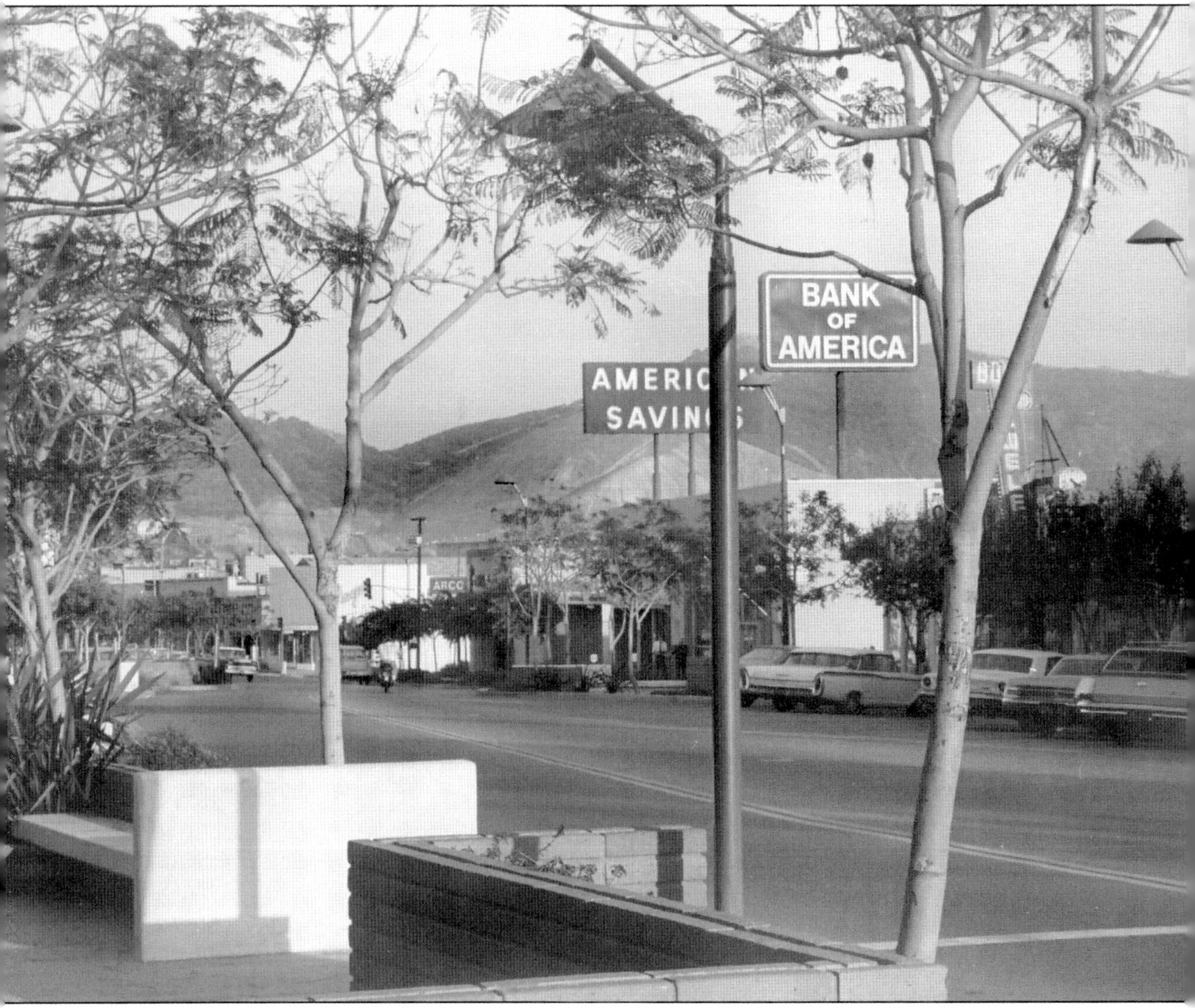

This is a view of the south side of the 2300 block of Honolulu in the early 1970s. Bank of America had moved to this location in 1953. The American Savings building is now occupied by Chase, and Bill Bailey's has since been torn down to become a parking lot. The Arco station at the corner (where Coffee Bean and Quiznos are now) was directly across the street from Faye's (now Starbucks). (Courtesy of Pat Grant.)

The Top Hat bar (2321) featured a spectacular sign on the outside wall, but in spite of its metropolitan image, it served Chinese food. This photograph from 1967 shows the new trees and part of the outdoor bench area for the new shopping park. The Top Hat closed a year or two later, replaced by Avignone's, which is still in business.

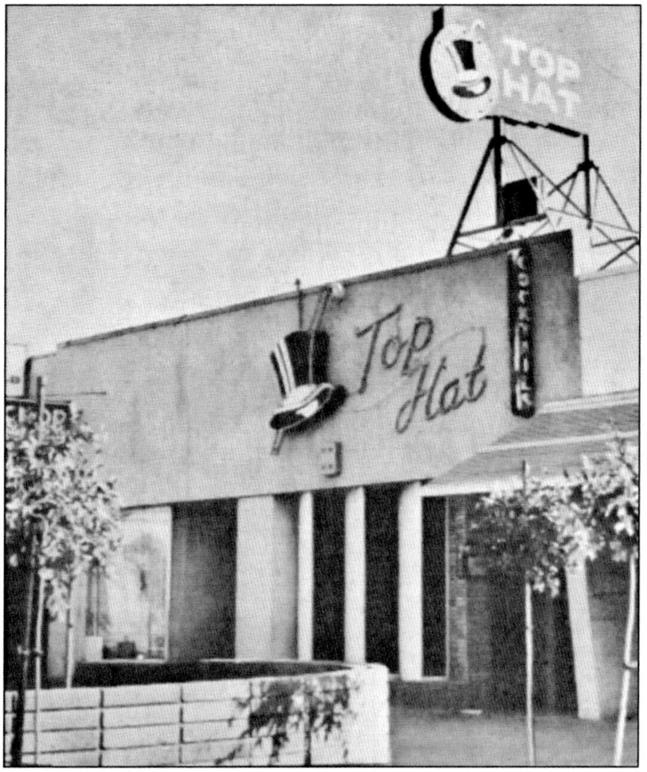

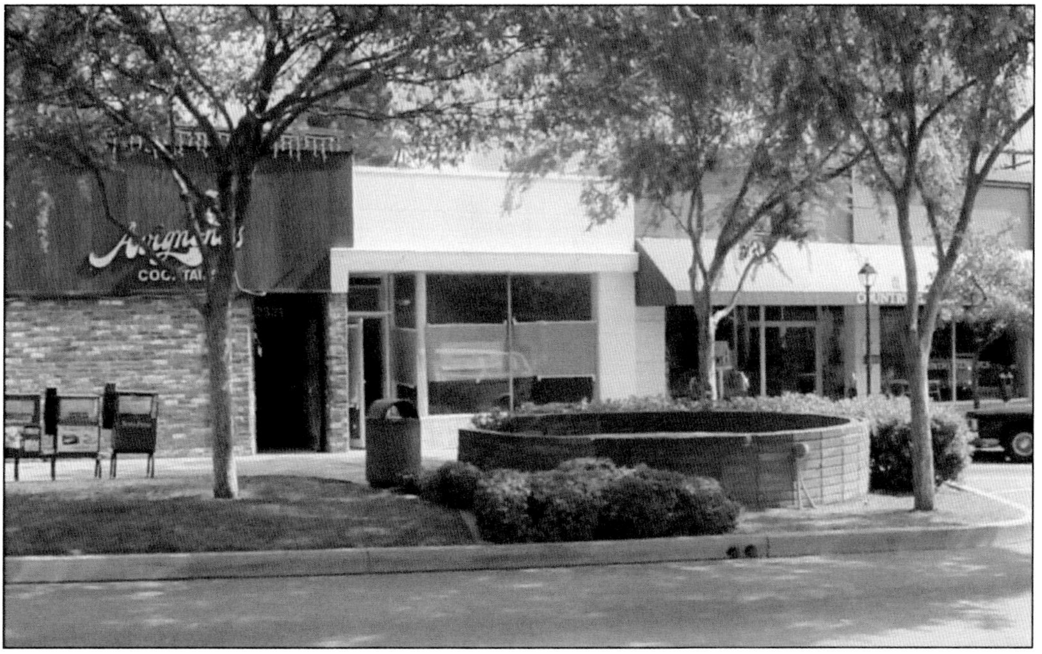

In 2003, Mary Dawson was in the process of opening Revelation TOPS in the space at 2321 1/2, between Avignone's (on the left) and Country Classics, which had moved into the former Montrose Hardware storefront in the 1980s. Country Classics was in business for about 30 years but closed during the economic downturn in 2009. (Courtesy of Mary Dawson.)

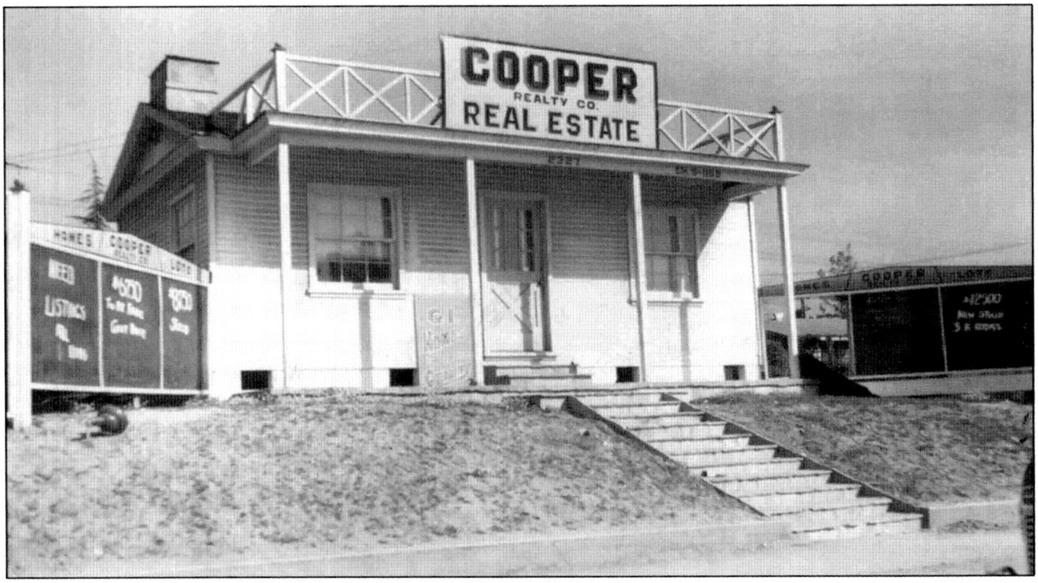

Lee Cooper moved to La Crescenta in the 1940s and made his living on the post–World War II housing boom. He opened his real estate office (2327) in one of the old houses on Honolulu Avenue west of Ocean View Boulevard, next door to the Zwick home. Cooper later moved his business outside the shopping park, and the house was replaced with retail stores.

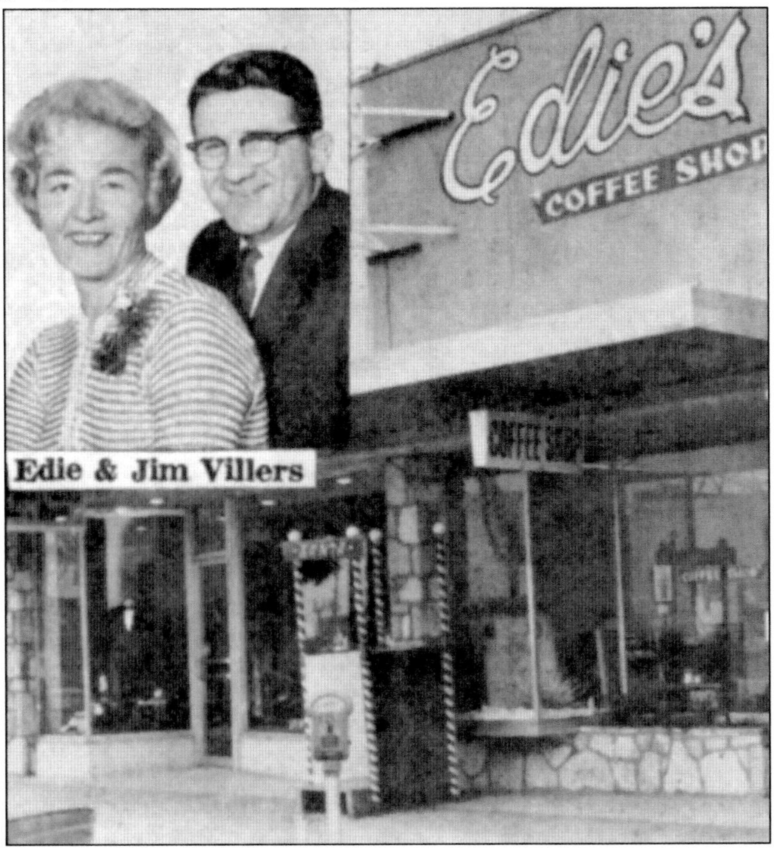

In the rear of Edie's Coffee Shop (at 2272 Honolulu Avenue) was a room with a small table around which local merchants and city employees ate and debated local politics. One of the waitresses, Bertha "Berty" Poole, hung a "Little City Hall" neon sign over the door. Edie moved to 2327, and in 1968, Berty bought Edie's and renamed it City Hall Coffee Shop.

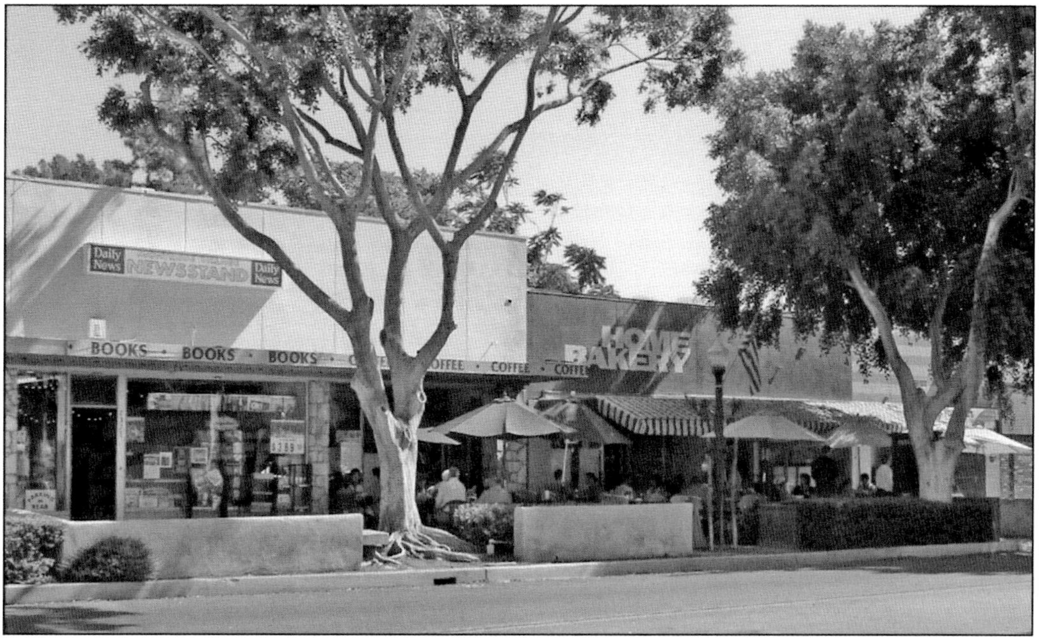

Started by Wilma Morgan and a fixture in the community since 1947, the Montrose Bakery moved to 2325 Honolulu Avenue in 1957. It has changed owners and names a few times since, such as Montrose Bakery and Café, Home Bakery (as seen here in 2007), and Montrose Bakery and Old Town Sandwich Shop. Current owner Henry Baeca bought it in 1988 and cannot remember when or why the name was changed.

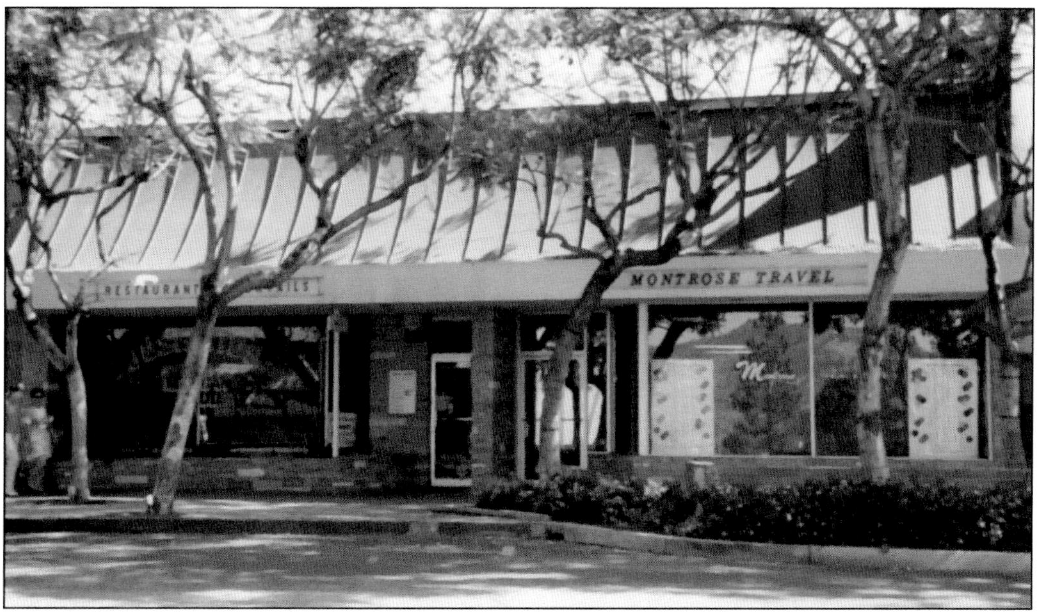

Joselito's (2345) is on the left and Montrose Travel (2343) is on the right in this 1979 photograph. Montrose Travel started in 1956 and stayed relatively small for about 30 years. In the late 1980s, the business started going through the roof, literally, as they added a second story to this building in 1990. Montrose Travel has expanded into several buildings and is now a $140 million business. (Courtesy of Joe McClure.)

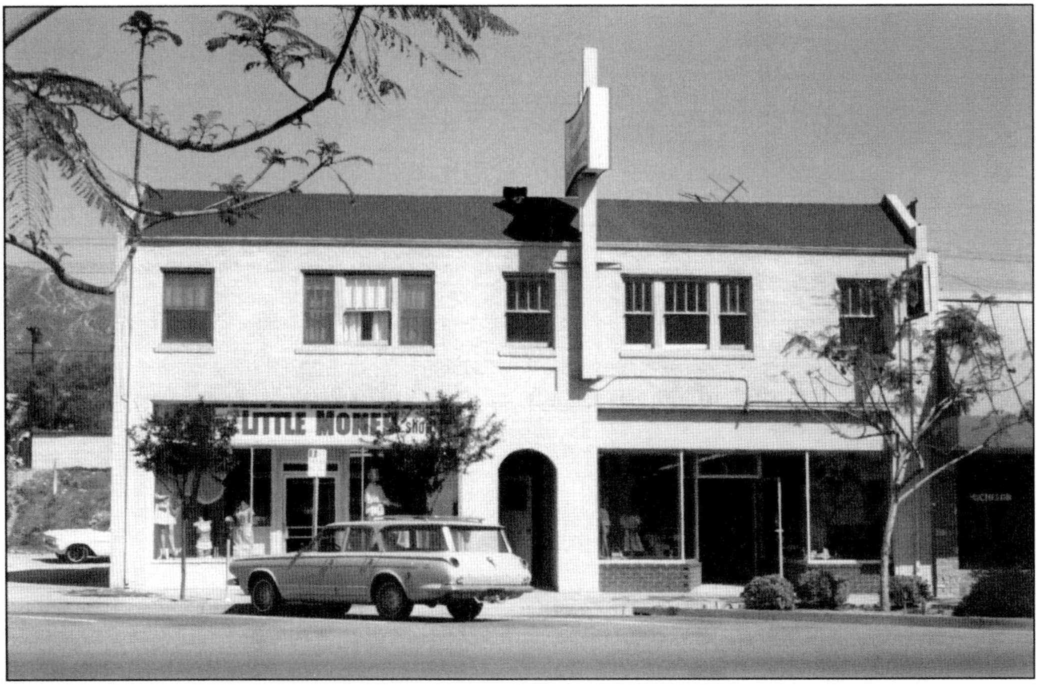

This is another building (2349) that Faye Snow owned. In fact, she lived in the apartment on the upstairs right. She also operated two stores out of the first floor: Faye's Fashionette (on the right), which specialized in clothes for teenage girls, and the Little Money store, which sold cheaper clothes than her other high-end stores. The building was condemned after the Sylmar earthquake, so Faye moved into one of her other buildings, tore down 2349, and replaced it with the large two-story women's department store below, which opened on Thursday, October 31, 1974. The store had 14,000 square feet of retail space and 22 employees. Montrose Travel bought the building in 1999. (Courtesy of Pat Grant.)

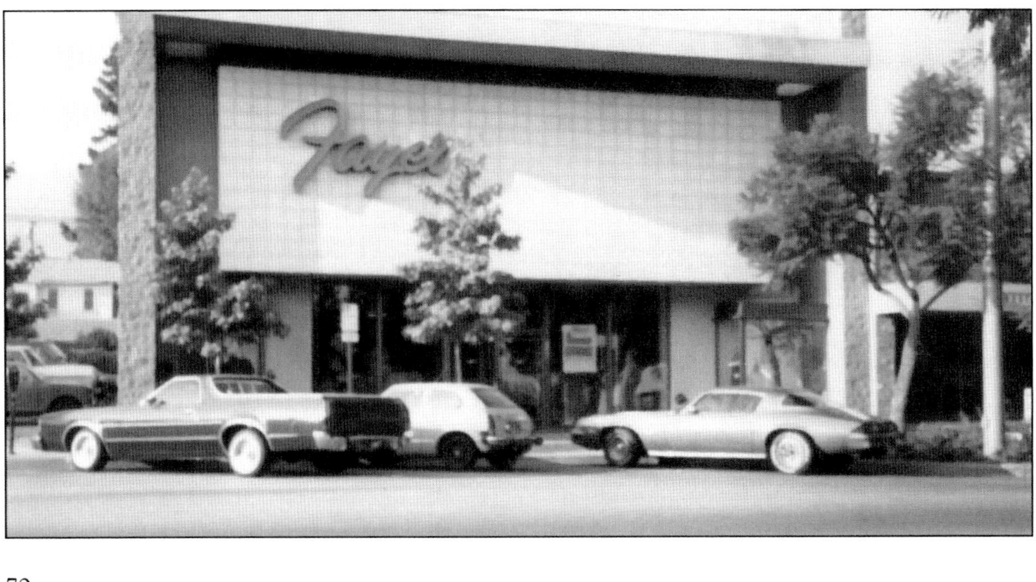

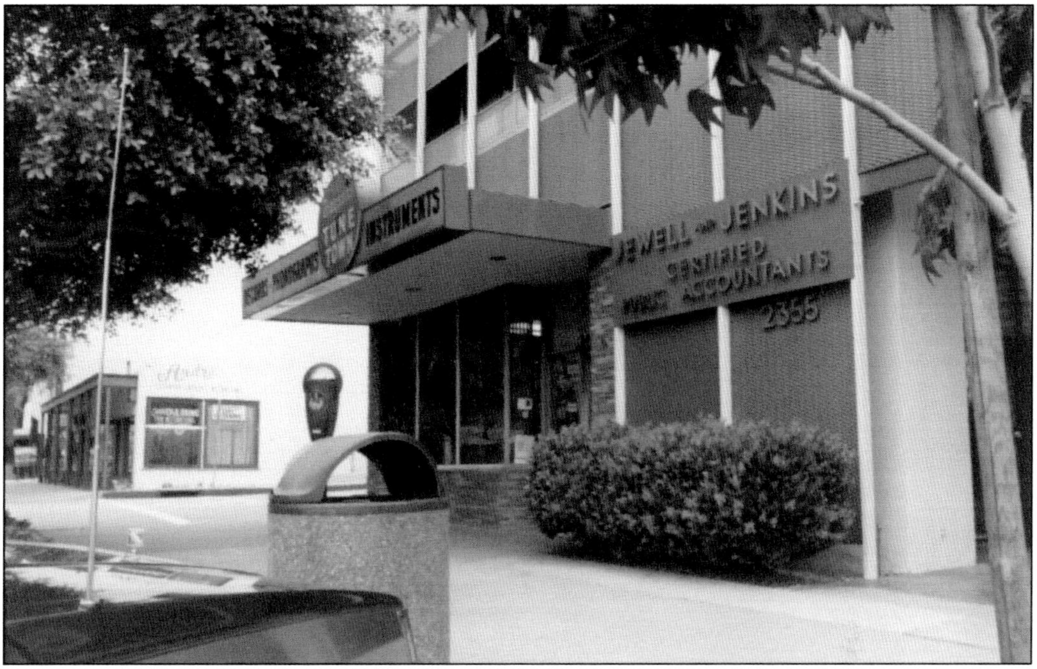

Val Micheli had been a successful touring musician, playing saxophone and clarinet, using the stage name Val Grayson. When he and his wife, Adeline, settled down in La Crescenta in 1953, they opened Grayson's Tune Town at 2312, selling records. In 1960, they moved to the building in the top photograph (2357) and expanded their merchandise to include phonographs, car stereos, and some musical instruments. In 1985, the Graysons built the two-story building at their current location at 2415 Honolulu Avenue (below). Their business has evolved dramatically from selling only records. Recently, their primary business has been selling guitars and musical instruments for local high school bands, along with offering music lessons. (Courtesy of Ken Grayson.)

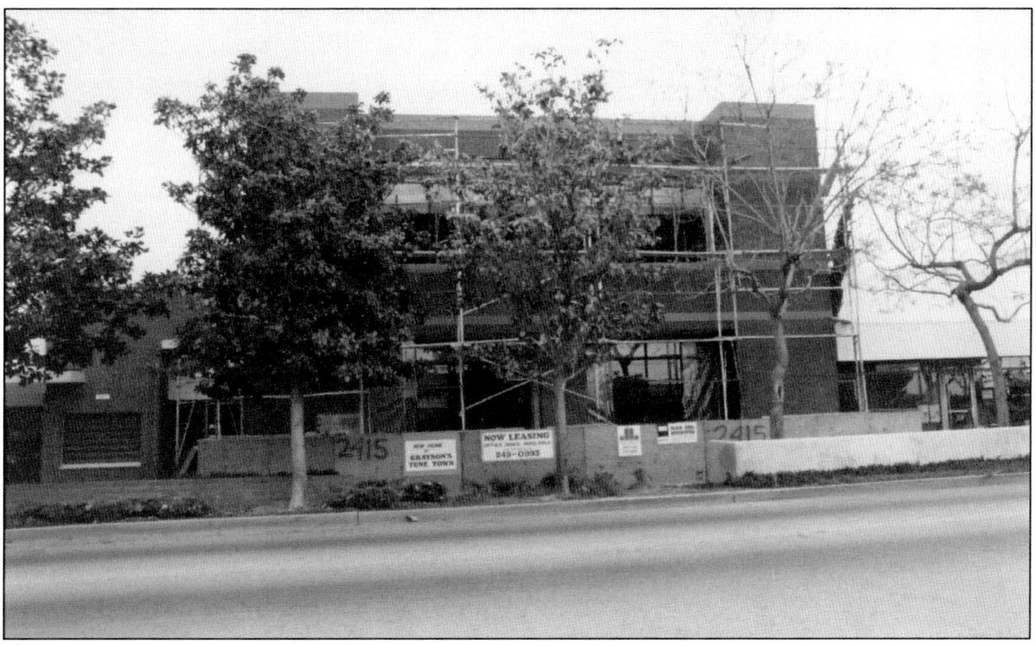

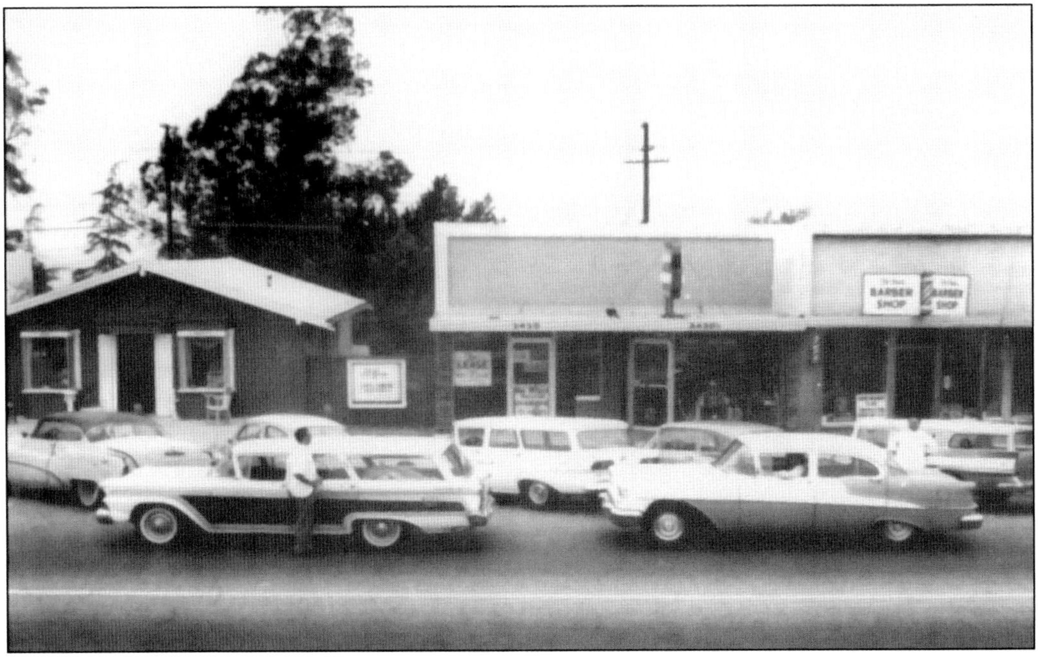

On the south side of Honolulu Avenue, the 2400 block still had one of the original houses (2418) being used as Pat Jones Furniture in the late 1950s and early 1960s. Today, the building in the center is home to The Hair Works (2420) and The Town Barber building (2422) is home to Pattye's Closet.

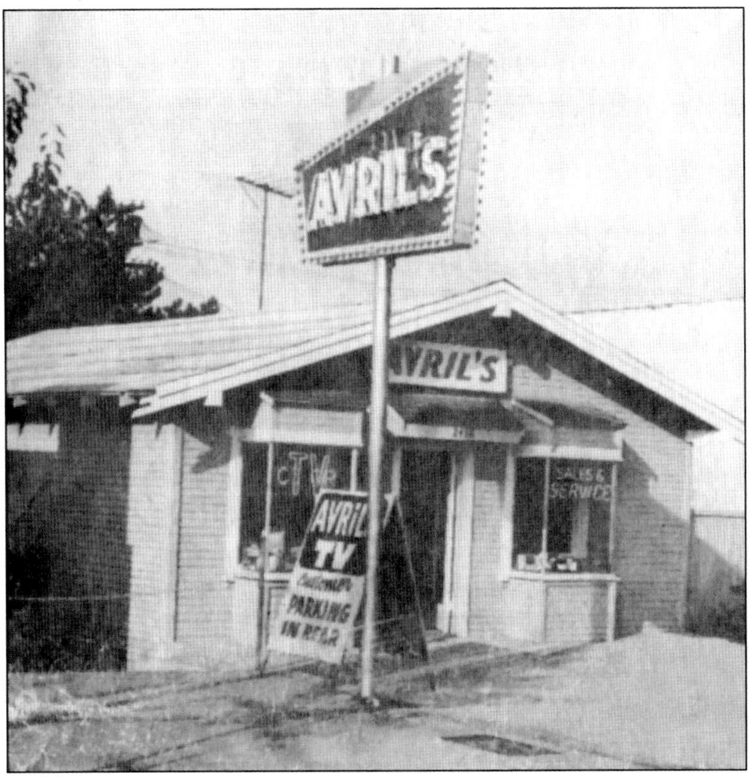

Electricians Norm and Walt Avril came to Montrose in 1934 to help residents rebuild after the great flood and never left. They bought a small appliance repair shop in 1945 and moved the store up and down Honolulu Avenue five times. This is the same house in the above photograph, at 2418. The house was torn down in the early 1970s and Avril's moved again but went out of business in 1992.

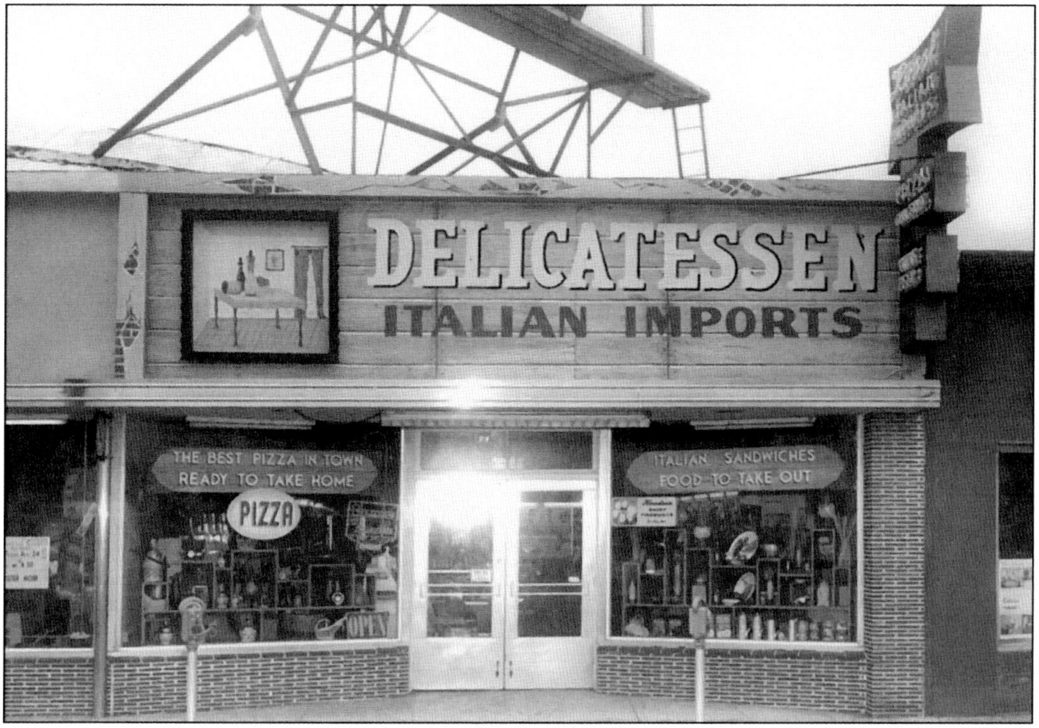

This was Rossi's Delicatessen and Italian Imports (2478) in 1963. The Rossis had come to California from the East Coast with their good friends the Dundees (owners of Kona Kai and Scotch Mist Restaurants) and the LoGuercios (owners of Bert's Market). All of them established successful businesses, with the Rossi family also owning the popular Three Oaks Restaurant. Several Italian restaurants have followed in this space, including the current one, Giuseppe's Pizzeria.

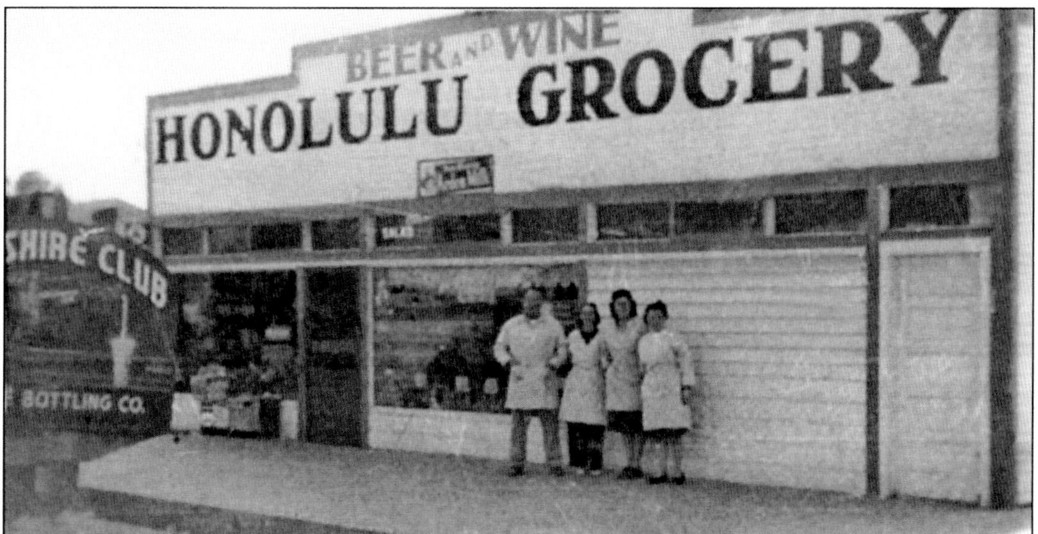

Honolulu Grocery was located on the south side of Honolulu where Orangedale Avenues dead-ends into it. The store had wine casks from which customers could fill their own bottles. Old-timers say that the smell of vino wafted out to the sidewalk. The property later became a car dealership and a parking lot and is now a Trader Joe's.

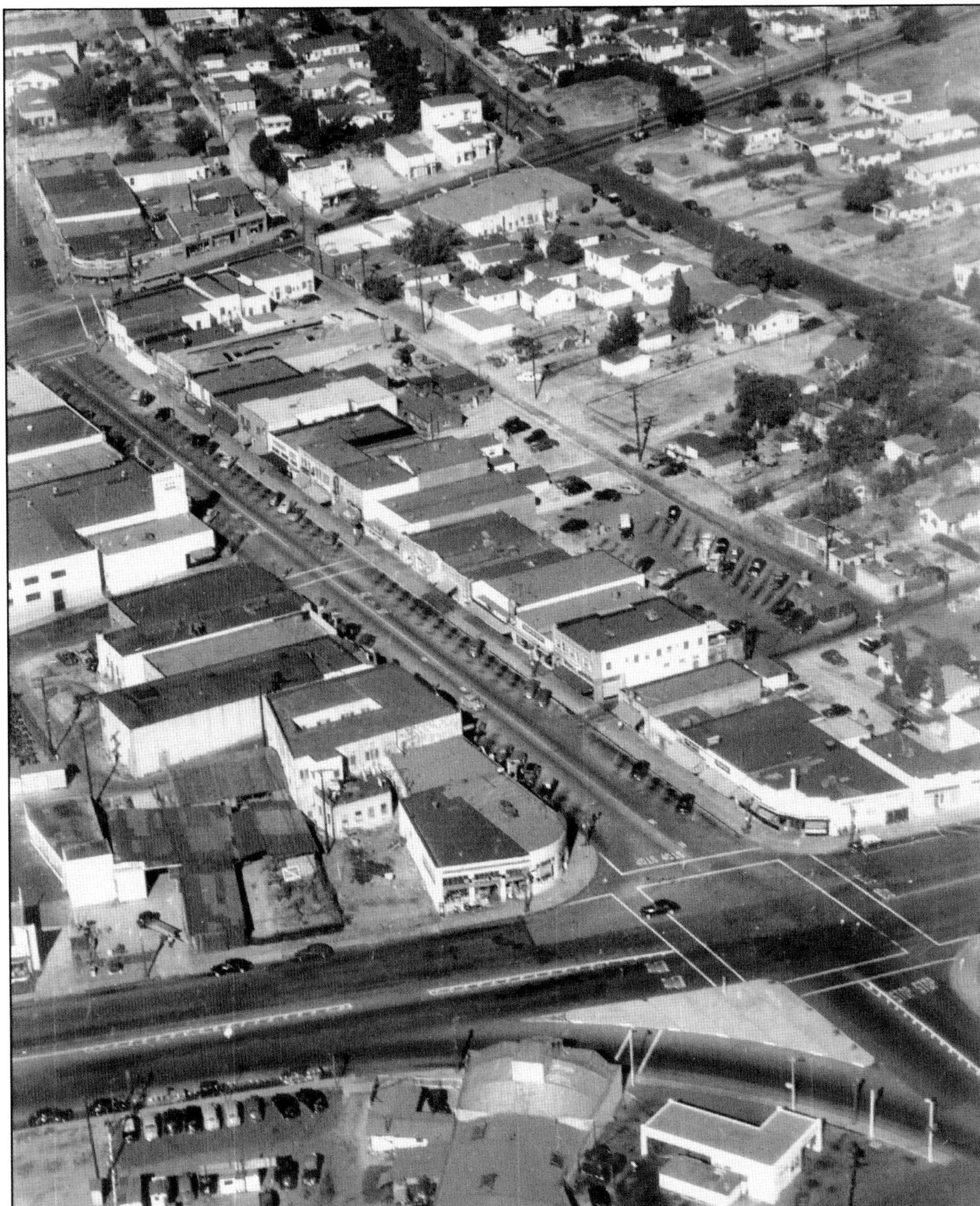

These aerial photographs from the early 1950s offer an interesting angle on many of the historical items discussed elsewhere in this book. Starting from the bottom is the intersection of the streets with four names. The spire is still on the pharmacy, which has not yet been combined with the building on the north. The atrium of the Montrose Hotel is clearly visible. Thompson Brothers Cleaners has moved behind the Reinhard Building. The Shopping Bag tower sign still faces only east. The trees on the east side of Ocean View Boulevard have been removed.

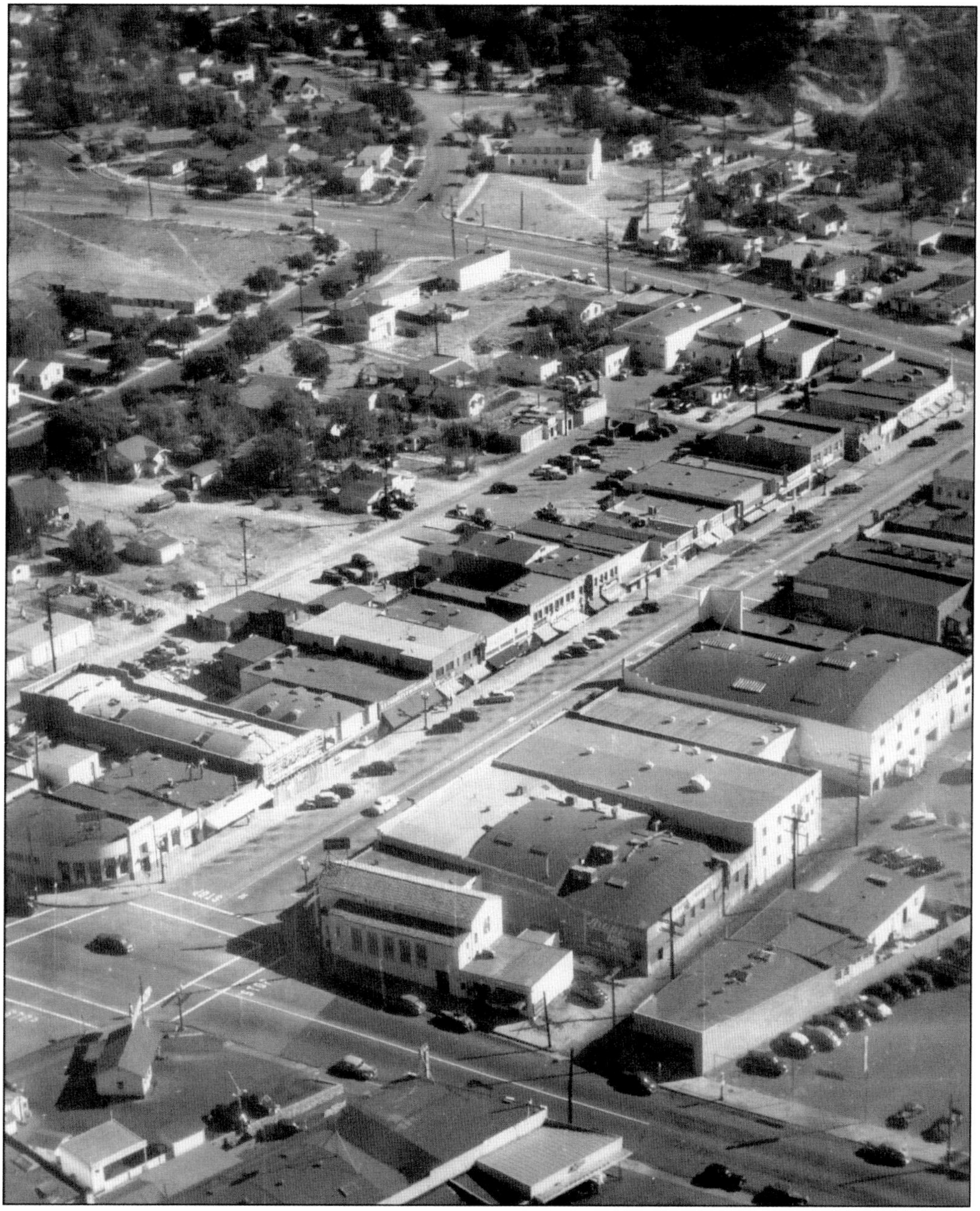

Looking northeast, the Richfield gas station is visible at the southwest corner of Honolulu Avenue and Ocean View Boulevard. The Bank of America is still in the Crescenta-Cañada Bank building, which means this was taken before 1952. The back side of the Shopping Bag tower sign is clearly visible. The old Montrose lamp posts are still standing. One of the necessary components of the shopping park renovation was buying the houses on Florencita Drive just behind the stores on Honolulu Avenue; the houses and lots (that are now parking lots) are clearly visible in this photograph.

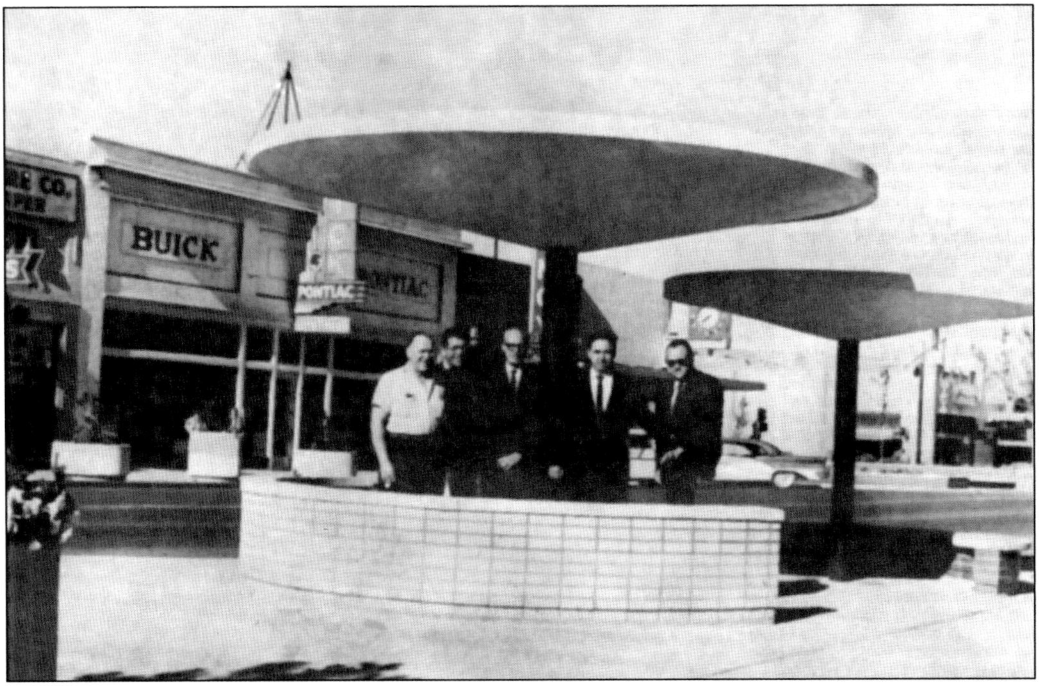

In the late 1950s, business in Montrose was suffering, the same as it was in business districts across the country, due to the popularity of suburban shopping malls. Locals discussed the idea of closing Honolulu Avenue to car traffic. Instead, Hugo Ebmeyer, Bob Cooke, Cliff Banks, Tom Jeffers Jr., and Don Carpenter (pictured from left to right) and others visited Grand Junction, Colorado, to see what that city had tried in an effort to turn its fortunes.

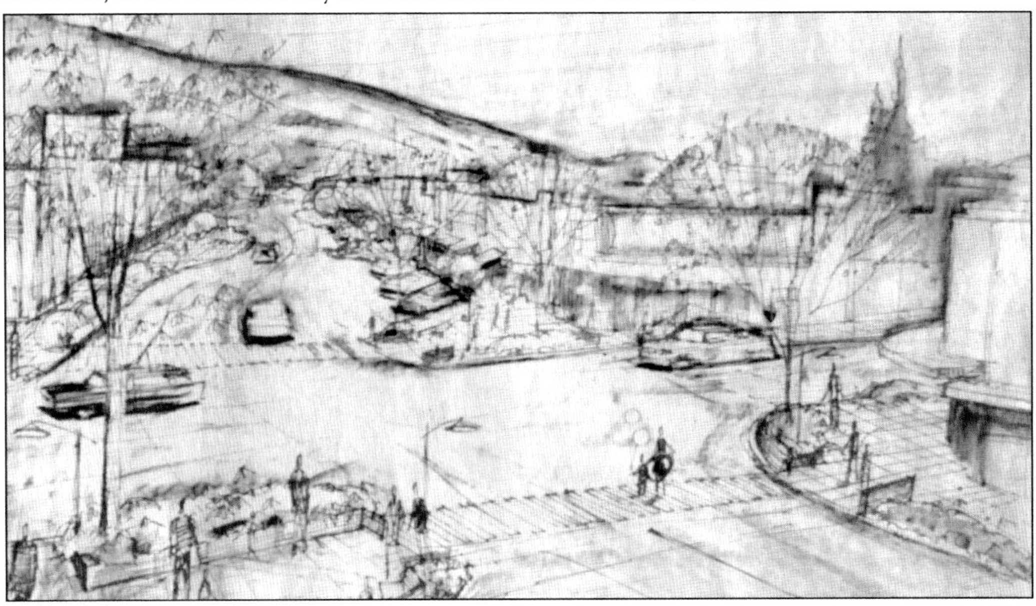

This is one of the sketches that Jack Simison made as the concept for the new shopping park. This is looking west, in front of the intersection of Honolulu Avenue and Ocean View Boulevard. The final design did not match this exactly, but it came close, and the trees and park-like setting are what transformed Montrose into the relaxing place it is to shop and stroll, even 40 years later.

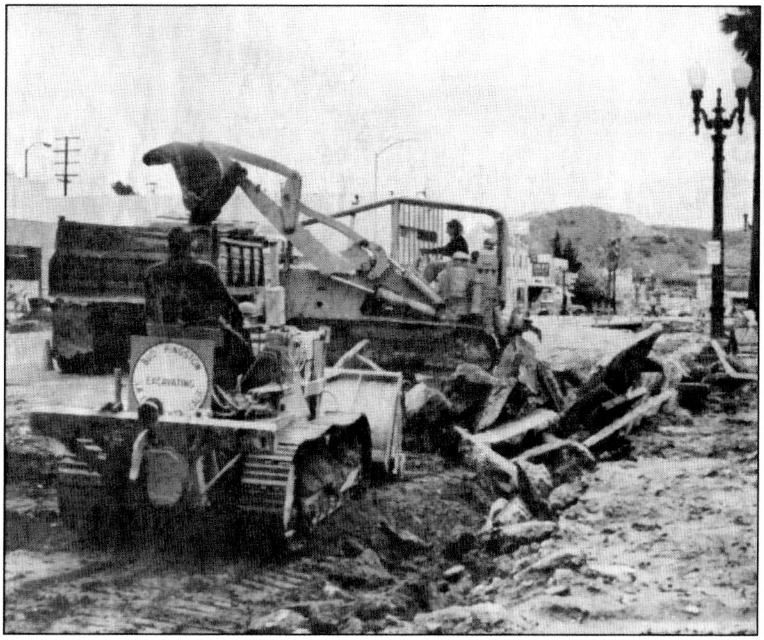

The renovation of the shopping park was approved at the end of January 1967 and demolition started in March at the west end. Rains delayed the progress, which forced merchants in the 2300 block to deal with the muddy mess for months. In the top photograph, crews are breaking up the sidewalk and curbing on the south side of Honolulu Avenue, just west of Wickham Way, with Grayson's Tune Town and Faye's Fashionette visible in the background across the street. (The old streetlamp at this location had not been replaced in the 1950s.) In late May, aboveground construction finally began; below, the forms are installed and concrete is being poured in about the same area as the top photograph. Seeing how far this is cutting into Honolulu Avenue gives one an appreciation for how daring this concept was.

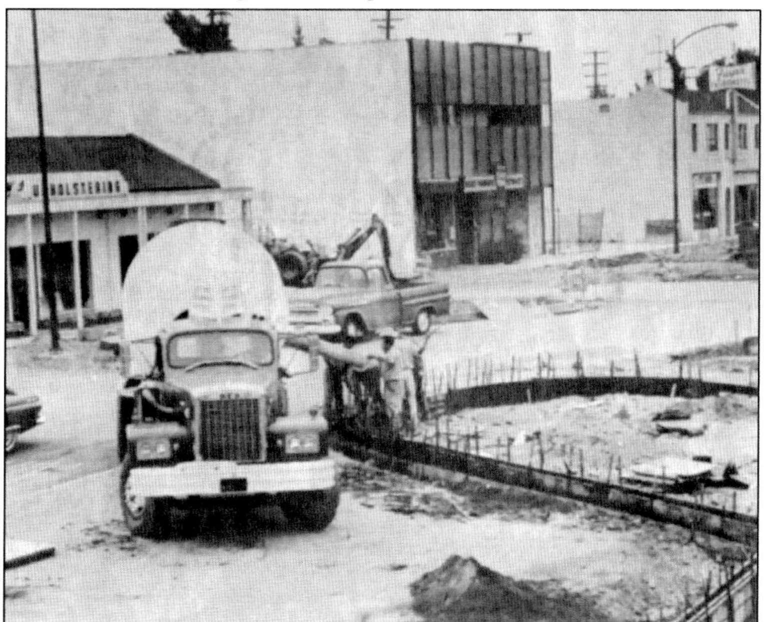

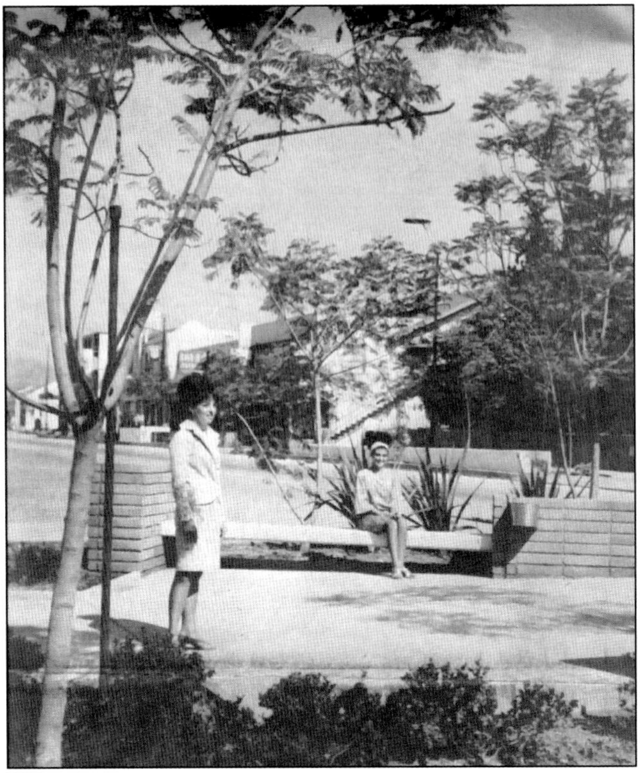

The renovated Montrose Shopping Park was dedicated on Friday, September 1, 1967. To promote it, the *Ledger* put out a special edition featuring interviews with many merchants and photographs of the construction. They included photographs of women and children resting on the new benches. Here, Cynthia Barkley (left) and Sally Badalamenti relax in the 2300 block; behind them are the Bar-B-Q Roundup, Faye's Fashionette, and Grayson's Tune Town.

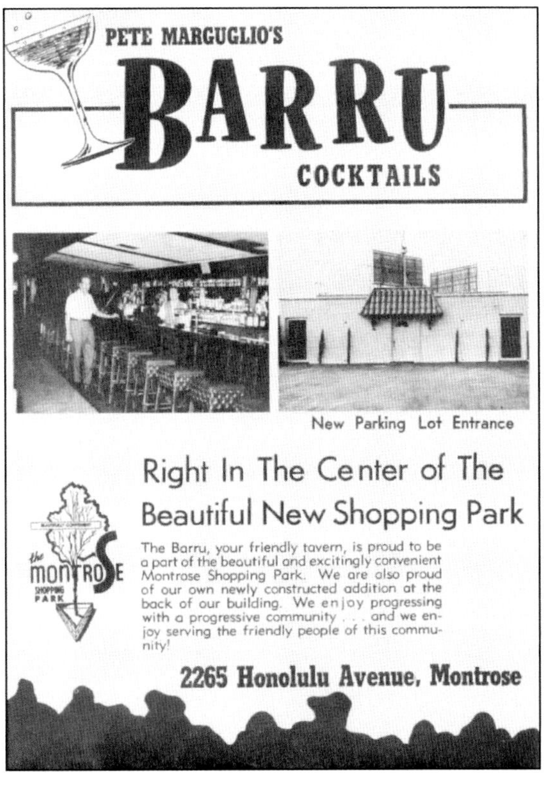

One of the main objections to the redesign of the shopping park was the lost parking spaces. The city of Glendale bought the houses behind the shopping park and replaced them with parking lots, but most stores did not have rear entrances, so the shop owners had to spend a considerable amount of time and money to build them. In 1967, The Barru was so proud of its new rear entrance that it featured it in advertising.

Three

PETALS AND LEAVES
THE SURROUNDING AREA

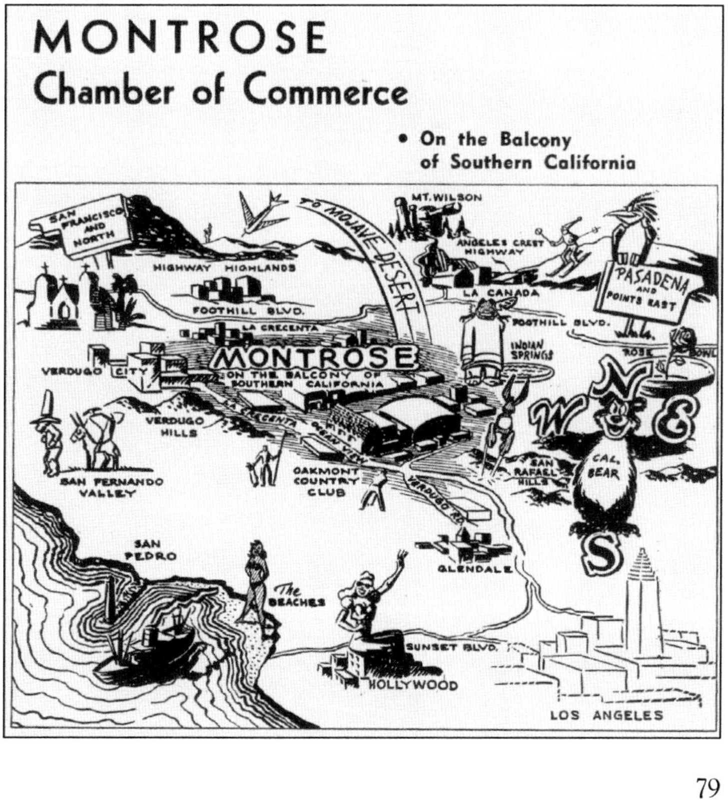

This Montrose Chamber of Commerce directory cover from 1955 shows Montrose not just "on the balcony of Southern California" but pretty much at the center of it. Even Verdugo City and Highway Highlands seem to have skyscrapers. This chapter takes a look at a few places of interest that lie around the fringes of the shopping park. (Courtesy of the Montrose Chamber of Commerce.)

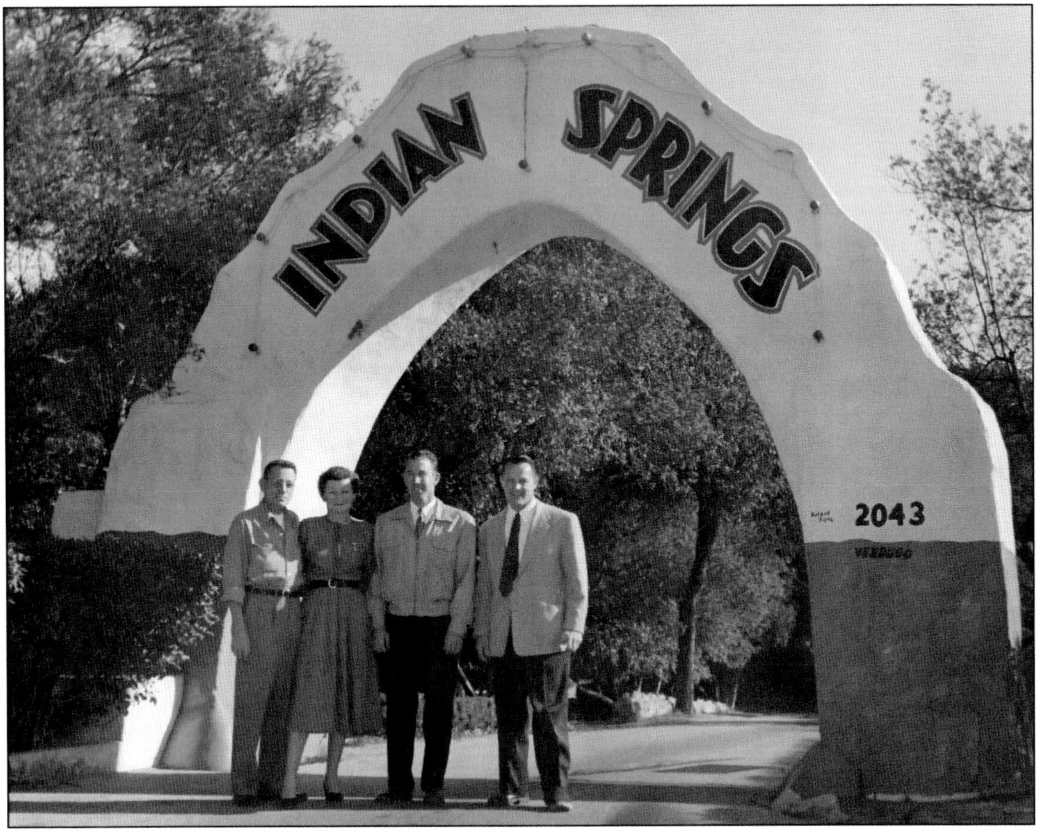

When talking about "old Montrose" with Baby Boomers who grew up in the area, nothing brings back fonder memories than Indian Springs, a swimming pool and recreational park in a shaded glen below Verdugo Boulevard, just east of the shopping park. Standing under the Indian Springs arch in the late 1940s are Mr. and Mrs. Monte Friend, Bill Reinhard, and Lyle Draves. (Courtesy of Lyle Draves.)

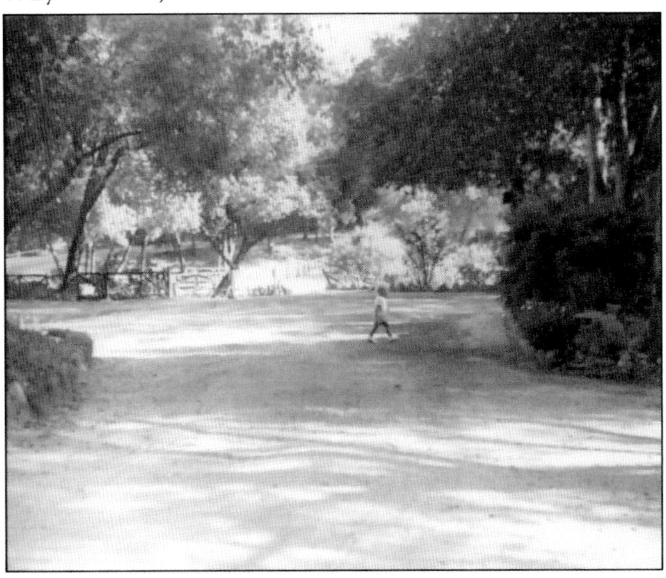

For thousands of years, this oak-filled canyon was possibly the only spot in the valley that had close to year-round water. Tongva Indians lived here at least part-time until chased out by Spanish settlers in the late 1700s. In the 1920s, local resident (and part Blackfoot Indian) Charles Bowden had an idea to turn the glen into something special. (Courtesy of Lyle Draves.)

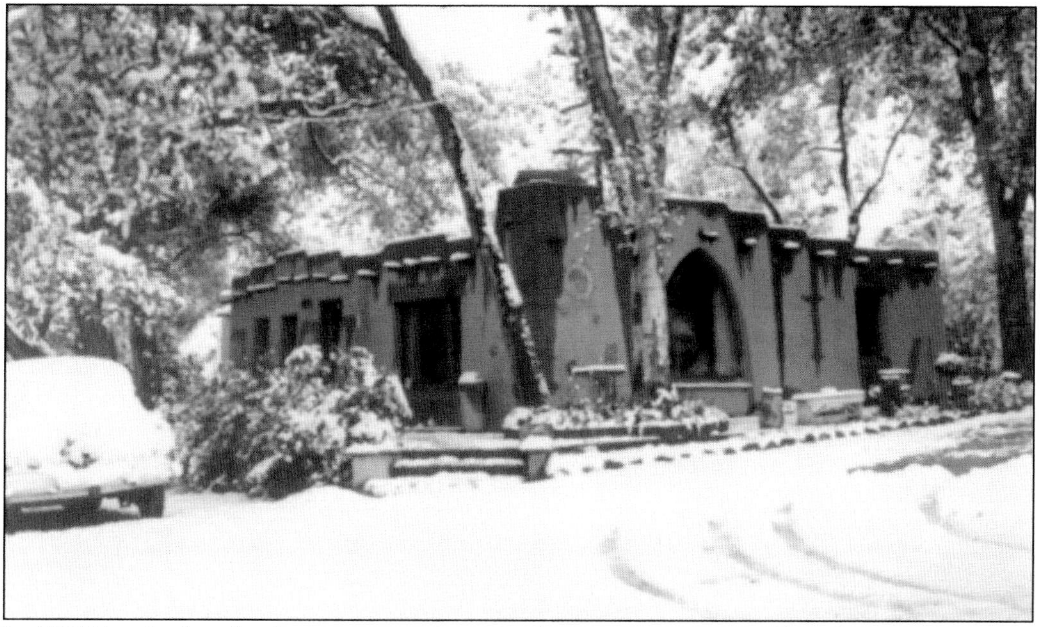

In 1927, Bowden bought the property and on March 16, 1928, announced his plans in a front-page story in the *Crescenta Valley Ledger*. He said his crew was already transforming the grounds into "a place of beauty, rest, and recreation." He named it Indian Springs and planned to preserve Native American customs, even building a new home (shown here) using "real Indian architecture." (Courtesy of Kathryn Halford.)

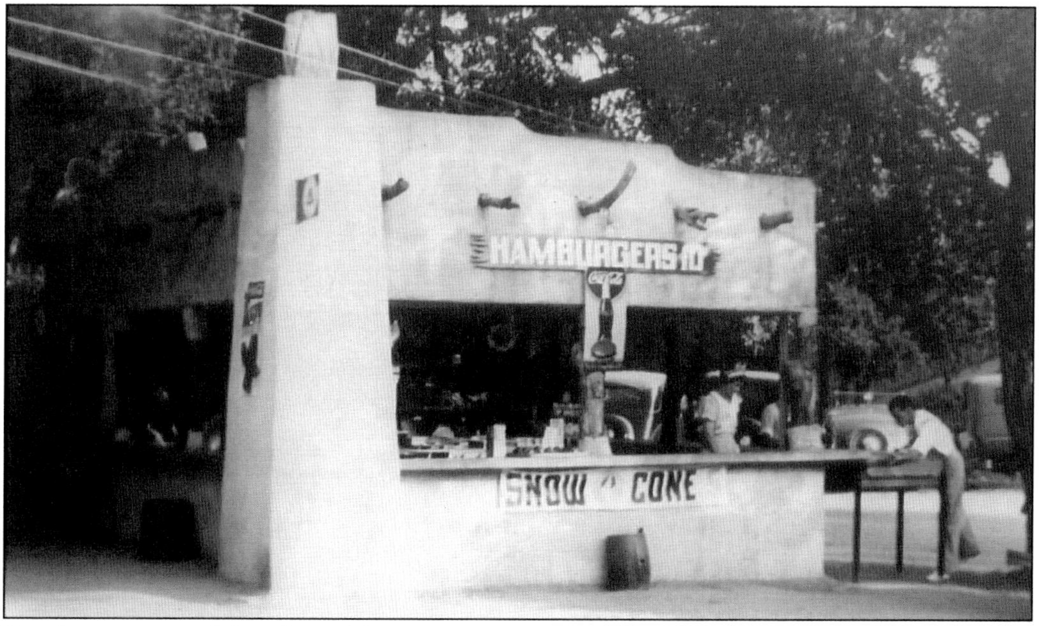

Bowden announced that the park's major attraction would be a huge swimming pool. In addition, he promised "tennis courts, basketball courts, open-air fireplaces and all the other features to make up the ideal recreational park. Rippling brooks will meander through the grounds, the source of the water supply being two natural springs which are located on the property." He never built the courts, but this is the "real Indian architecture" hamburger stand. (Courtesy of Lyle Draves.)

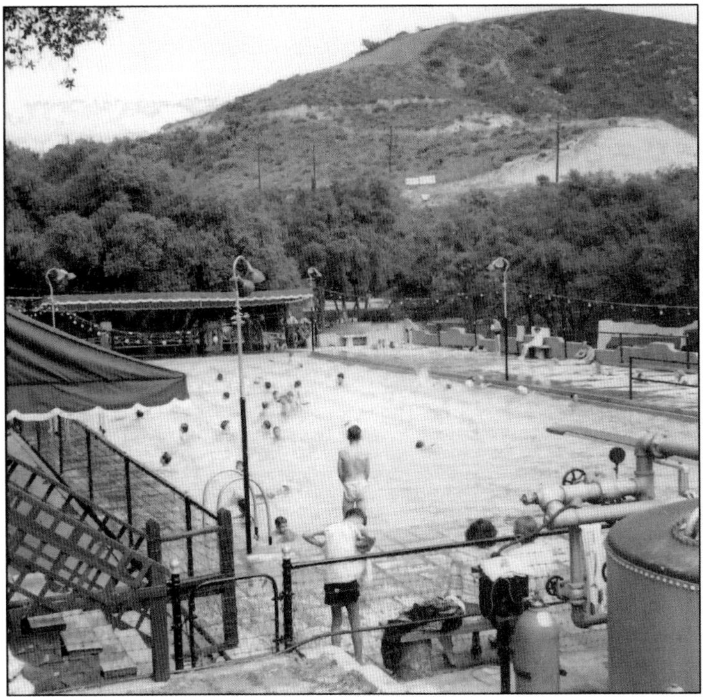

Indian Springs opened on May 18, 1928, with a crowd estimated to be as high as 2,000. Bowden had promised visitors, "You will be thrilled from the moment you enter through the magnificent archway and down the winding road to the Pueblo Indian Village." He put on a tremendous show with a glee club, orchestra, Spanish troubadours, and dancers, and a water show in the pool. (Courtesy of Lyle Draves.)

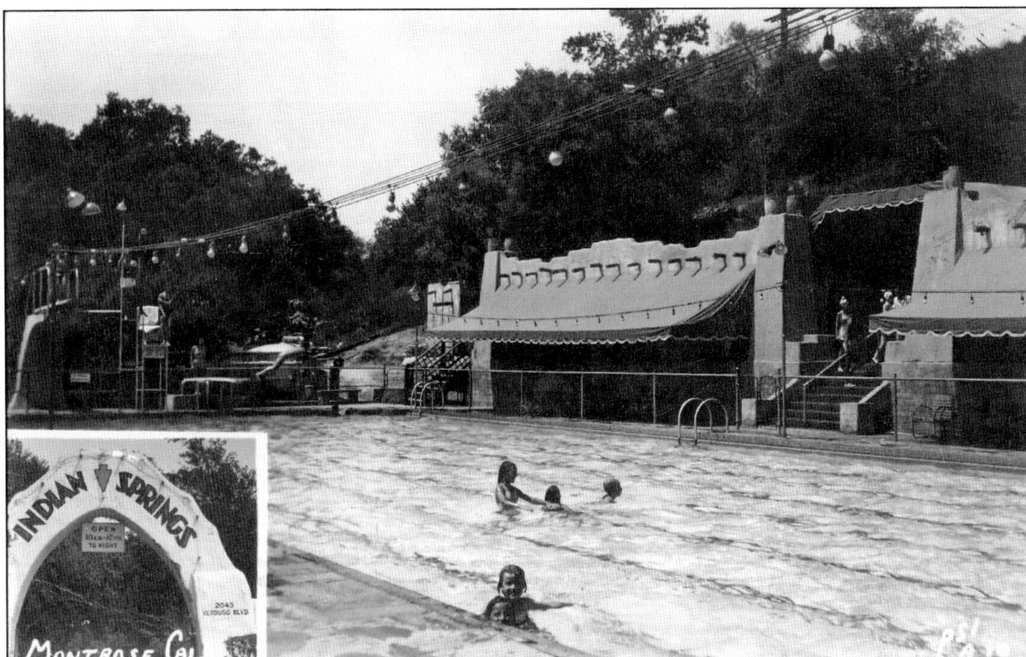

For decades, Indian Springs was the center of recreation for residents of the valley. Diving coach Lyle Draves took over the pool operations in the 1940s and coached his future wife, Vicki Manalo, into two gold medals at the 1948 Olympics in London. In 1951, they moved into the Bowman house on the grounds, and Vicki taught diving while raising four sons. (Courtesy of Pat Robinson.)

People came to Indian Springs for reasons other than just swimming. The picnic areas in the wooded glen were as peaceful as Bowman promised. Horse riding groups would ride through here. Meeting rooms on the grounds were in demand by a variety of different groups. There was even a dance floor, and locals remember music rising from the canyon every Saturday night. (Courtesy of John Newcombe.)

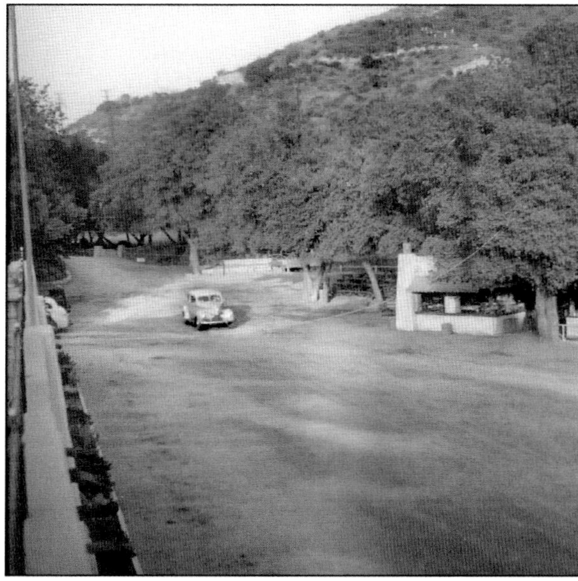

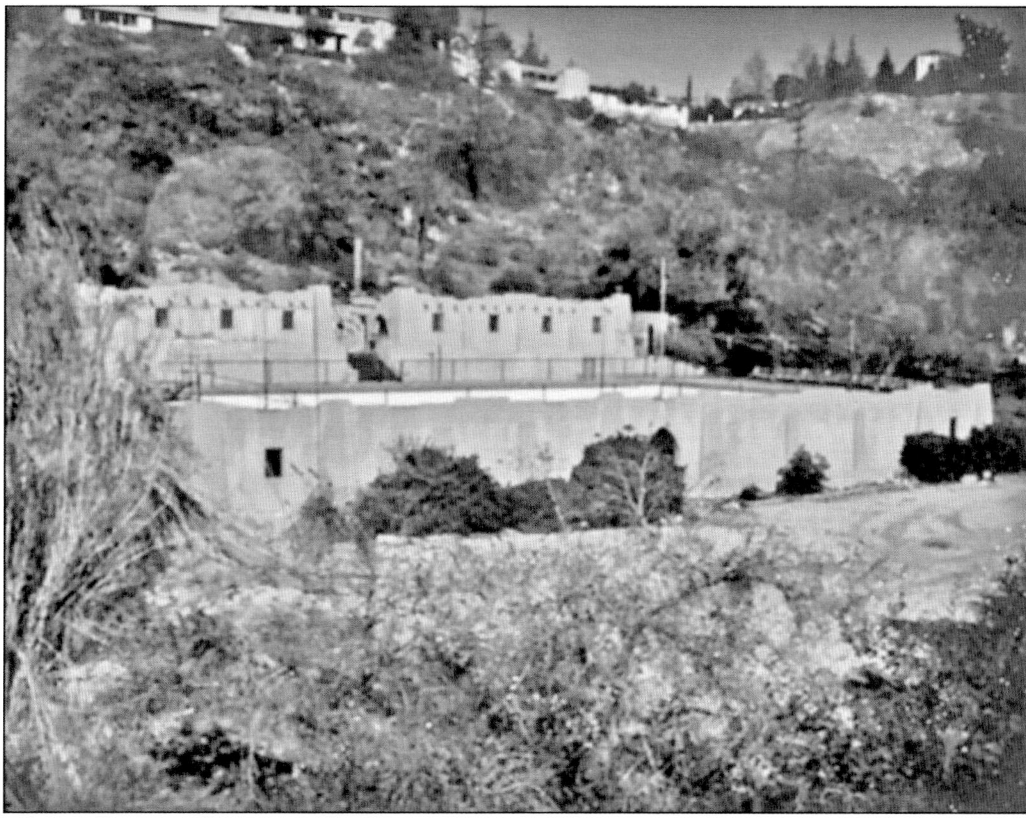

Monte Friend had bought the resort from Bowman sometime in the 1940s and hired Draves and Bill Reinhard to run it. In the early 1960s, J. Morgan Greene of La Cañada bought the property from the Friend estate and in 1966 closed Indian Springs, tore down the pool (seen here near the end), cut down the trees, and filled in the entire canyon with dirt from Greene's nearby Verdugo Hills Hospital construction. (Courtesy of Floyd Farrar.)

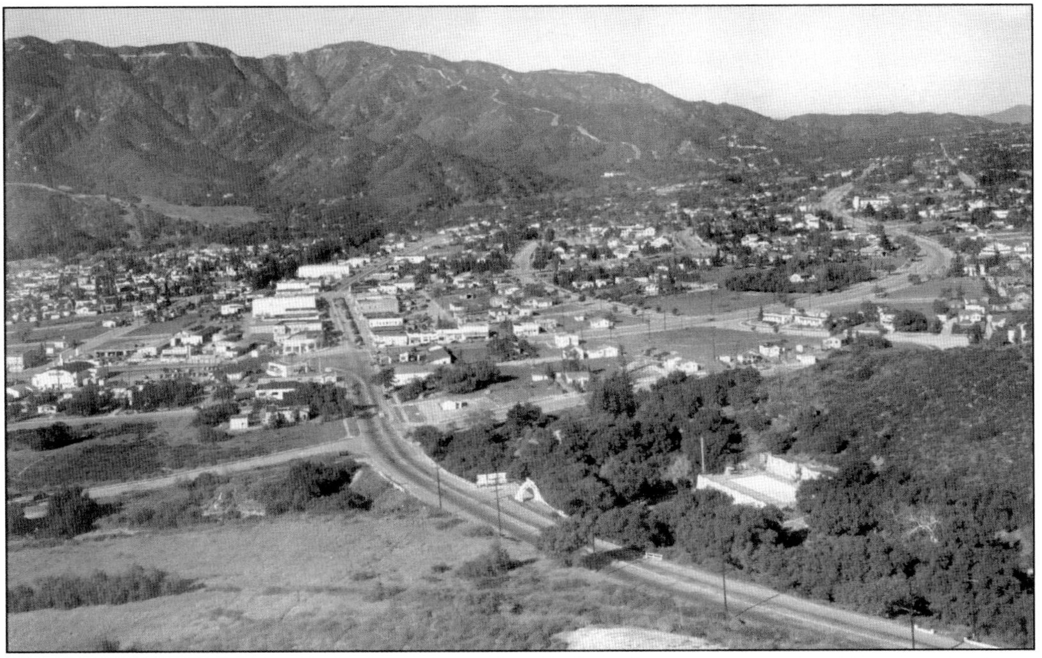

This photograph from the 1930s shows how close Indian Springs was to the Montrose business district. It is clear what attracted Bowman to this glen of oak trees and why he found it peaceful. What is not clear is how this treed canyon was allowed to be destroyed. Or course, that is looking at it in 2012. At the time, it was probably not an issue, perhaps even considered "progress."

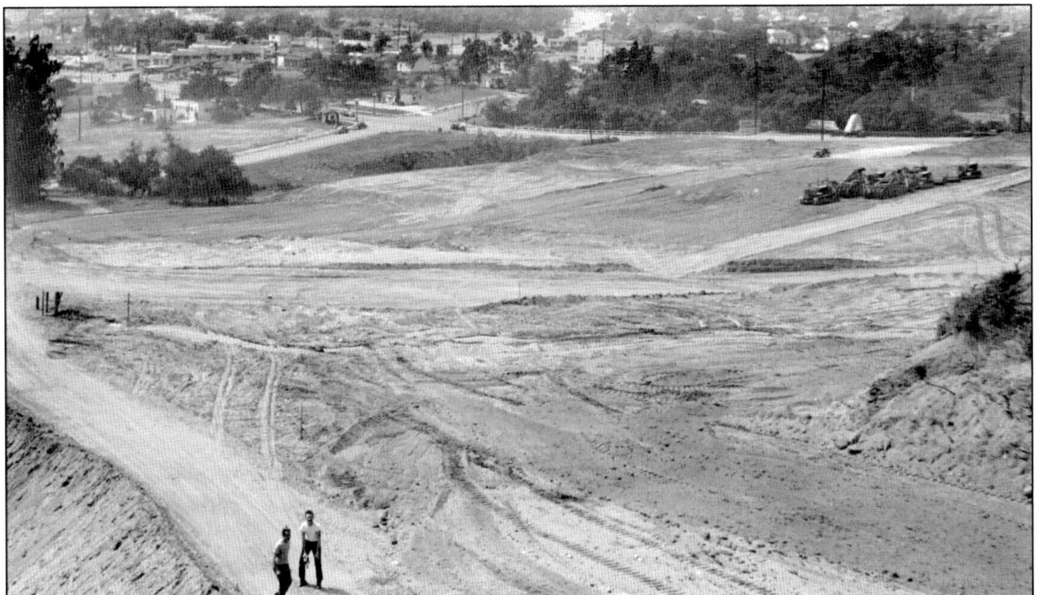

After World War II, soldiers who had been stationed in Southern California decided to stay and live here, causing another building boom. This large field, which had remained almost untouched in the years since the opening day barbecue that took place on part of it, was leveled and covered with multi-family units. That is Verdugo Boulevard and Park Place in the background, with the Indian Springs arch near the right rear.

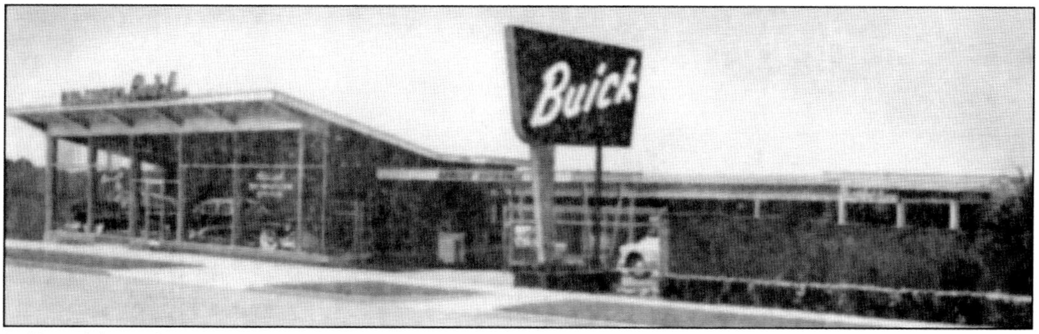

Bill Golden, the youngest Buick dealer in America, opened Golden Buick in this modern new showroom in 1952 at 2100 West Verdugo Boulevard, just west of the field shown on the opposite page. This distinctive building has since been used for a number of different retail ventures, but they have seemed out of place in the glass house that once proudly displayed the 1952 Buick Roadmaster with its "Fireball 8" engine.

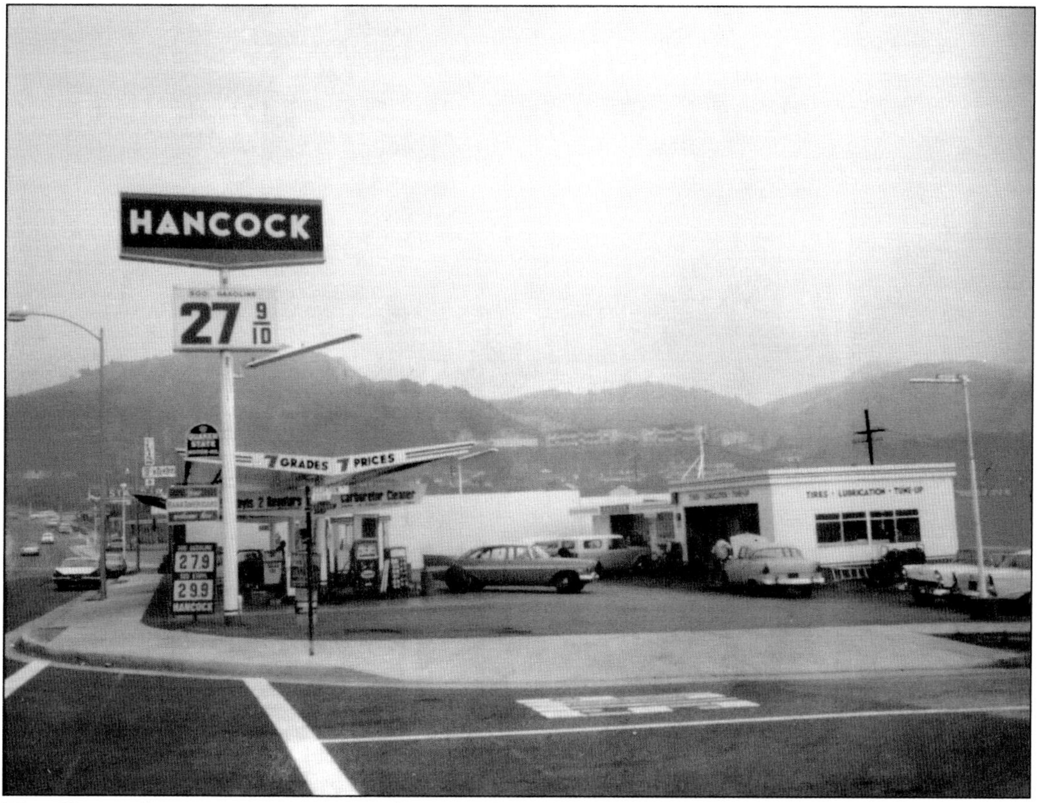

This Hancock service station at Verdugo Boulevard and Clifton Way is roughly where the 4,000 visitors gathered on opening day. (The sloped roof of the Golden Buick showroom is visible behind the BankAmericard sign.) Unlike many of the dozens of gas stations that used to blanket the area, this one is still in operation, under a different name.

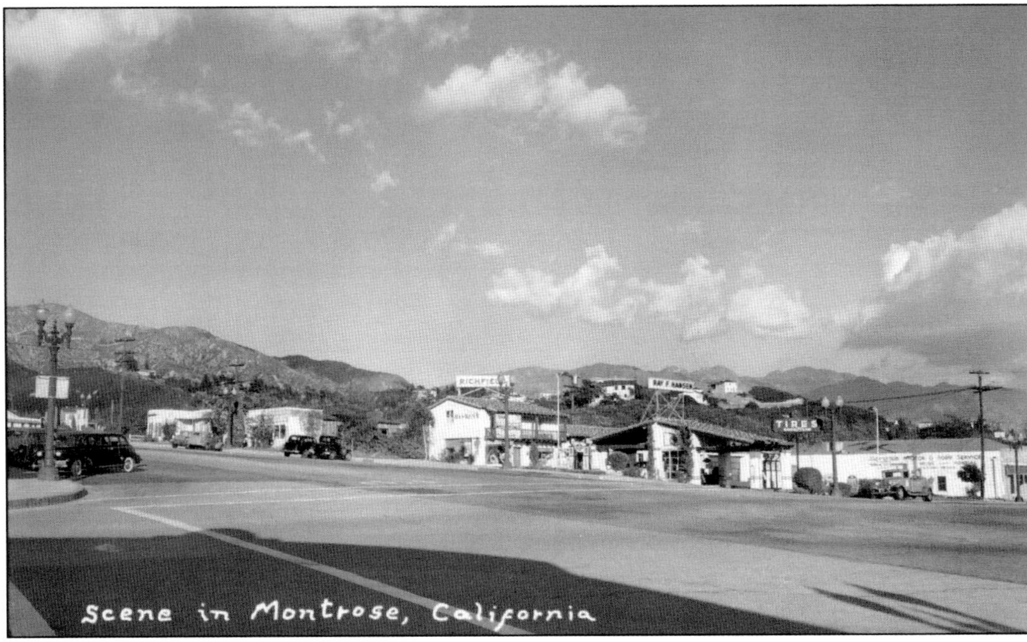

While the gateway corners on the west side have been photographed repeatedly, the opposite corners have not generated as much attention. This early 1950s view (above) looking north shows the four different streets that intersect at the gateway to Montrose: Verdugo Road (bottom), Verdugo Boulevard (right), Montrose Avenue (top), and Honolulu Avenue (left). The gas station at the northeast corner is where Fred Anderson's real estate office was on the day of the barbecue (shown on pages 15–16). Below is the southeast corner (also pictured on page 28) around 1967. Ray M. Andersen moved here from Minnesota in the 1930s and started working at Swanson's Furniture, where he eventually became partner. He took over the business in the early 1960s and eventually turned it over to his son Ray B. Andersen.

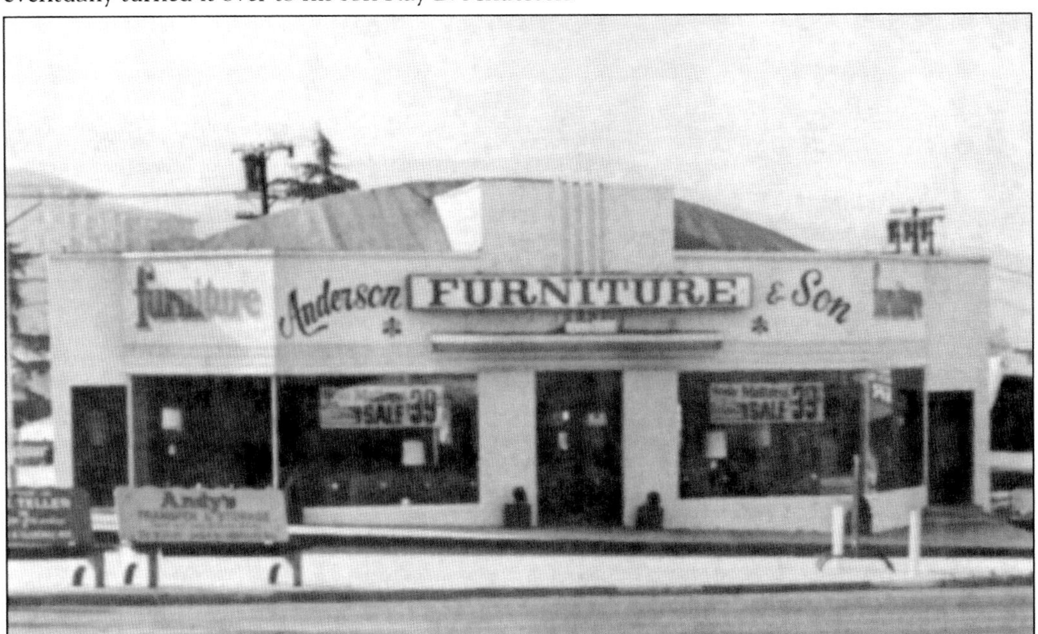

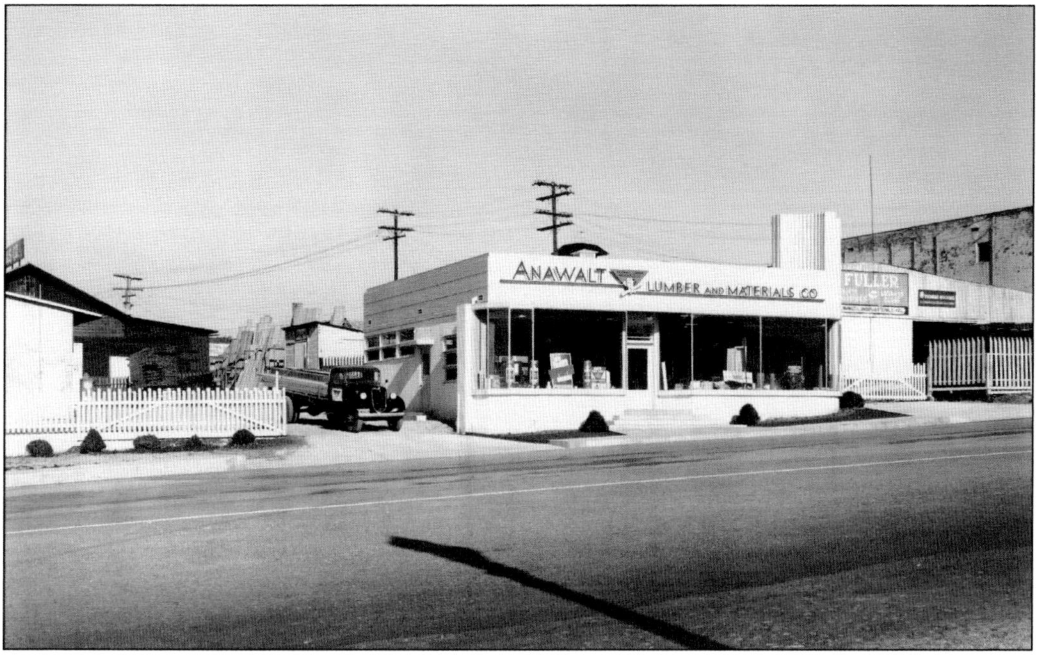

Anawalt Lumber, on the west side of Verdugo Road just south of Honolulu, is the oldest continuously run business in Montrose. It started as Johnson-Anawalt in 1920, but Johnson sold his share during the first year, and it has remained in the Anawalt family ever since. In 1967, the *Ledger* ran a story on the oldest businesses in Montrose. Of the nine listed, only two remain: Anawalt's and Andy's Transfer. (Courtesy of Thomas Anawalt.)

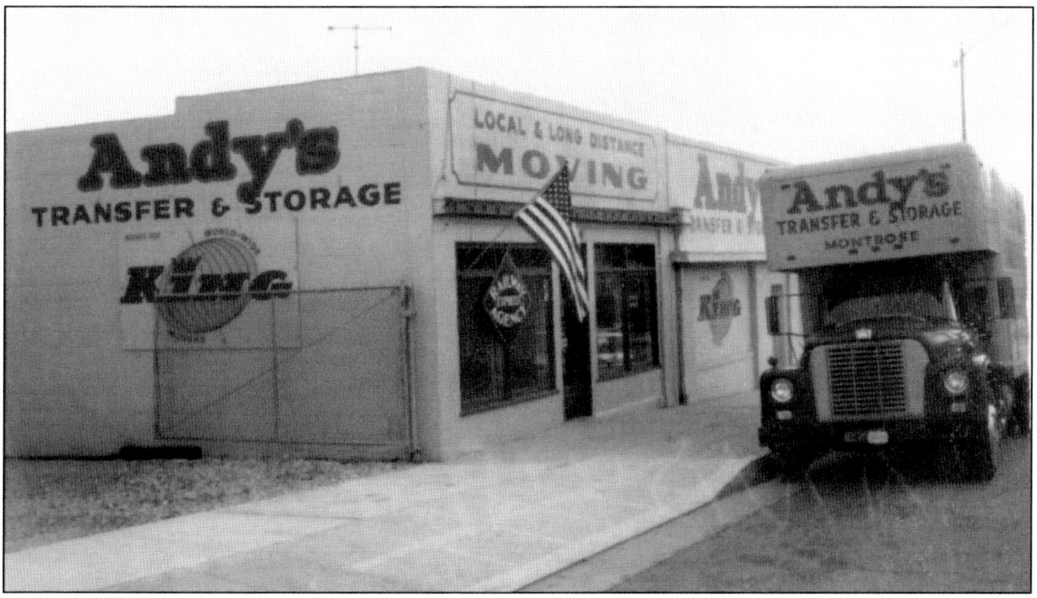

Andy's Transfer was started in 1921 by Dick Anderson, transporting construction materials from Los Angeles to the Crescenta Valley. Anderson sold it two years later, and the company expanded into household moving. In 1945, the company was sold again, and expanded into storage. In 1948, it moved from Honolulu Avenue to 3464 North Verdugo Road and has continued to expand into a global enterprise. But it has kept Andy's Transfer in the name for 90 years.

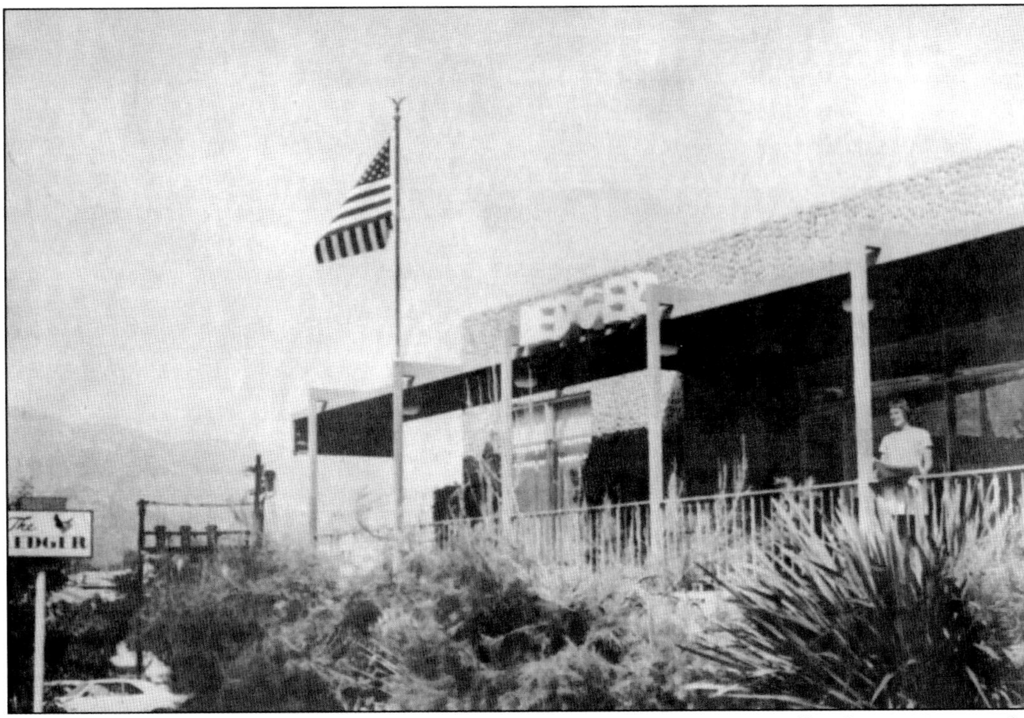

The *Ledger* newspaper was the main hometown paper for the Crescenta Valley from 1922 into the 1980s. This small paper won scores of awards for excellence under the leadership of the Carpenter family, who owned it through nearly its entire lifespan. It moved many times and built this office at 2219 Broadview in 1965.

In the late 1890s, William Sparr planted citrus orchards on his acreage in the lower portion of the Crescenta Valley. During the land boom of the 1920s, Sparr decided his land was worth more than his fruit, ripped out most of his trees, and subdivided his property in 1922. His real estate office was donated to Glendale and is now the Sparr Heights Community Center.

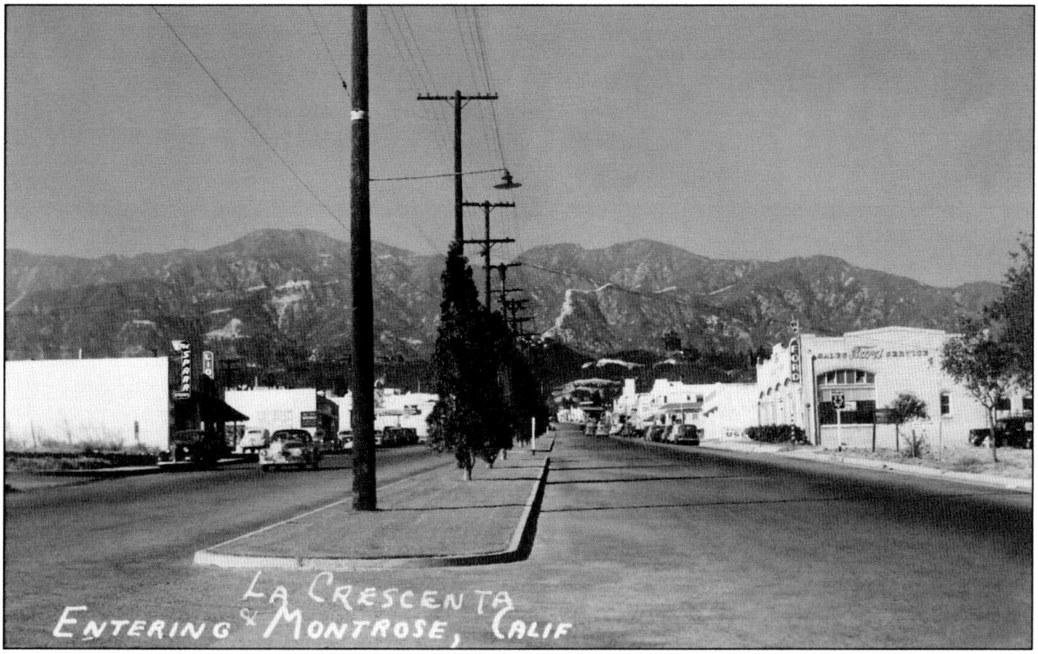

This wide median on Verdugo Road south of Montrose was the track bed of the Glendale & Montrose Railway. Almost immediately after the G&M went out of business, the rails were removed for scrap, and the wooden ties were cut up as firewood for the needy of La Crescenta. Local residents transplanted trees from their own yards to beautify the median. (Courtesy of Mark Havlik.)

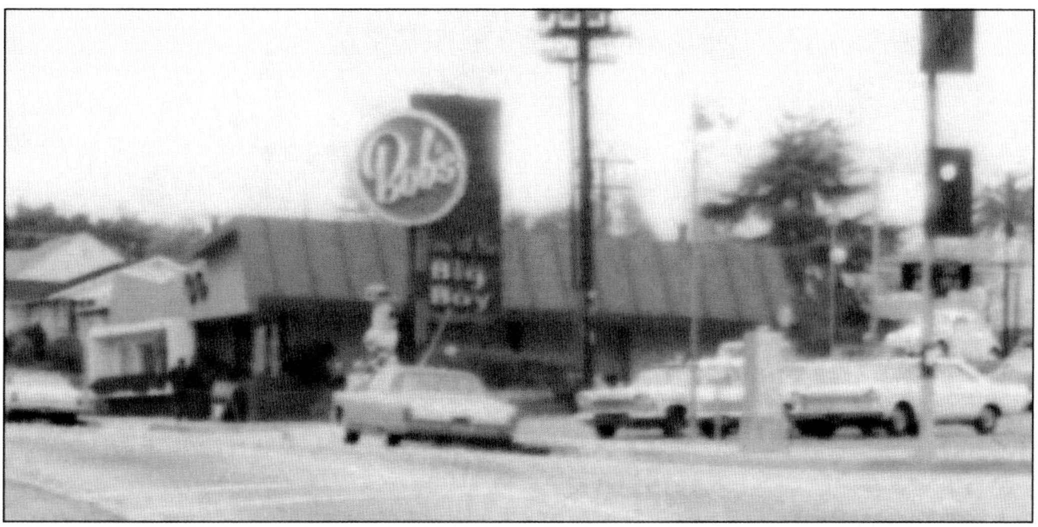

Another favorite of Montrose-raised Baby Boomers was Bob's Big Boy restaurant on La Crescenta Avenue half a block west of Verdugo Road. The Bob's chain underwent management changes in the mid-1980s and closed several restaurants, including the Montrose one, much to the chagrin of local high school students. The building was home to another restaurant for a while and is now being used for a preschool. (Courtesy of Mark Havlik.)

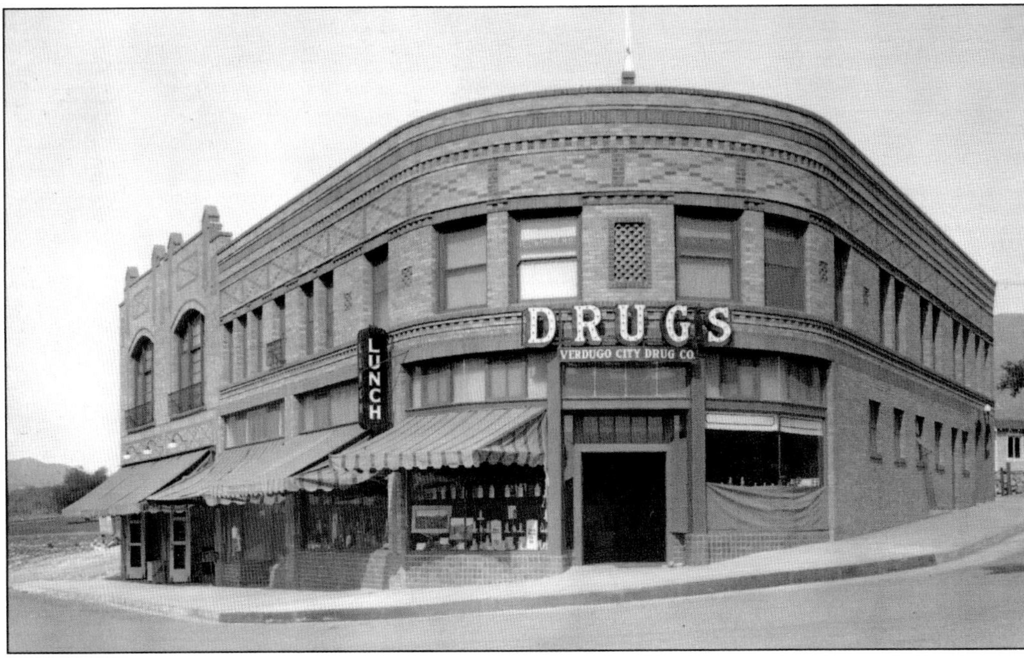

In 1925, real estate entrepreneur Harry Fowler launched the 10-acre development Verdugo Park, soon after changed to Verdugo City. It is no skyscraper as depicted on page 79, but the centerpiece of Verdugo City was the two-story Fowler building featuring a drugstore, offices, and an auditorium–ball room–social center at the northwest corner of La Crescenta and Honolulu Avenues. Verdugo City also had a post office, a gas station, and a grocery store.

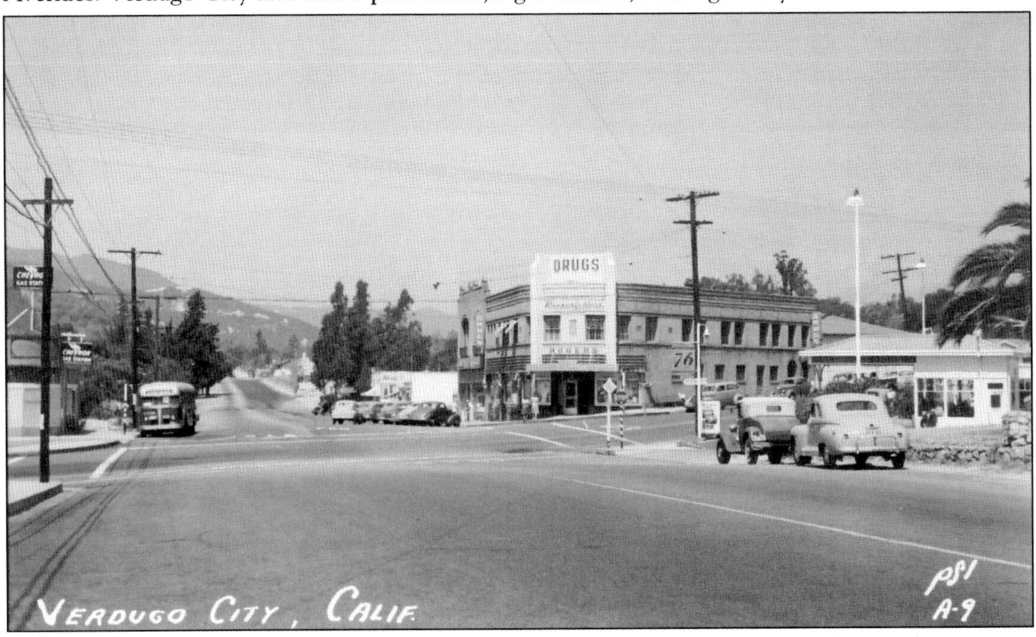

In the 1940s, the owner of the building tried to modernize it by putting a large, white stucco piece at the corner as shown in this 1947 photograph. The intersection at that point had two gas stations and two drugstores. Verdugo City was annexed by Glendale in the early 1950s. (Courtesy of Mark Havlik.)

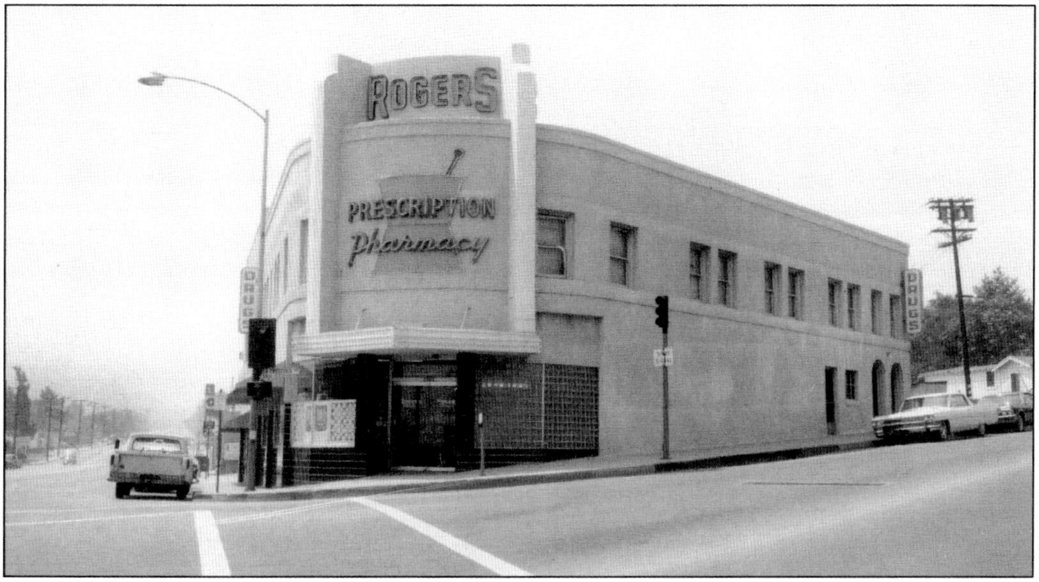

At some point after that, the entire building was stuccoed over. In addition to the Roger's Pharmacy, the building was also longtime home to the Trade-Rite Market, which was owned by Bill Bailey, one of the founders of the local Rotary Club and responsible for many improvements in the valley.

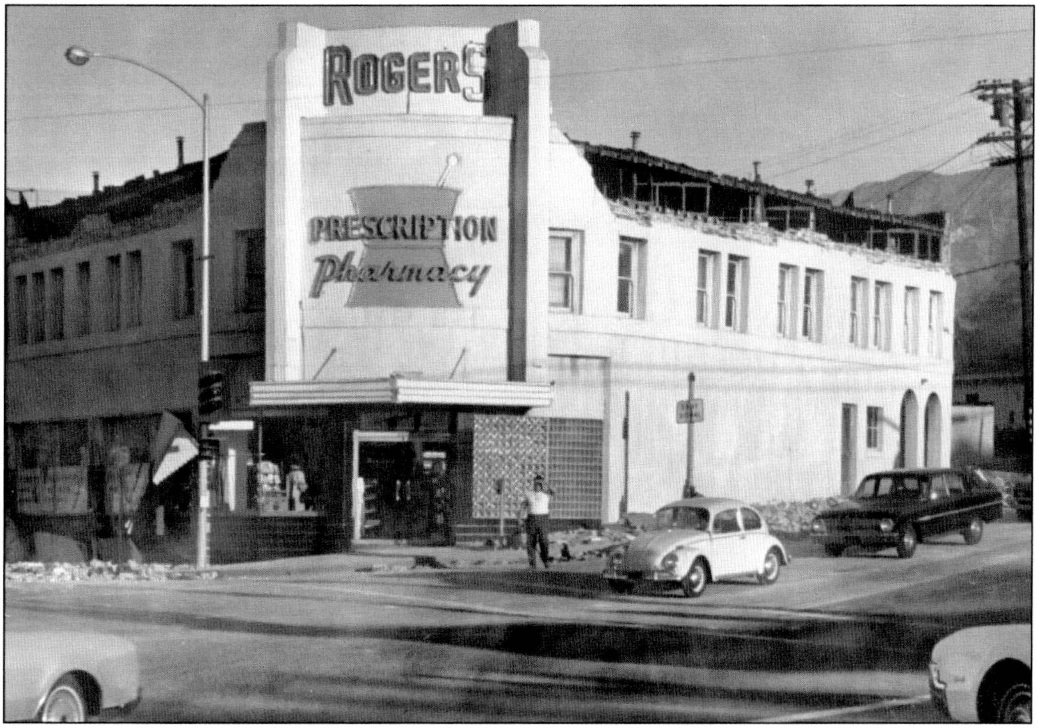

In spite of the stucco covering, the 1971 Sylmar earthquake damaged this beautiful building beyond repair and it had to be torn down. Shown here after the earthquake, the structure's upper walls had rained down on the sidewalks below. Verdugo City had lost its identity—but it still has its own post office, which means it still exists!

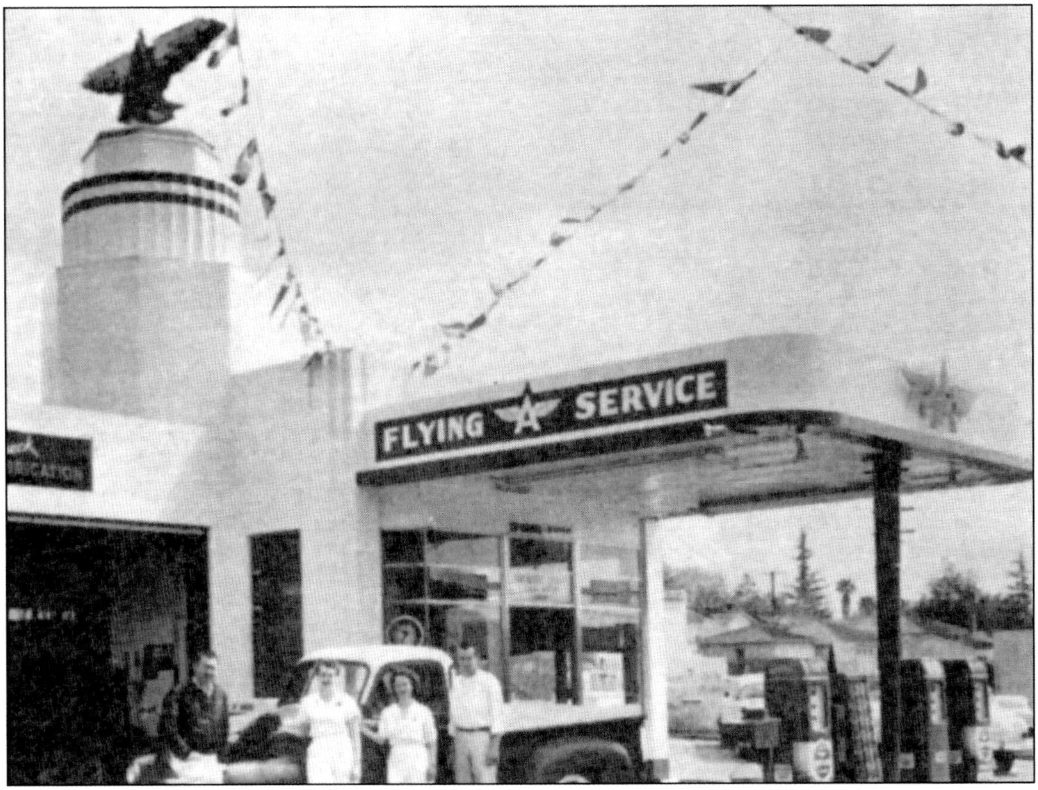

In 1958, the corner of Ramsdell and Honolulu Avenues was graced by a Flying A service station, which locals remember fondly because of the tower mounted on top of the office. At the top of the tower was a huge A with neon-lit wings. The A stood for Associated Oil Company.

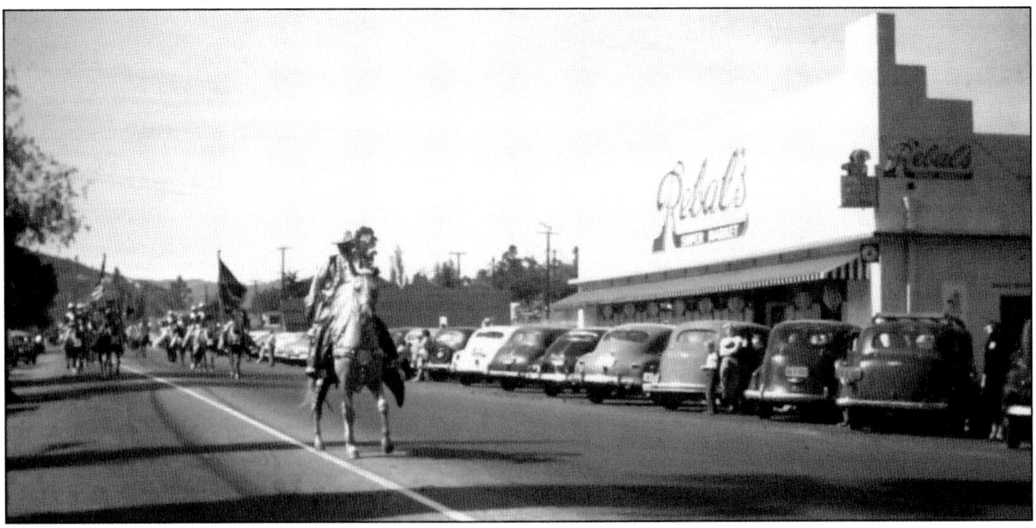

The valley had its own wacky merchant in the person of Fred Rebal, who, in 1946, opened Rebal's Mad House "where a fast nickel beats a slow dime." He billed his full-service market at 2931 Honolulu Avenue as the store "that made Verdugo City famous." In this photograph, the Western Days rodeo parade is passing in front of the store on its way to the shopping park. (Courtesy of Ray King.)

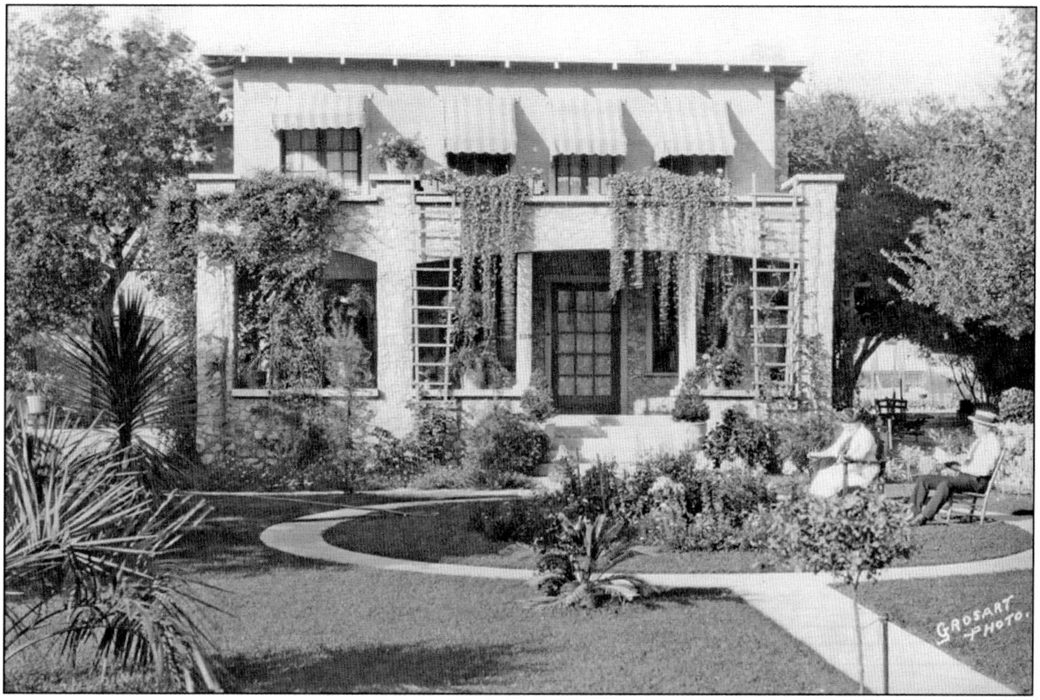

In 1923, Agnes Richards started Rockhaven Sanitarium at 2713 Honolulu Avenue as a "safe haven" for women with mental illnesses. She created a peaceful atmosphere with beautiful gardens and home-like settings to provide patients with a sense of dignity. Richards died in 1967, but Rockhaven stayed open until 2006. In 2008, the city of Glendale purchased the property with the intention of turning it into a library and community center.

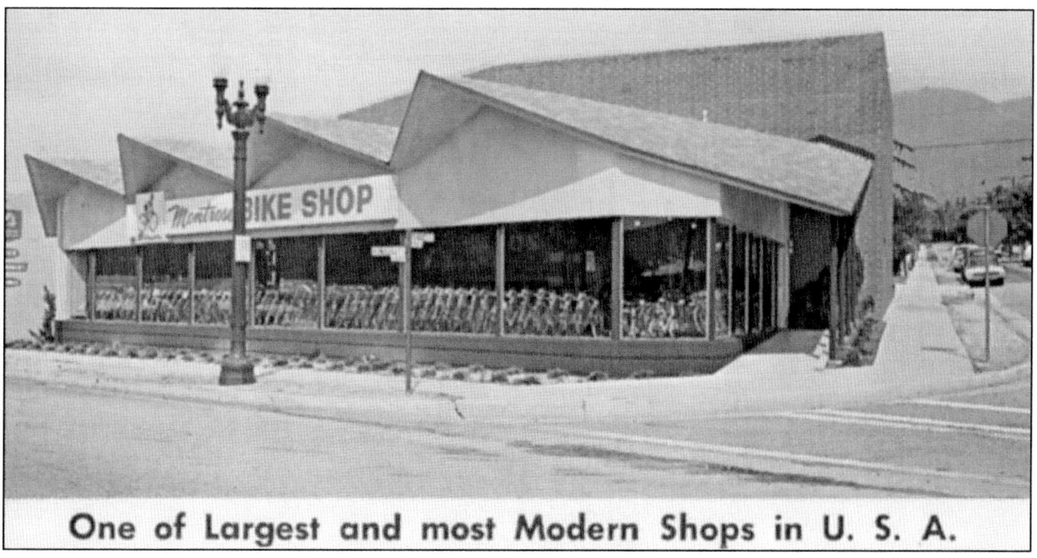

The Montrose Bike Shop moved to 2501 Honolulu Avenue in 1954. Owners Bob and Beverly Hansing had to choose between several predesigned plans that the Schwinn bicycle company offered, and they chose this beauty. Their son Dennis took over the store in the late 1960s, and Jonathan Livesay bought the shop (but not the building) in about 2007. Some say a covenant in the building's property title states that this must always be a bike shop.

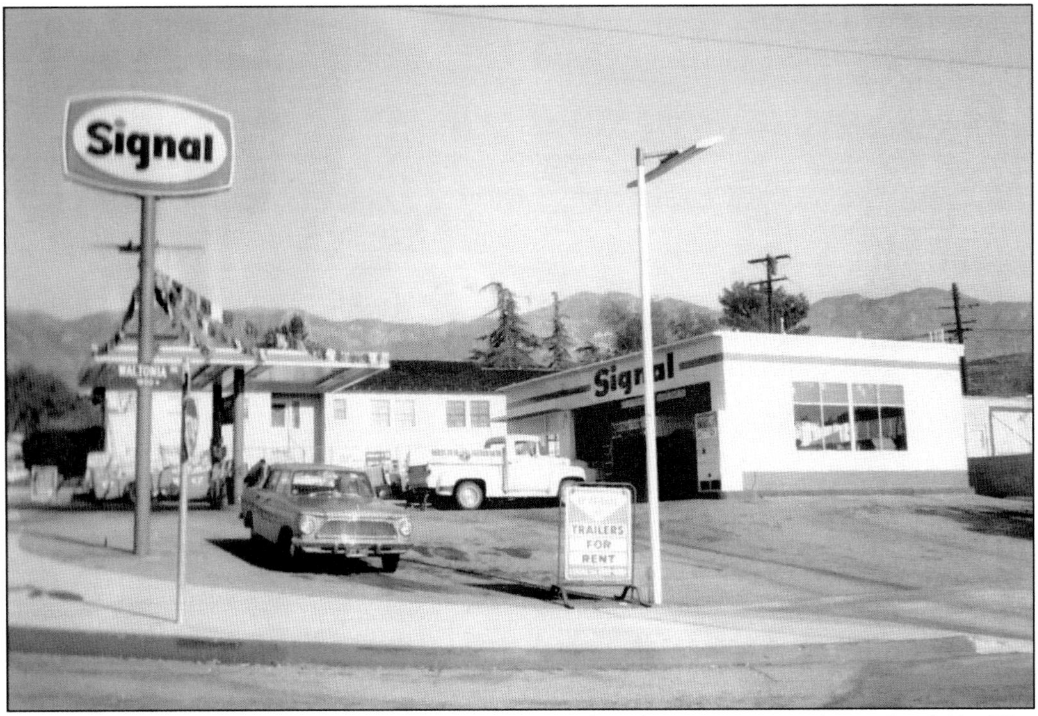

This is the northeast corner of Montrose Avenue and Waltonia Drive in the early 1960s. The Signal Oil and Gas Company was named for Signal Hill in Long Beach, and its motto was "Go Farther with Signal Gas!" But by 1965, the company was not going any farther with gas and closed all its stations to focus on aerospace as Allied-Signal. This corner is now occupied by a medical office building and looks nothing like this.

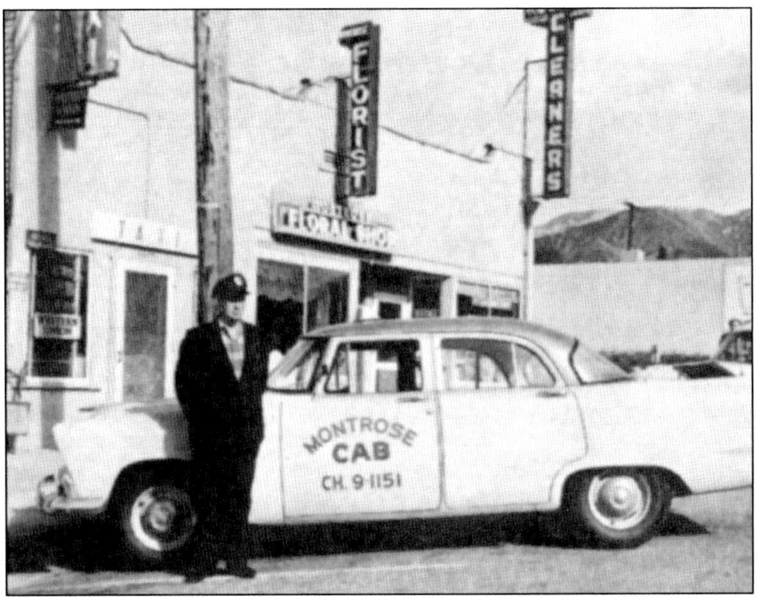

This loop around the edges of the shopping park ends at the Montrose Cab Company, which had its dispatch office in this small retail building at 2034 Montrose Avenue, a half block north of Honolulu Avenue. It also handled Western Union Telegrams. This building was demolished to make way for a bank, which in turn was demolished to make way for the current occupant, Carl's Jr.

Four

Color and Thorns
Fun and Not-so-fun Montrose

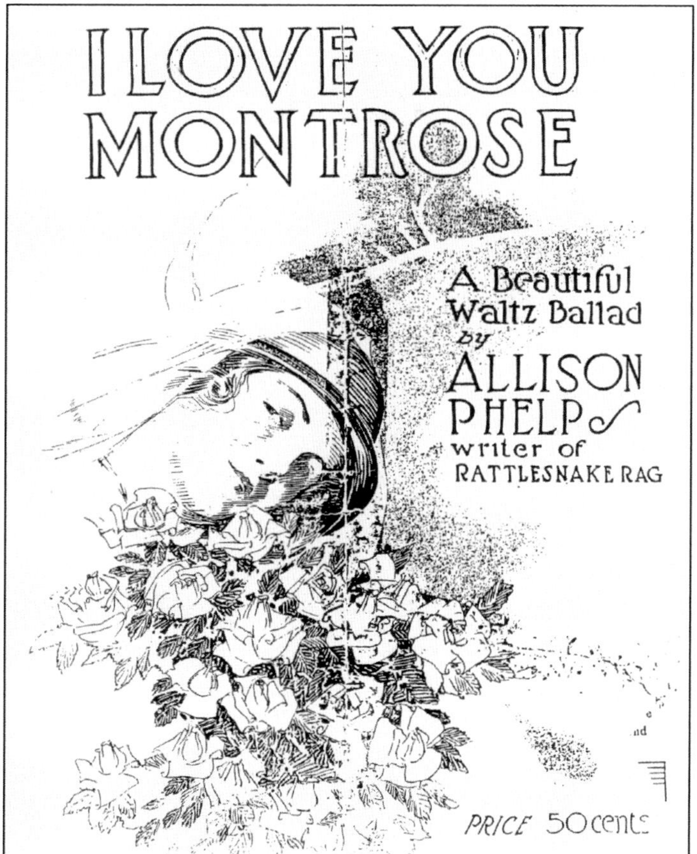

Woody Guthrie got national attention with his song about the Montrose flood, but for some reason Allison Phelps's "I Love You Montrose" was not a big hit. "I love you, sweet Montrose, Your mountains, your canons and vales, I love all your beautiful shadows, And the sun as it purples and pales. Sweet Montrose, I love only you." This chapter looks at some of the things to love, and possibly hate, about Montrose. (Courtesy Chamber of Commerce.)

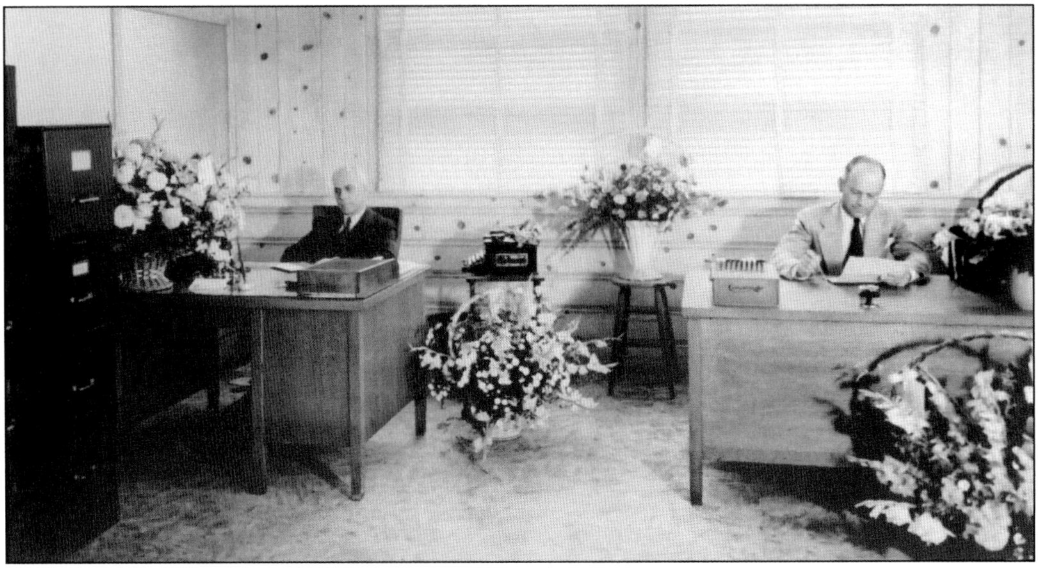

Fred "H.F." Anawalt (left) founded Anawalt Lumber in 1920; his son Bernard (right) worked closely with him from the beginning. Anawalt's was one of the many lumber yards in Montrose that supplied materials for the 1920s building boom, but it's the only one still in existence. H.F. passed on the business to Bernard, who passed it on to his son "Buzz" (Bernard Jr.) who passed it on to his son Bill, the current owner. (Courtesy of Thomas Anawalt, Bill's son.)

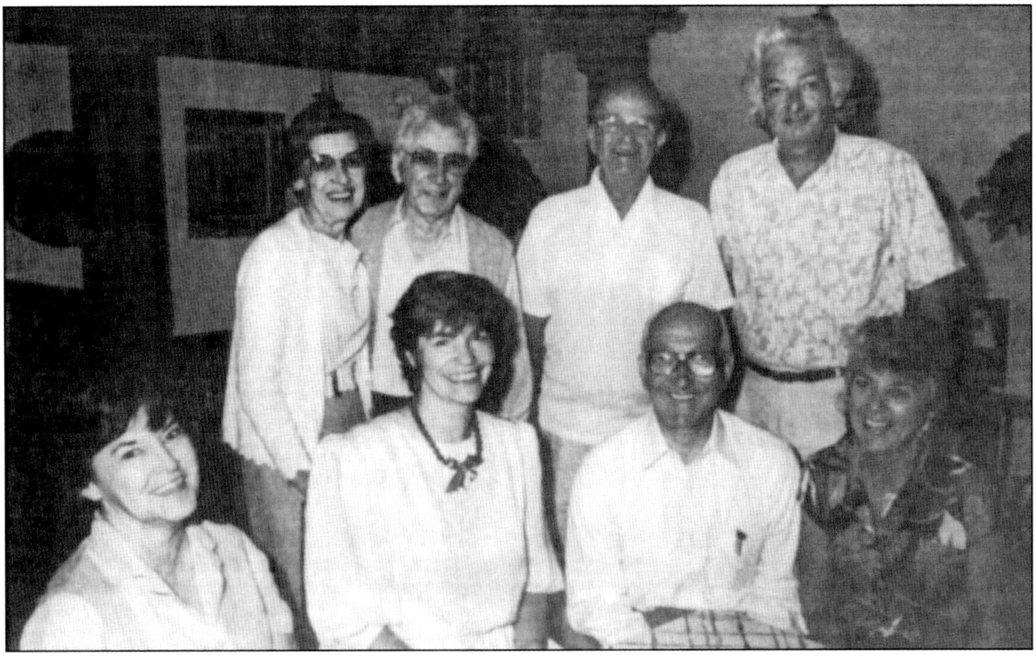

In 1987, this stellar committee of Montrose Shopping Park Association (MPSA) members planned the party in honor of the 20th anniversary of the shopping park renovation. They are, from left to right, (first row) Delores Dickenson, Jo Ann Balteau, Val Grayson, and Sandra Swanson; (second row), Margaret Bellamy, Jay Drayman, Frank Roberts, and Walt Hackman, who was president of the MPSA at the time. (Roberts had been president of the MPSA for nine years.) (Courtesy of Pat Grant.)

The Montrose Bowl opened in 1936. At that time, pins had to be reset by hand, and many young Crescenta Valley residents clipped their fingers in the machinery as part of a first job. The Edwards family owned it until the 1980s. Bob Berger started leasing it in 1982 and finally bought it in 1988. It is open mostly for private parties and film shoots.

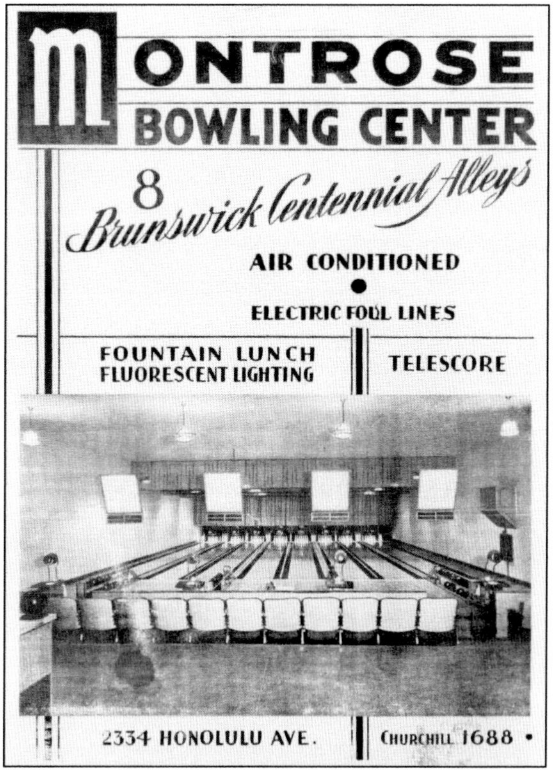

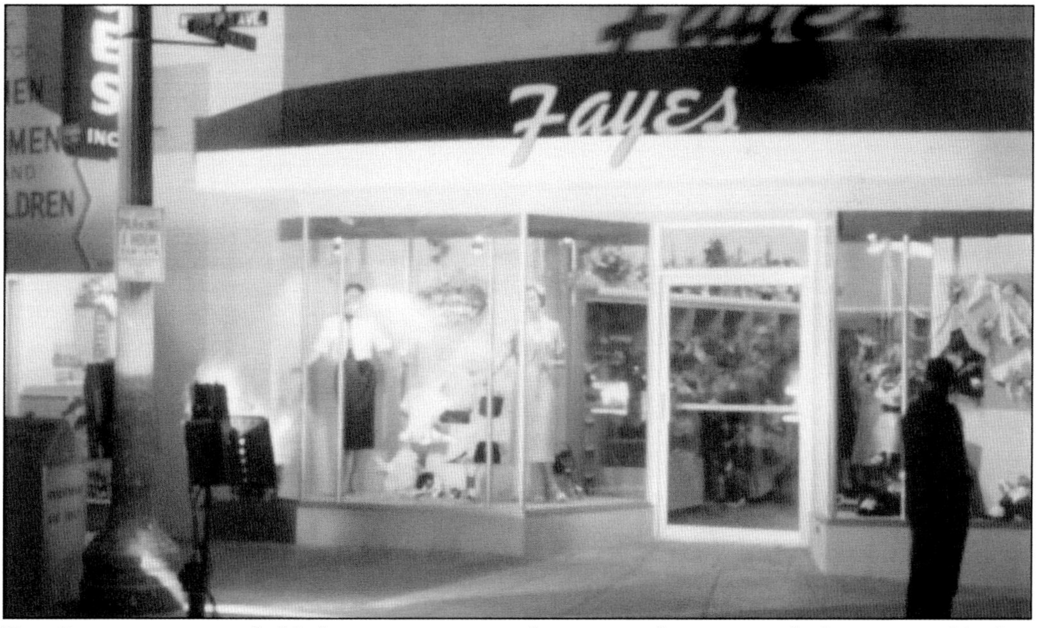

Faye Snow was a remarkable businesswoman with a tremendous sense of what women liked to wear. Starting with a small store and one employee in 1950, she created an apparel enterprise as she expanded to four Montrose stores. In 1954, she moved into the former Crescenta-Cañada bank building and on opening weekend (shown here), 2,000 people came in spite of torrential rain. (Courtesy of Pat Grant.)

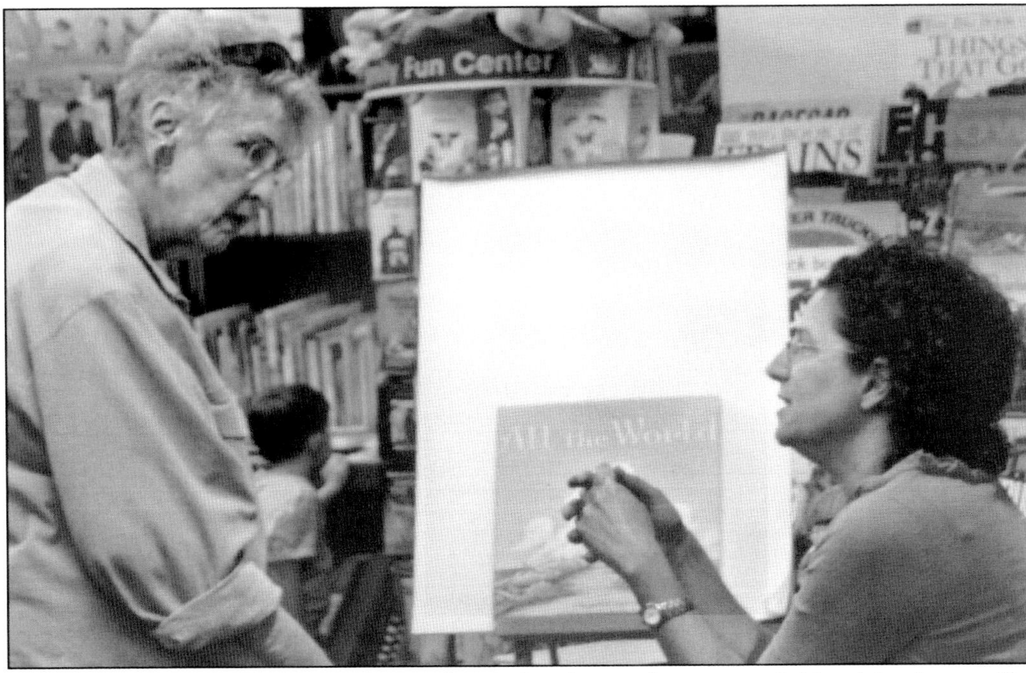

Once upon a time there was a young mother with a dream of owning a children's bookstore. She shared this dream with a friend of hers, who told her, "You open a bookstore, and I'll build you a building." The young mother was Jane Humphrey, and she opened Once Upon a Time at 3457 North Verdugo Road in 1966. She moved into the shopping park in 1971. Humphrey (left) is shown here with children's author and illustrator Marla Frazee. (Courtesy of Maureen Palacios.)

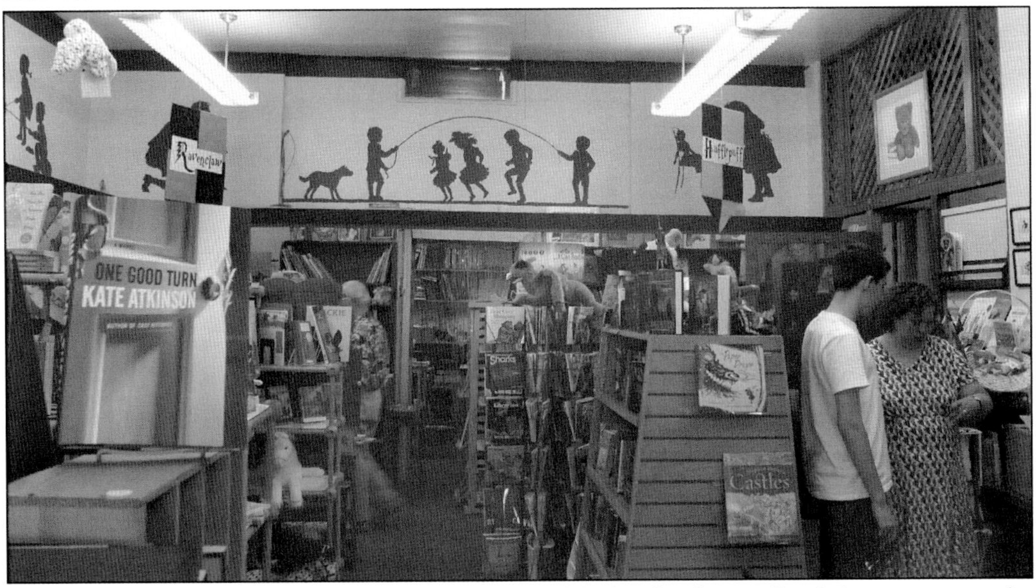

Once Upon a Time moved twice in the shopping park before landing in Faye's former store in the former bank in 1980. Humphrey admitted that the store was not a real money-maker, but she felt she was doing something meaningful by introducing youngsters to the joys of reading. By 2003, Humphrey was ready to retire so she tried to sell the store. There were no takers, and it looked like she would have to close the business.

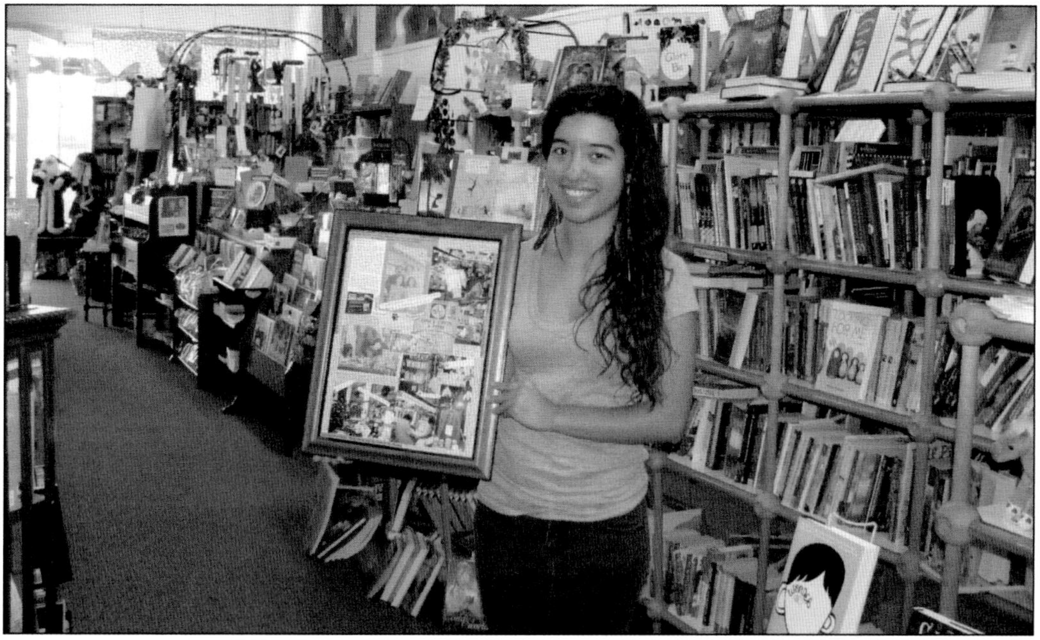

Jessica Palacios, then age nine, read about this and wrote a letter to the local paper, pleading with someone to buy the store. "Where am I going to get my fifth Harry Potter book if there is no Once Upon a Time?" Her entreaty was answered—by her own mother, Maureen, who bought the store shortly afterward. Here is Jessica in 2012 with a collage of photographs and her letter to the editor.

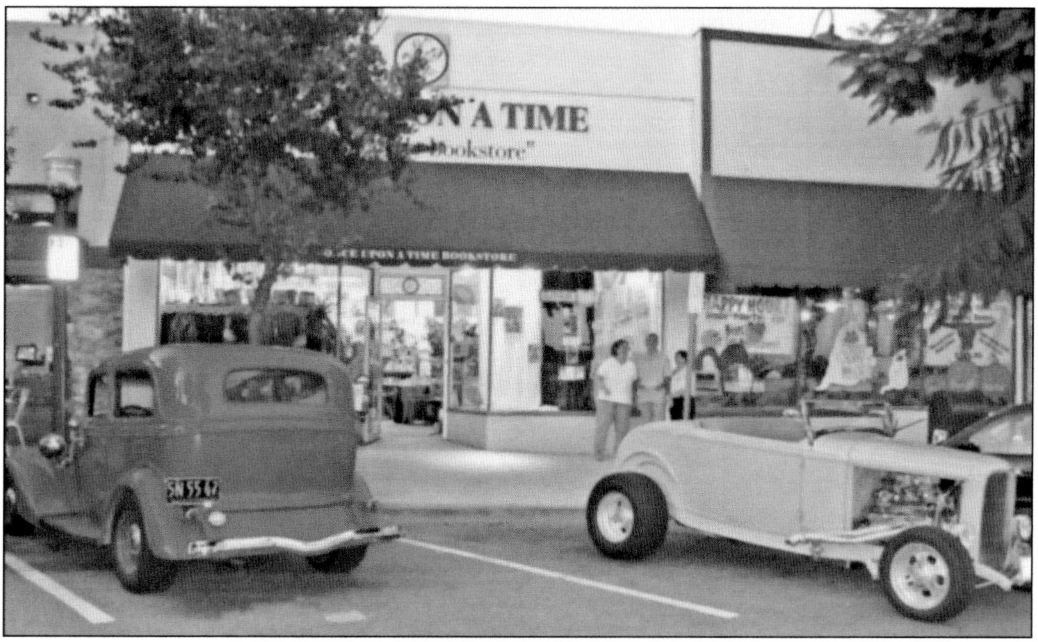

In 2007, Once Upon a Time moved again to 2207 and is now the oldest still-operating children's bookstore in the country, which is a major achievement considering Humphrey had to compete with mega bookstores and Palacios has to compete with Amazon. She does this by hosting book signings, "pajama story time," and adult book clubs, among others. Without the community's support, though, Once Upon a Time could be just that.

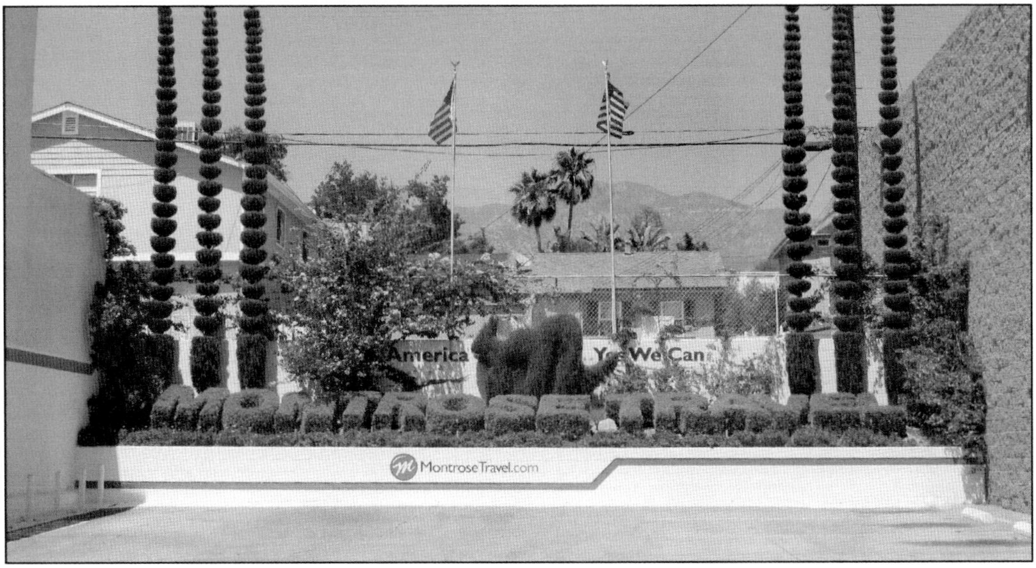

As Montrose Travel grew and needed more office space, some locals complained that this service company was taking away valuable retail space and ruining the charm of Montrose. Others came to the company's defense. To do its part for the shopping park, Montrose Travel has kept the exteriors of its buildings well maintained and even added this charming topiary garden at the end of its parking lot.

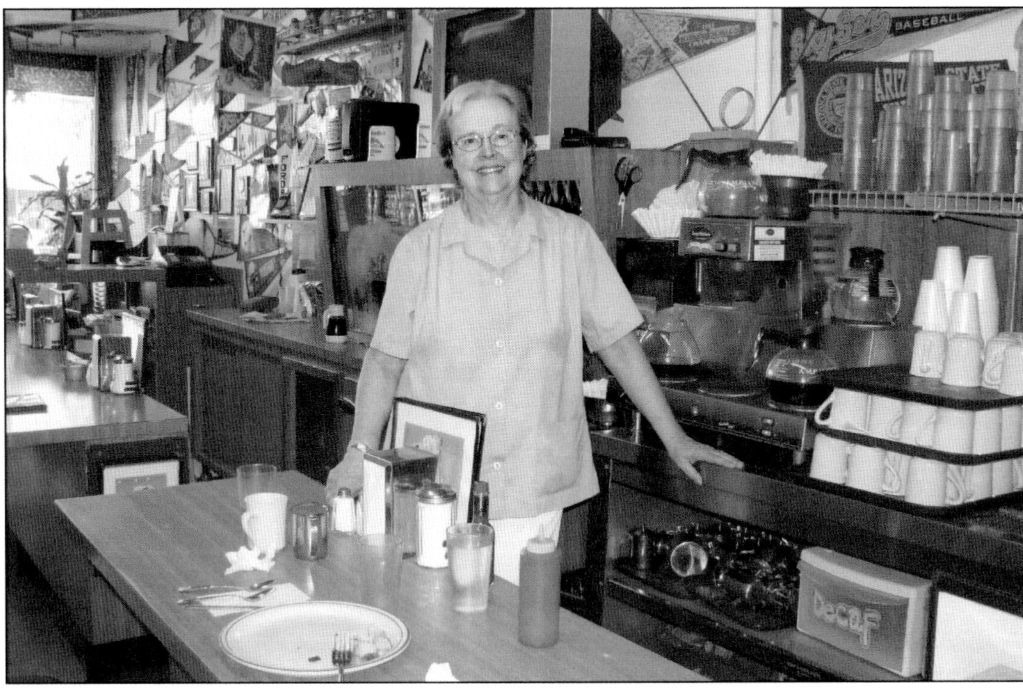

Wanda Bergstrom has been a waitress at City Hall Coffee Shop since 1972 and still comes in for the morning shift five days a week. She is a big Dodgers fan and one day put up a pennant. A customer came in and asked where her Ohio State pennant was. She told him she would put it up if he brought one in. He did, and today the walls are covered with pennants of customers' favorite teams.

During Prohibition, the Crescenta Valley was still wooded enough to provide cover for people making their own liquor and close enough to Los Angeles to keep plenty of Southern Californians "happy." In this photograph from the 1920s, the local justice of the peace Judge Dyer watches as gallons of confiscated moonshine are poured down the gutter on Ocean View Boulevard in front of the sheriff's department.

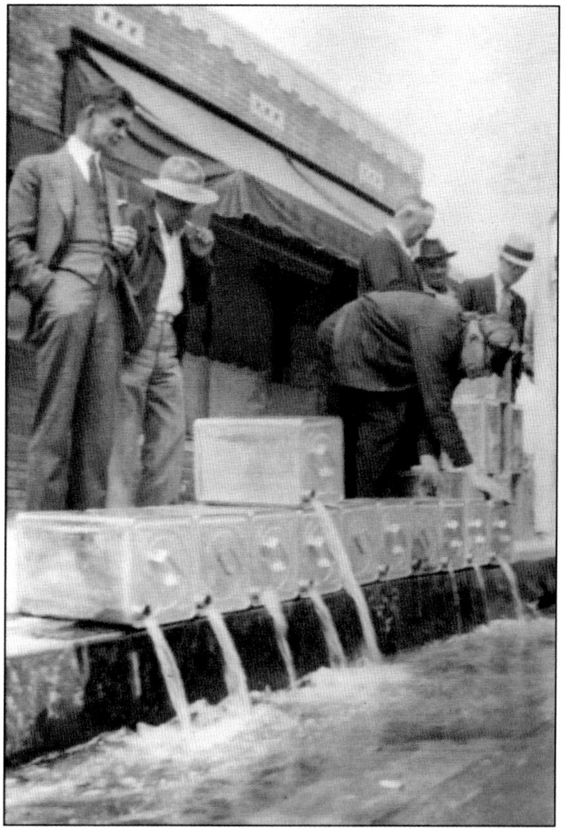

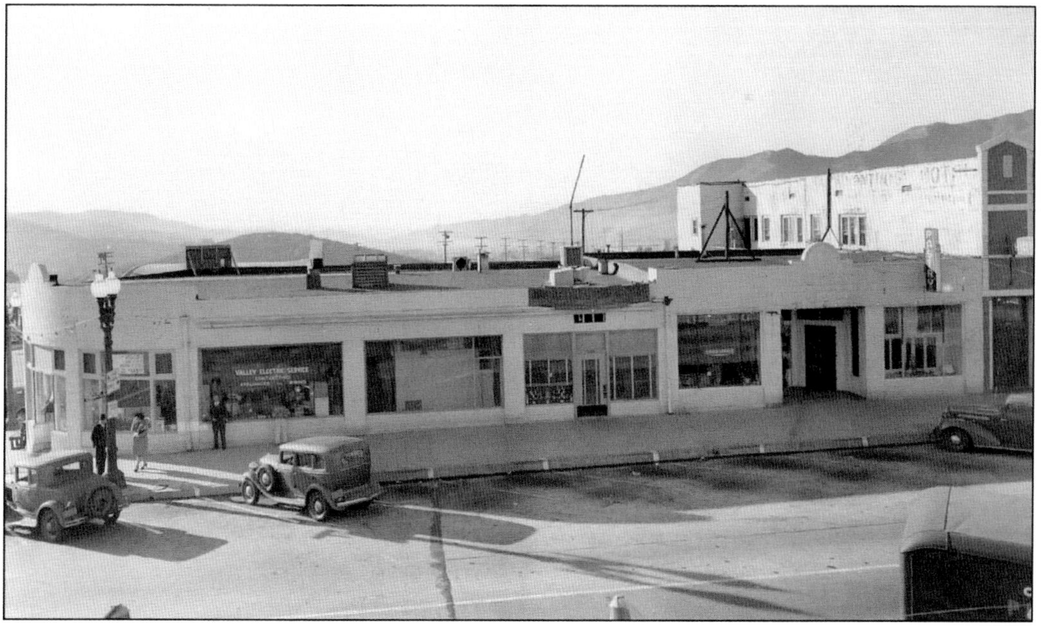

The Trail Café in the western part of the Potts building was notable for being the first establishment in Los Angeles County to serve alcohol legally when Prohibition ended in 1933. Some local cynics say this is because it was also serving alcohol illegally before Prohibition ended.

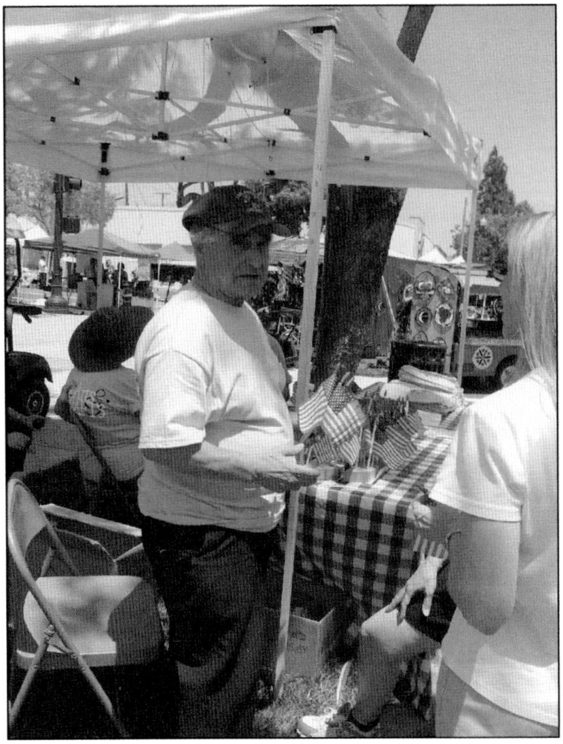

Vito Cannella, an Italian immigrant and longtime Montrose barber, was so bothered by flag burning demonstrators during the Vietnam War that he teamed with Bill Bailey and rallied support for a National Flag week, which Congress approved on June 9, 1966. Every year, the president issues a proclamation designating the week in which Flag Day (June 14) occurs as National Flag Week. Vito is shown here passing out flags in 2006.

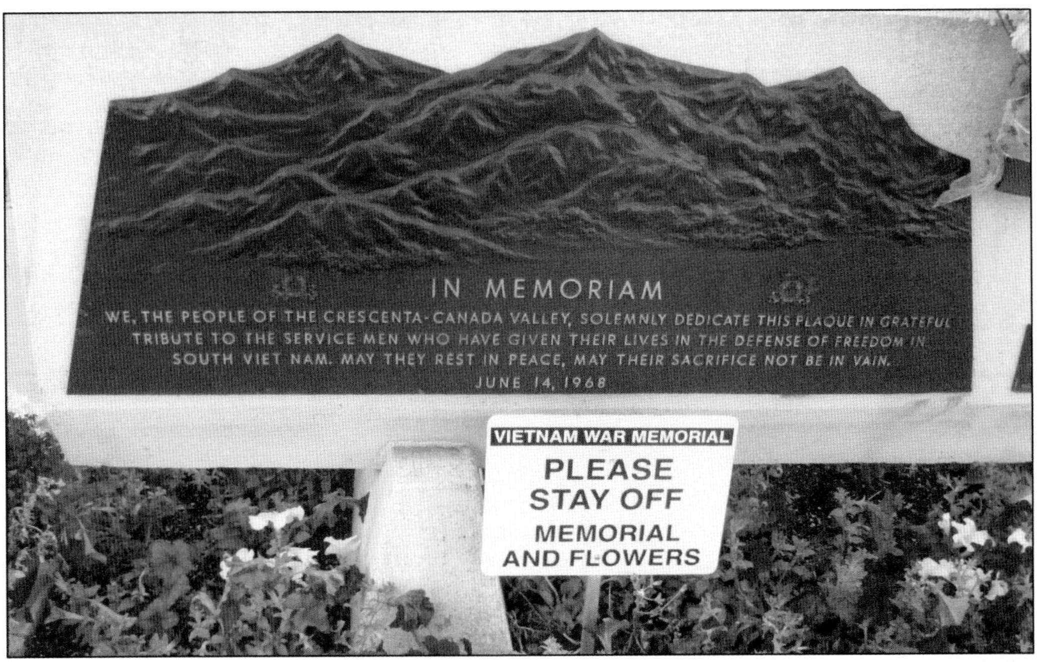

Built in the plaza at the northwest corner of Honolulu Avenue and Ocean View Boulevard, the Montrose Vietnam War Memorial was the first in the United States to honor soldiers who gave their lives in that conflict. The *Ledger* newspaper's Don Carpenter challenged the community to fund this effort, and the response was so great that the *Ledger* actually had to ask citizens to stop sending money. The excess funds were used to maintain the memorial.

In that same plaza, on July 4, 1975, as part of the country's year-long bicentennial celebration, state senator Frank Lanterman helped the Montrose–Verdugo City Chamber of Commerce dedicate this bronze frieze that memorializes Don Jose Maria Verdugo and the Rancho San Rafael land grant that was the start of the Crescenta Valley. (Courtesy of Chamber of Commerce.)

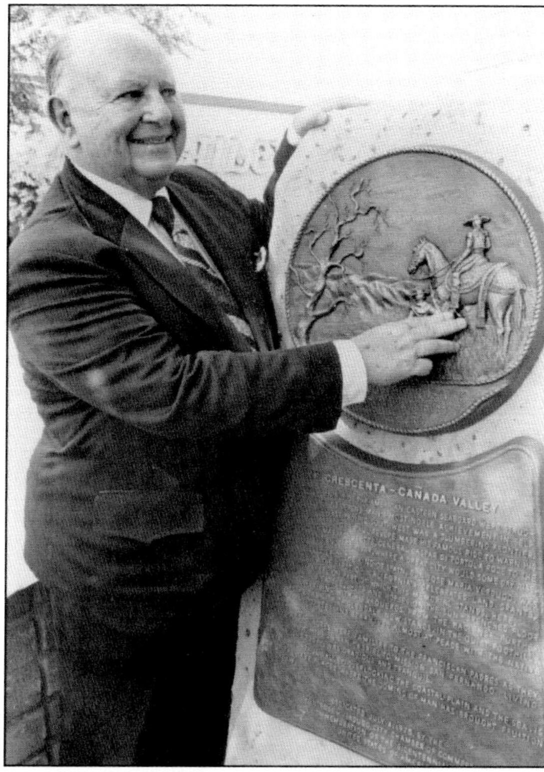

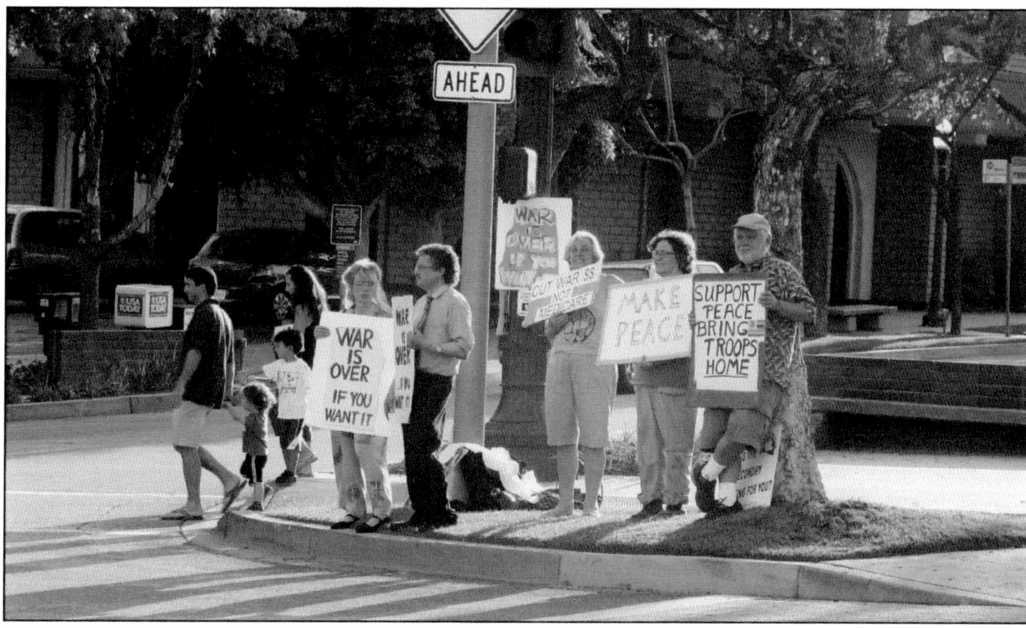

To protest the wars in Iraq and Afghanistan, the Montrose Peace Vigil started in 2006 at that same corner. It has met every Friday evening since, no matter the weather. In 2008, local veterans started staging a counter protest to "support our troops" at the southeast corner. It was then that the shopping park started taking down the American flag before the peace vigil and re-hanging it on Saturday.

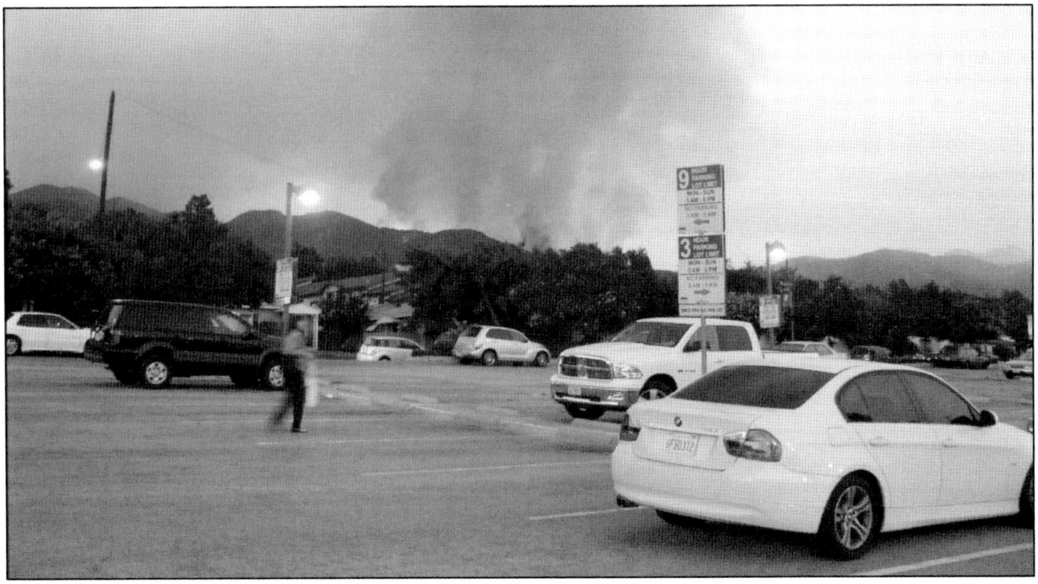

The hills and mountains around Montrose have caught fire many times over the years, though the shopping park has never been threatened. In August and September 2009, the Station Fire raged in the San Gabriel Mountains, seen here from the parking lot on Florencita Drive. Ash from the fire fell upon Montrose like snow.

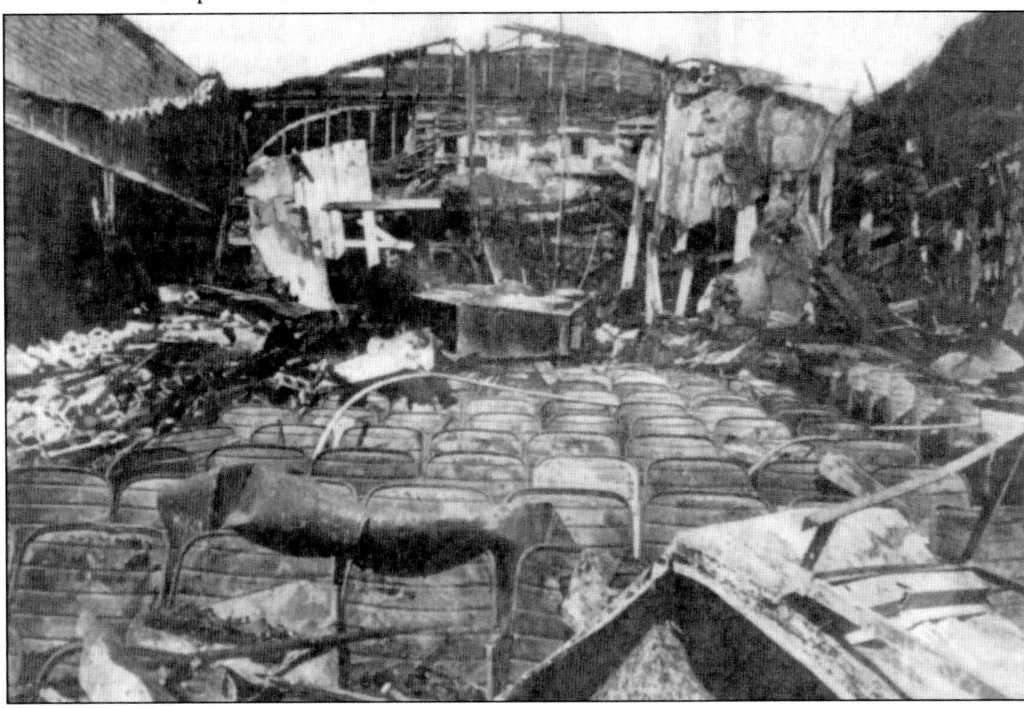

The Montrose Theater burned down under suspicious circumstances in 1987. Arson investigator John Orr from the Glendale Fire Department was at the scene early on. Orr was later found guilty of being a serial arsonist, with one of his fires started along the 210 Freeway about half a mile from the theater. Local residents have long wondered if the Montrose Theater fire was another of Orr's, though he was never charged for it. (Courtesy of Pat Grant.)

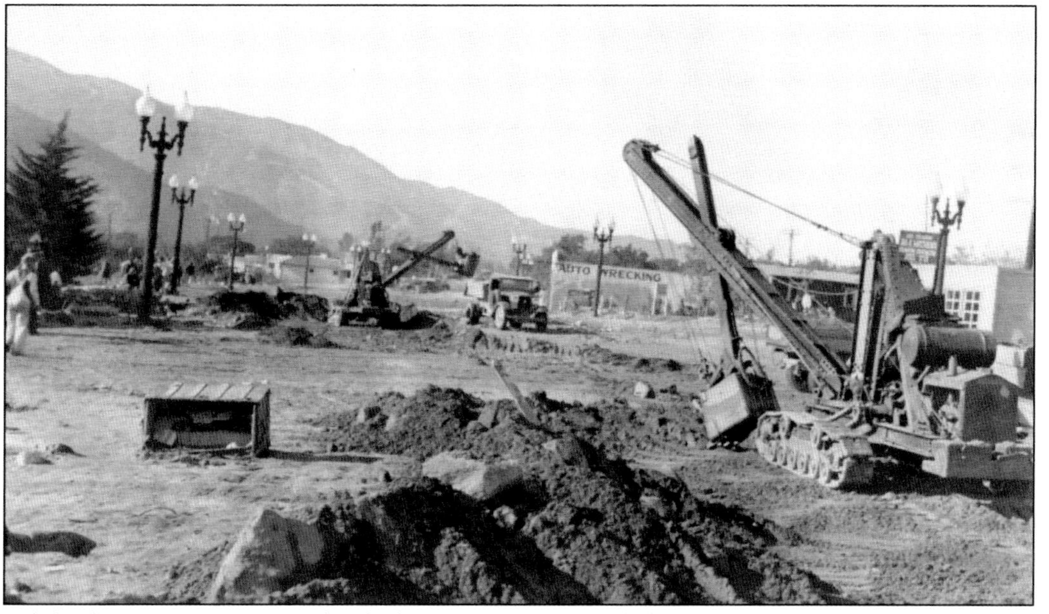

While the Great Montrose Flood of January 1, 1934, killed many and destroyed homes in the Crescenta Valley, the main damage to the shopping park was from the deep mud and debris. This is the intersection of Honolulu and Orangedale Avenues, where Trader Joe's is today. And residents think it is hard to get in and out of that parking lot now.

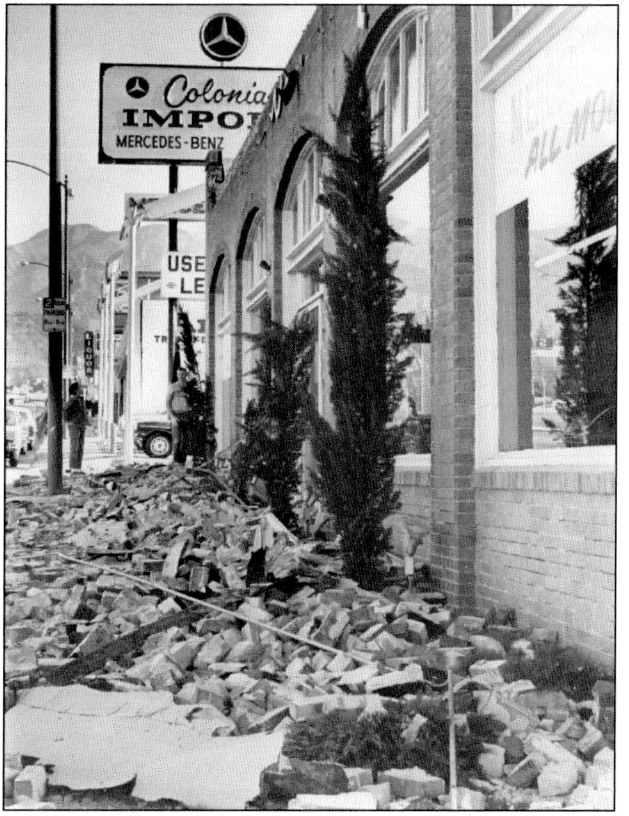

The February 9, 1971, Sylmar earthquake did more to change the look of Montrose than just about anything else. Dozens of brick buildings had extensive damage and had to be retrofitted. Most were covered in chicken wire and stucco, especially the ones shown in the parade photographs on pages 46 and 48. However, Montrose was lucky enough not to lose any significant buildings because of it.

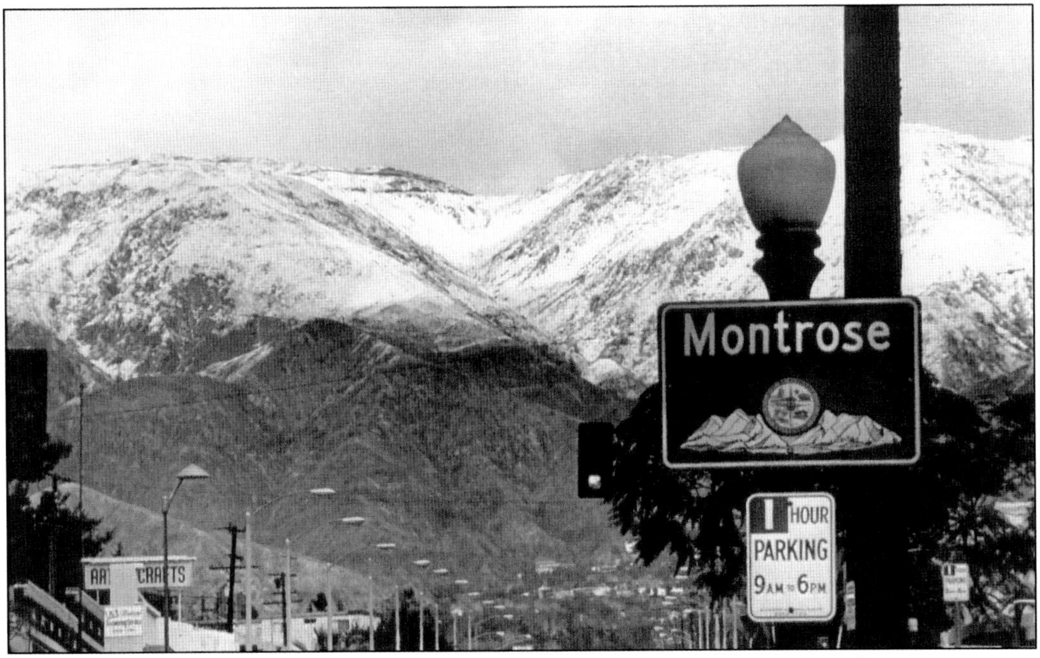

One of the great pleasures of living in Montrose only happens every two or three years: snow on Mount Lukens and the nearby San Gabriel Mountains. This photograph from the late 1970s looks north on Ocean View Boulevard with the old Montrose sign clearly visible. Three styles of street lamps light this block (see pages 108–109).

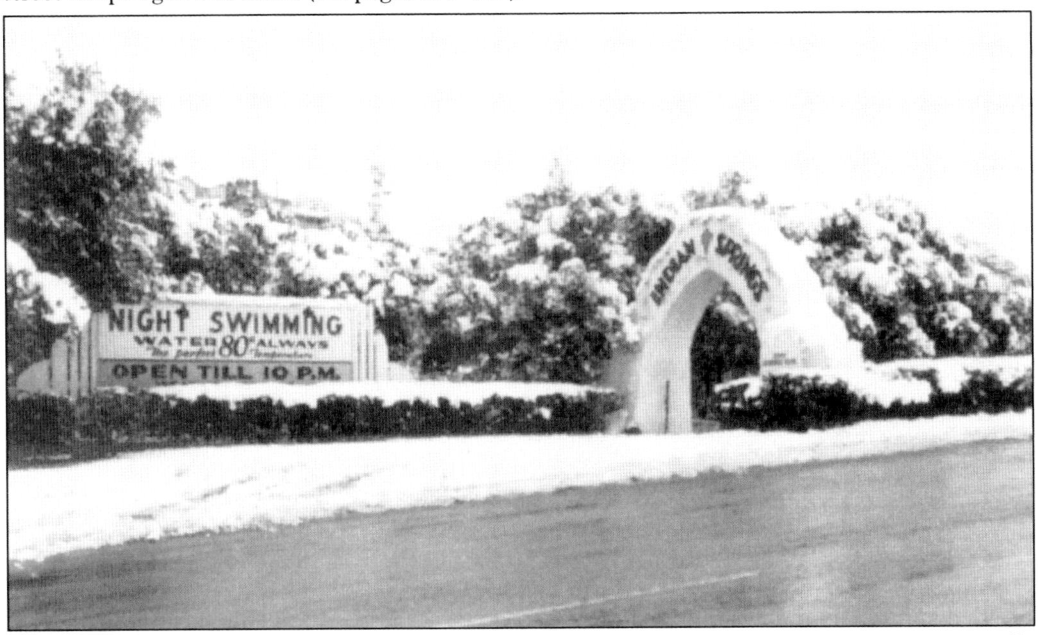

While snow sometimes falls in the areas above Foothill Boulevard and snowflakes occasionally flitter but melt on contact in Montrose, the blizzard of January 10, 1949, was different. All of Los Angeles was blanketed with snow and five inches fell over the flatlands of Glendale. Here is the entrance to Indian Springs that morning, still advertising 80-degree pool water. (Courtesy of Kathryn Halford.)

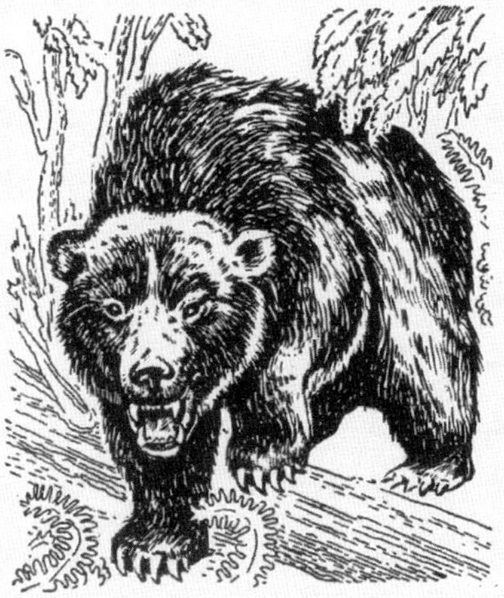

Last Bears Sighted

The last known bears in the Crescenta Valley were sighted in 1914 as a mother black bear and two cubs were reported on Briggs Terrace. Herbert T. Bathey, a local pioneer, was quoted in The Ledger in 1938, about the bear hunt that resulted.

"They were followed by hunters and their dogs from Dr. Utley's ranch to the old Bullock place in Verdugo Woodlands, where the hairy beasts were seen again in a tomato patch. Shot at, the bears doubled back on their tracks," and were chased, but lost in the upper reaches of the Big Tujunga Canyon.

Whether the bears were ever found and killed, Mr. Bathey did not say.

In 1938, residents thought there were no more bears in the area. Or at least that is what real estate agents were telling potential buyers in this notice. It is hard to believe no bears had been seen between 1914 and 1938, but they did not have Costco meatballs back then. In 2012, a bear nicknamed Meatball became a local celebrity as he scoured garbage cans near Montrose looking for this treat. (Courtesy of Chamber of Commerce.)

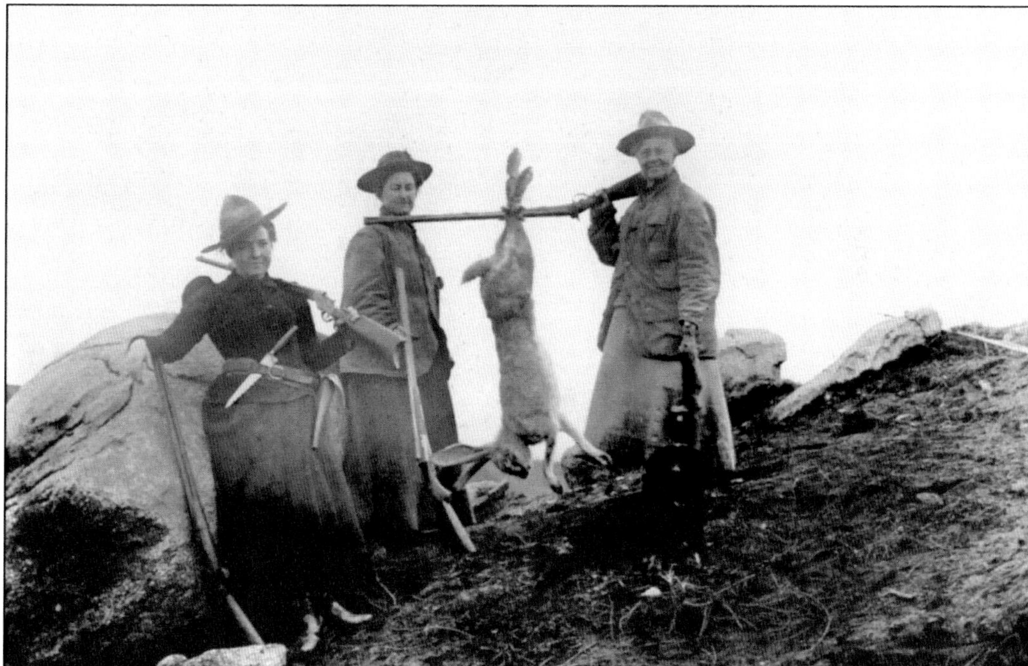

By 1926, selling rabbit pelts for coats was a big business, and one of the largest suppliers was J.R. Thorpe's Sierra Fur Farm at 700 Ocean View Boulevard. It had so many critters that it became a tourist attraction and hosted many parties. This photograph is from way before that year, as female hunters (Elizabeth "Libbie" Waterman is second from left) show off their prize jackrabbit in the local mountains. (Courtesy of John Newcombe.)

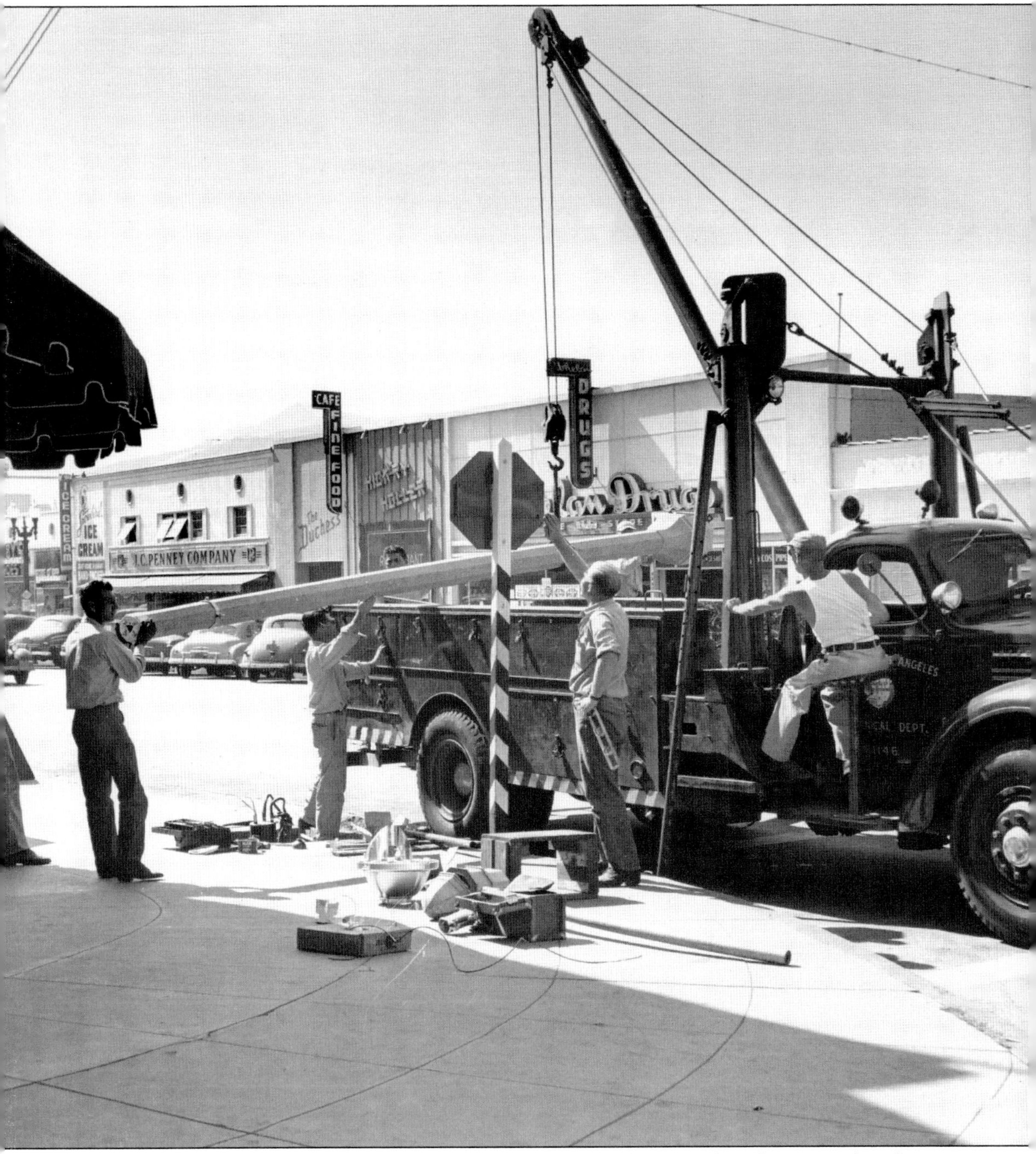

Montrose has had five styles of electric street lamps over the years, but the original and current ones look the same. In the 1950s, most of the original street lamps were removed and replaced with utilitarian concrete post lamps. This is a new concrete pole going in at the northeast corner of Honolulu Avenue and Ocean View Boulevard. Of equal interest are some of the shops in the background: The Snowbird Ice Cream parlor, which was the first name of Baskin-Robbins (this was only its third store); J.C. Penney; The Duchess; and Hick-ry Holler.

When the shopping park was renovated in 1967, these "futuristic" (well, what people called "futuristic" in the 1960s) sunhat-style street lamps replaced the concrete posts. They were much taller so they did not need as many of them as they did with the original lamps. (The new ones are visible in the photographs on pages 65 and 66)

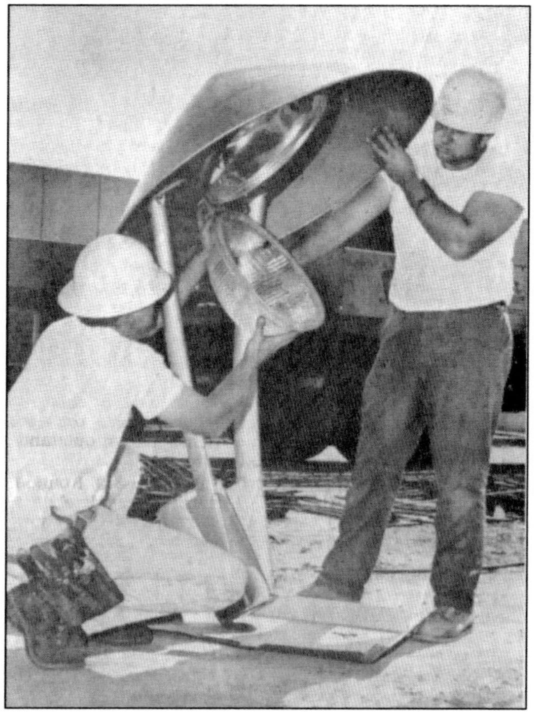

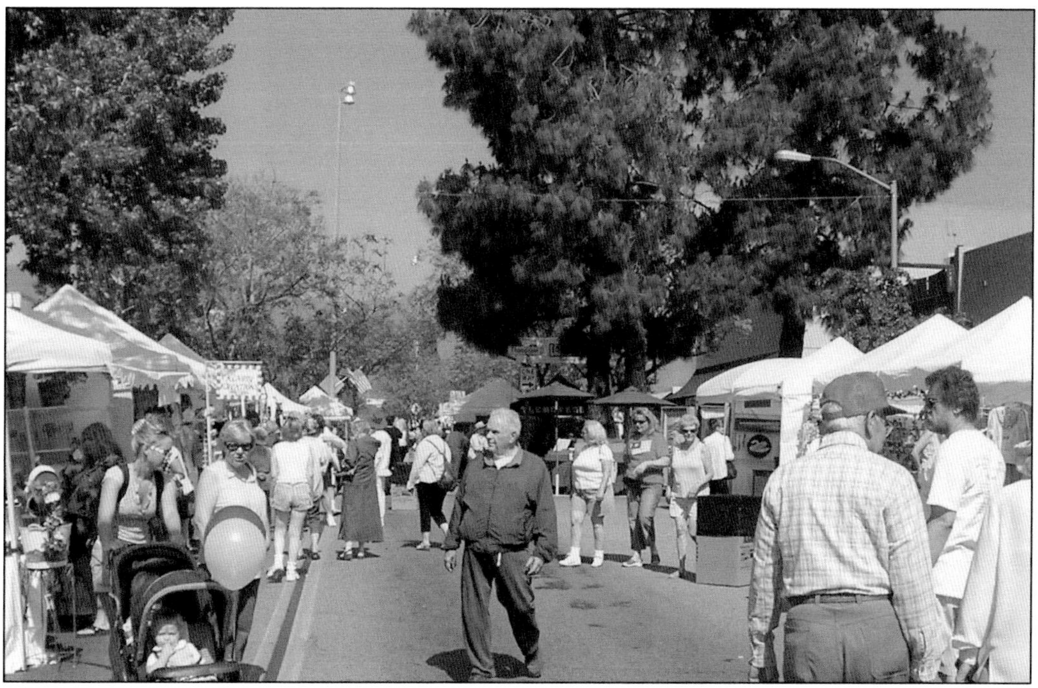

The energy crisis of the late 1970s prompted cities to switch to more efficient sodium vapor streetlights, and in the 1980s, Montrose replaced the sunhat lamps with fewer (only nine) and even taller (60 feet) sodium vapor lamps (visible in the background.) In 2005, the shopping park successfully spearheaded a campaign to have Glendale replace the "tarmac lights" with new lamps made from the same molds as the original Montrose street lamps.

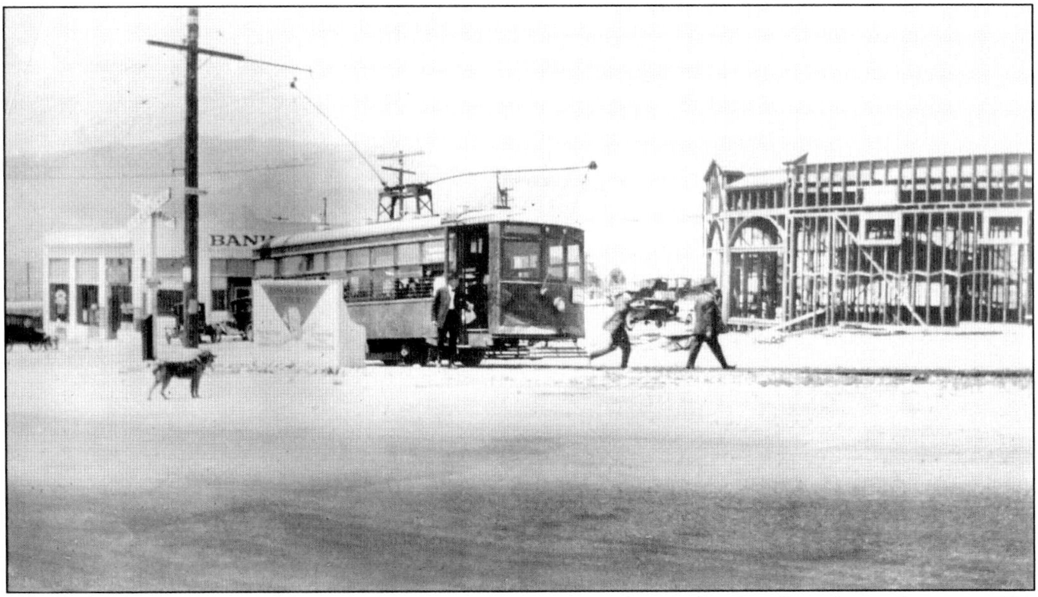

The G&M trolley car that most old-timers seem to remember is the "Dinky," shown here in 1923 dropping off passengers at Honolulu Avenue before heading up Montrose Avenue. The Dinky was smaller than other rail cars and had only one set of double wheels, centered under the car, making a ride on the uneven tracks feel like a trip at sea. High school kids used to gather at one end and try to rock the car.

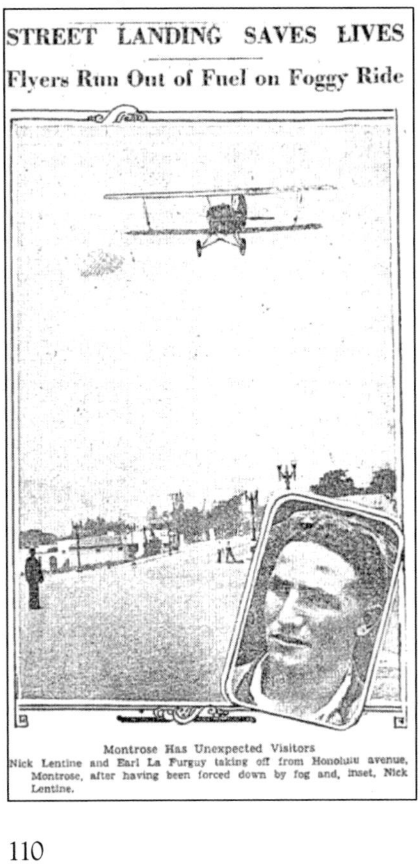

STREET LANDING SAVES LIVES

Flyers Run Out of Fuel on Foggy Ride

Montrose Has Unexpected Visitors

Nick Lentine and Earl La Furguy taking off from Honolulu avenue, Montrose, after having been forced down by fog and, inset, Nick Lentine.

In May 1931, Honolulu Avenue was the site of an emergency plane landing. Two young men out for a "joy ride" aboard a small plane at 2:00 a.m. realized they were low on gas. Through the fog, they saw the double line of lights along Honolulu and somehow landed the plane safely. More amazing, they took off from Honolulu the next day after refueling.

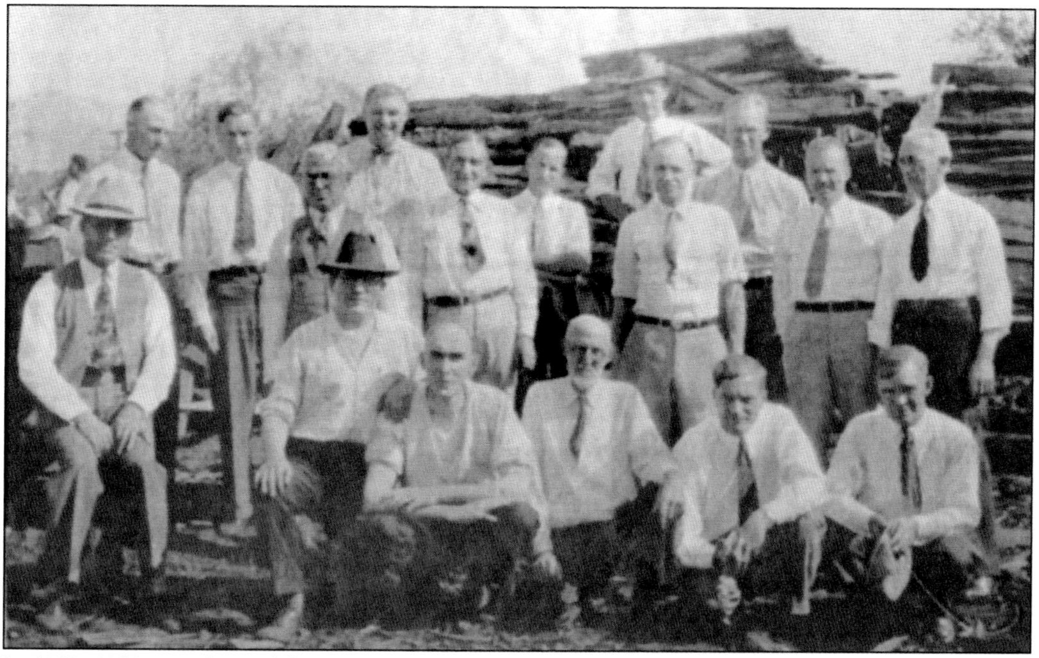

In 1929–1930, members of the Montrose–La Crescenta Kiwanis Club joined in an effort to provide firewood for needy families. After the G&M Railway went out of business, the club cut up the wooden railroad ties. Pictured here from left to right are (first row) R.Q. McDonald, Al Sullivan, Andy Clark, George Westum, and Jimmy Hicks; (second row) George Silver, William Crippen, Max Amelang, Floyd Peet, Robert Longman, C.M. Knox, Lee Merritt, Bernard Anawalt, Dr. Johns, Guy Carlton, Guy Weekly, and Dr. Wemple.

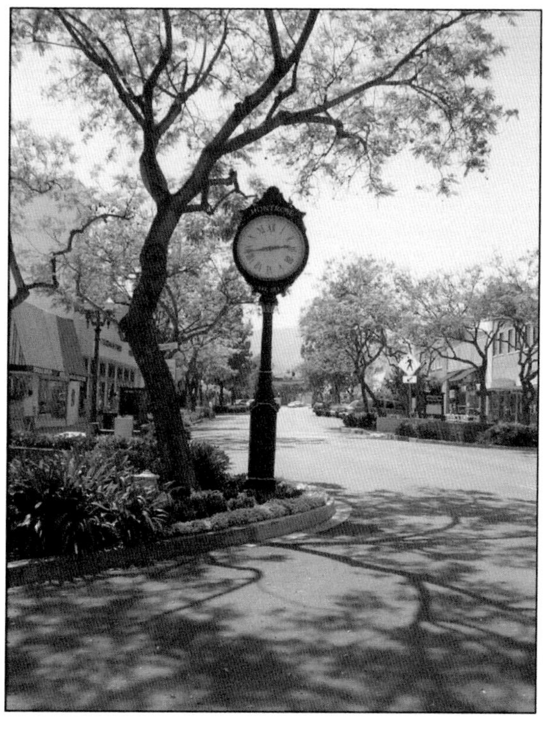

The Montrose Town Clock looks like it has been there since the beginning, but it is a new addition. Longtime Peet Stationers shopkeeper Anita Peet Geyer, upon her death in the late 1990s, bequeathed a sizable inheritance to Montrose. After much thought, the shopping park determined the best tribute to her would be a town clock. Many designs and locations were considered, and it was finally installed and started ticking on May 24, 2005. The clock almost instantly became the iconic symbol of Montrose.

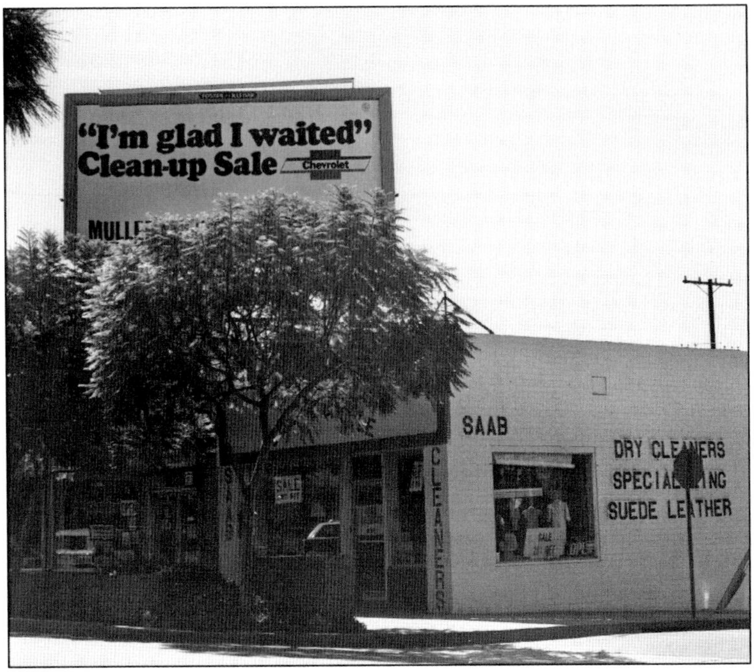

Montrose used to have a number of billboards, including this one on top of the store at the southeast corner of Honolulu and Las Palmas Avenues. To cut down on visual blight, Glendale passed a sign ordinance in 1973 that essentially made signs that stuck out from buildings "nonconforming." There was a 10-year grace period for owners to get their signs in compliance. (Courtesy of John Newcombe.)

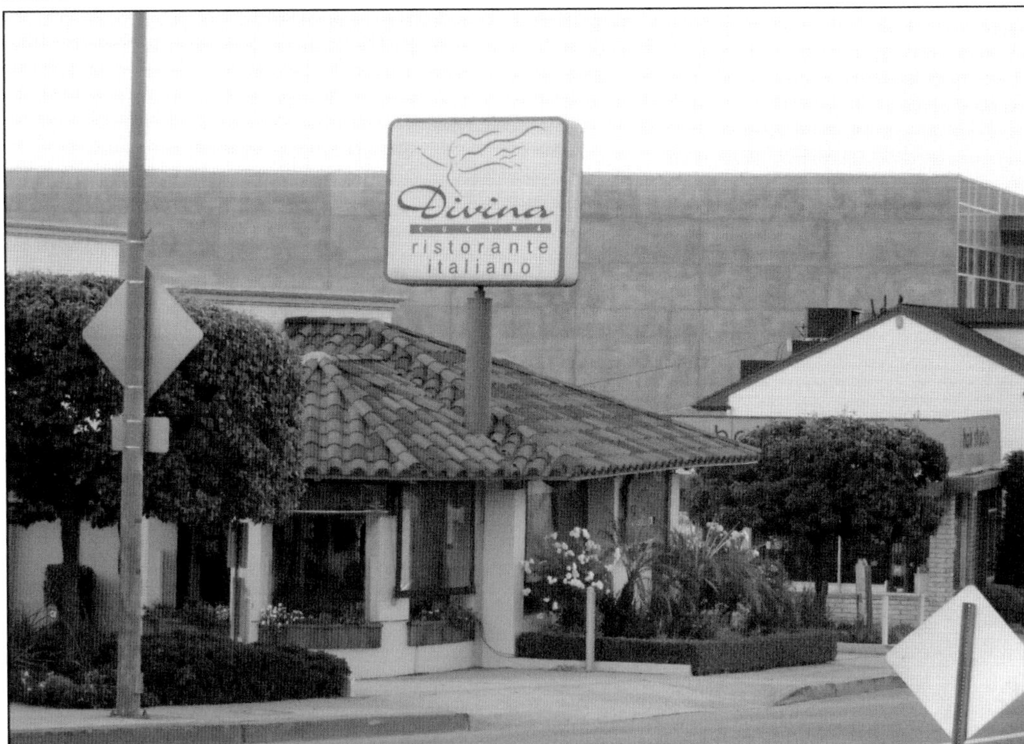

Divina Cucina Ristorante Italiano opened in 1996 at 3730 North Verdugo Road in the former Jessup Farm dairy building. When enclosing the patio in 2007, the owners made the former free-standing pole sign become a roof sign, which is technically against the law. Glendale threatened fines, but after a huge outpouring of support from the community, the sign was allowed to stay.

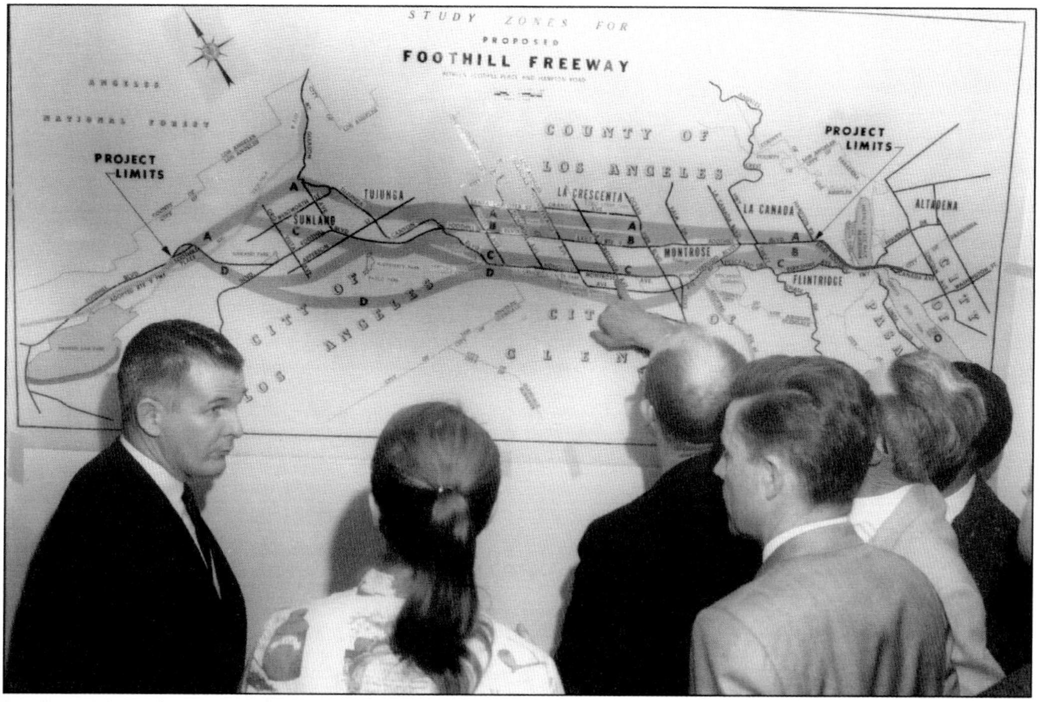

In the 1960s, the state of California decided that a freeway would cut through the valley roughly following the same path padres took between the missions 200 years before, from Pasadena to the San Fernando Valley. In this photograph, concerned citizens look at the possible placements. The bottom path option would have gone through part of the shopping park.

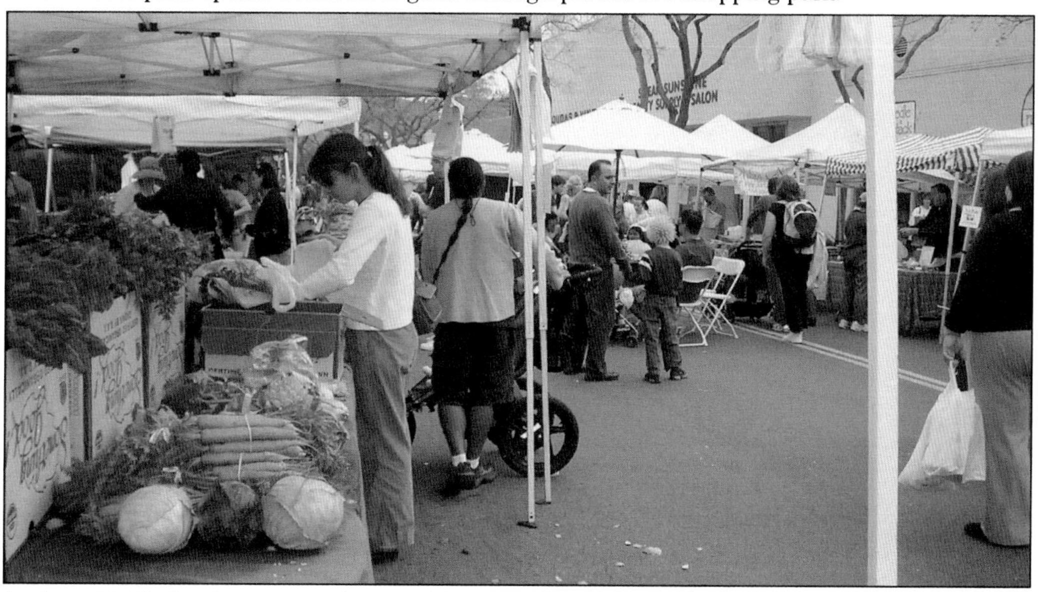

In about 2000, the shopping park started hosting a Thursday night farmers market and street fair. When the crowds started getting rowdy, the shopping park moved it to Sunday to make it more family friendly. The weekly Harvest Market has included pony rides, bounce houses, a climbing wall, a petting zoo, and other activities for kids, plus regular performances by Gremoli, a New Orleans–style jazz band.

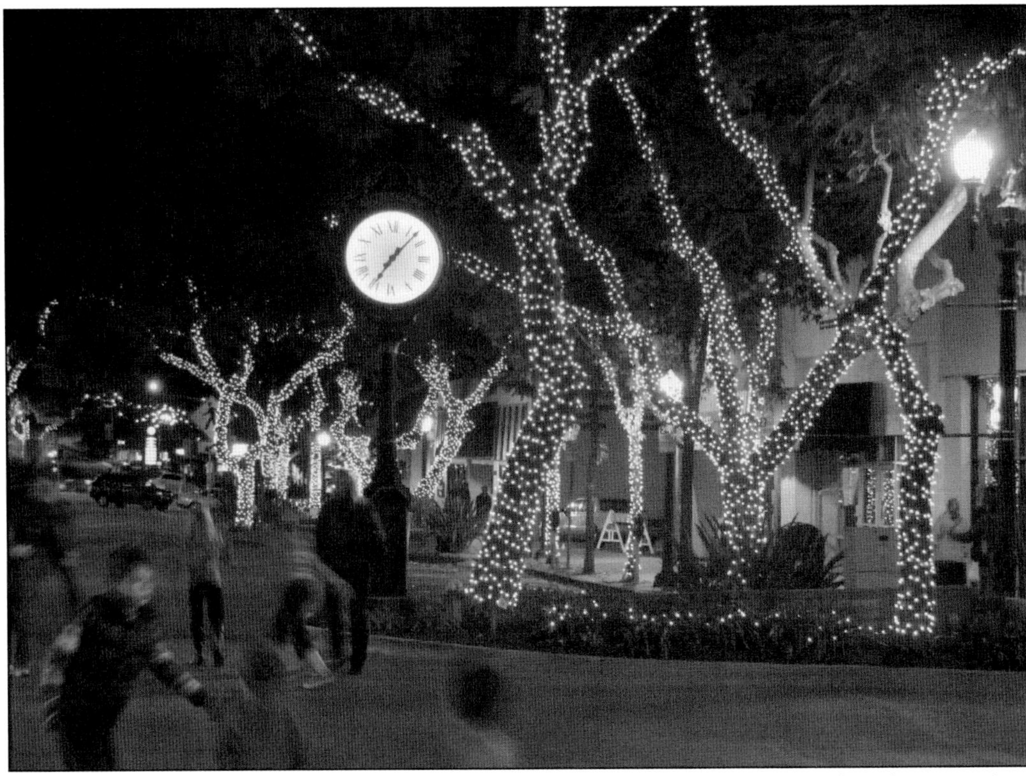

Almost once a month, the shopping park spices up the Harvest Market with a theme such as the Antique Auto Show or the Wags and Whiskers pet parade. For Halloween, it hosts trick-or-treaters. And from Thanksgiving to Christmas, the shopping park is turned into a winter wonderland with thousands of twinkle lights, a horse-drawn carriage, and Santa, of course. In 2011, snow was brought in!

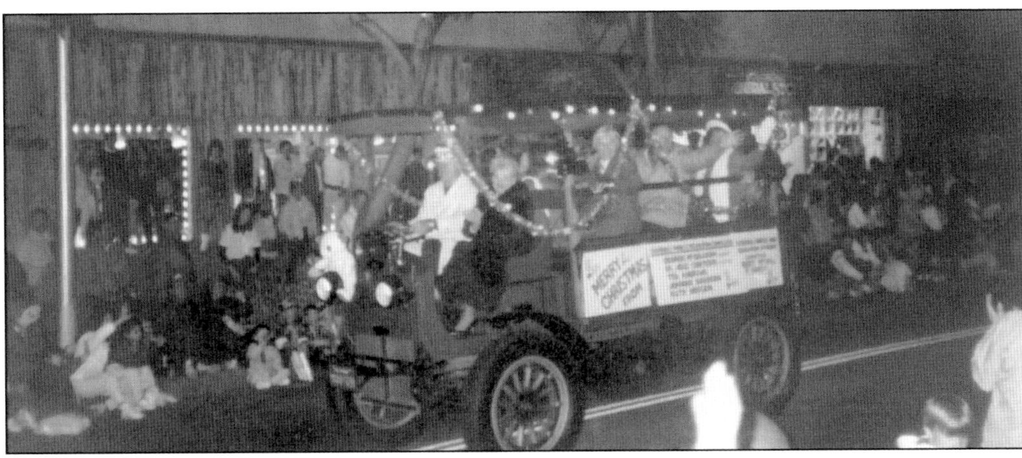

The Montrose Christmas Parade, originally an afternoon affair, was started by Dennis Morgan in the 1950s. After he moved from the area, the parade stopped—until 1976 when it was revived by "Mr. Montrose," Frank Roberts. It has been running continuously since, with close to 150 community service and youth groups, drill teams, and marching bands participating every year highlighted by Santa flying over the parade—in a helicopter.

La Cañada resident Dennis Morgan was a big movie star in the 1940s and 1950s and just as big a booster of the Crescenta Valley community. Morgan hosted celebrity baseball games to raise money to purchase and dedicate Two Strike Park in La Crescenta. Morgan was a regular visitor to Montrose and helped start the Montrose Christmas Parade. He is seen here with comedian Eddie Cantor.

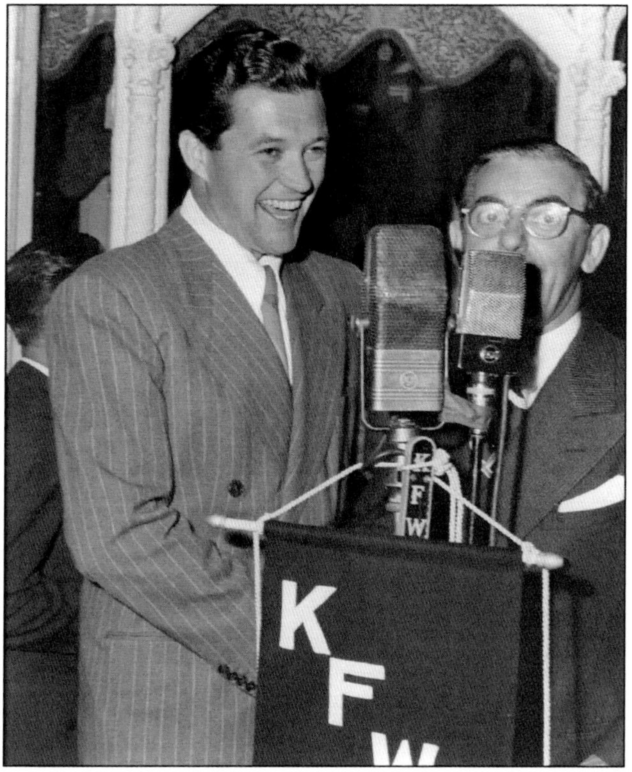

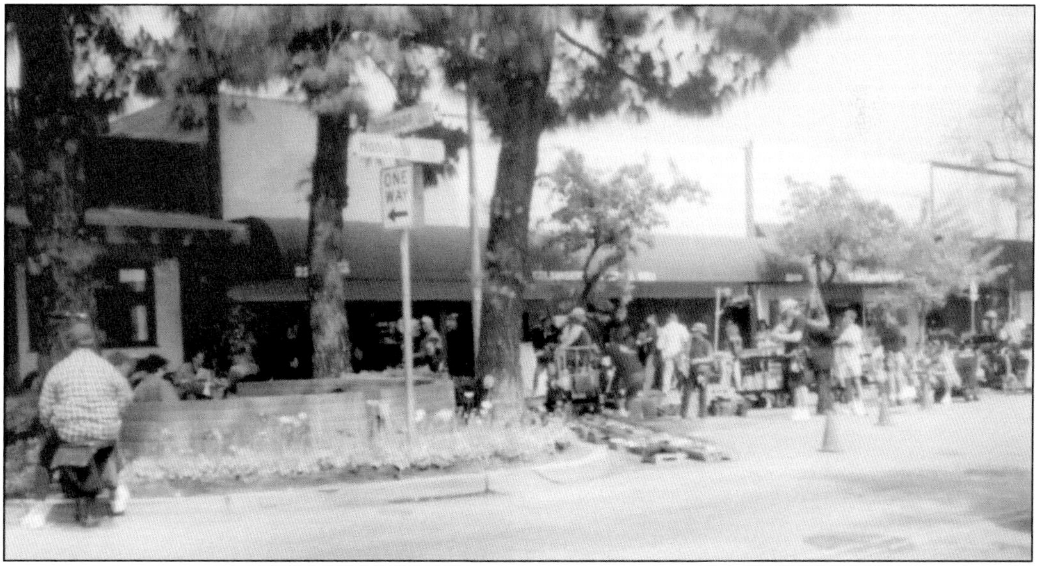

Montrose is the most-filmed location in the city of Glendale, with television shows and movies shot here regularly, including *Gilmore Girls*, *Seventh Heaven*, *Columbo*, *Magnum P.I.*, *Sons of Anarchy*, and *True Blood*. In 2000, this Hollywood crew was shooting a scene for a television show in front of the Star Café and Gelsinger's Meats. (Courtesy of Kerri Gelsinger Scott.)

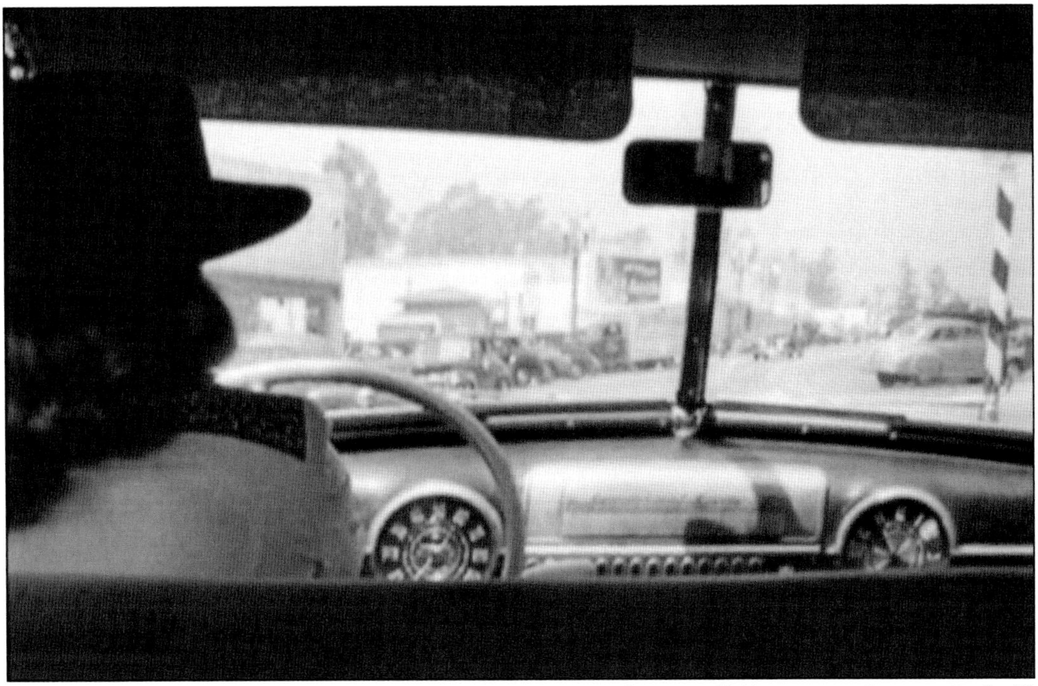

The 1949 film *Gun Crazy* contains one of the most unique shots in all film noir: a three-and-a-half-minute, continuous take of the lead characters robbing a bank in Montrose, all shot from inside their car. During the sequence, the car stops at Honolulu Avenue and Ocean View Boulevard while the driver gets out to rob the bank and his partner slides over behind the wheel. (Courtesy of Warner Bros.)

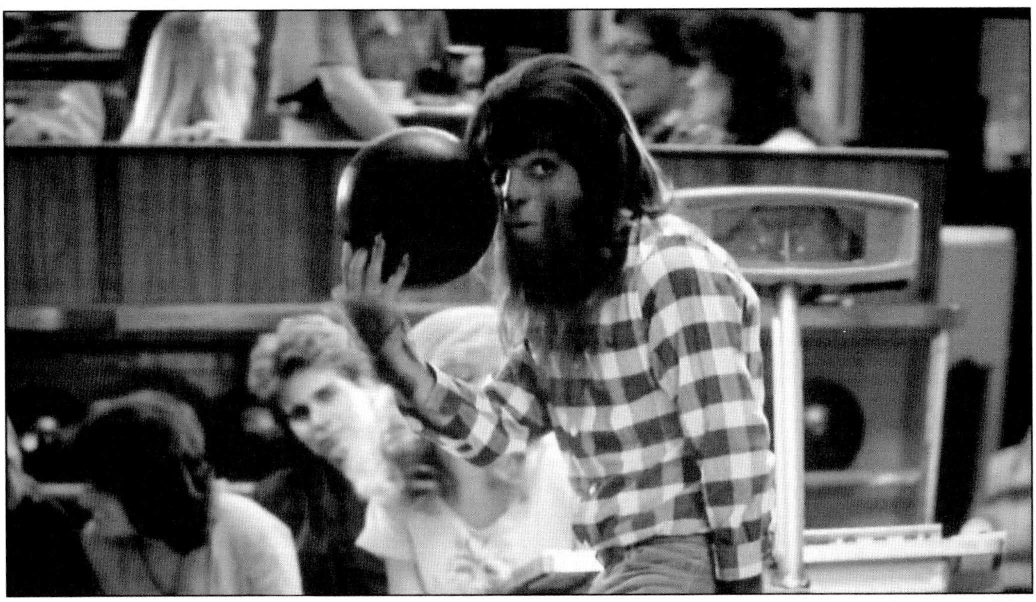

The 1985 comedy film *Teen Wolf* starring Michael J. Fox was a comic retelling of the 1950s film *I Was a Teenage Werewolf*. In it, Fox becomes an exceptional athlete and popular with the girls when he turns into a werewolf. The short bowling scene was filmed at Montrose Bowl. (Courtesy of MGM Home Video.)

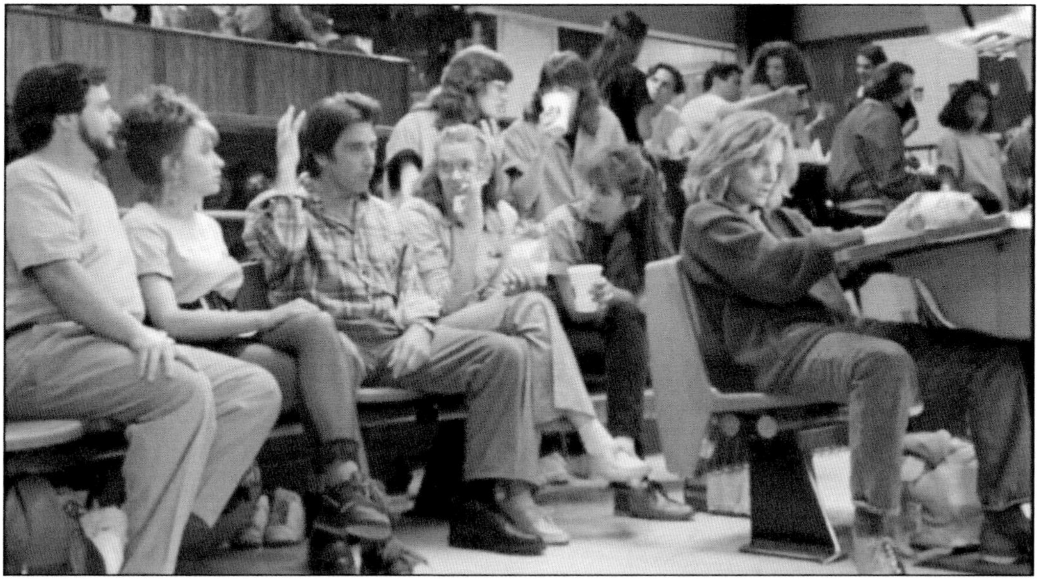

In the 1991 film *Frankie and Johnny*, the Montrose Bowl was the site of a lengthy scene starring, from left to right, Nathan Lane, Kate Nelligan, Al Pacino, Jane Morris, and Michelle Pfeiffer. Because of the many camera angles, Montrose Bowl plays a major part in this sequence. (Courtesy of Paramount Pictures.)

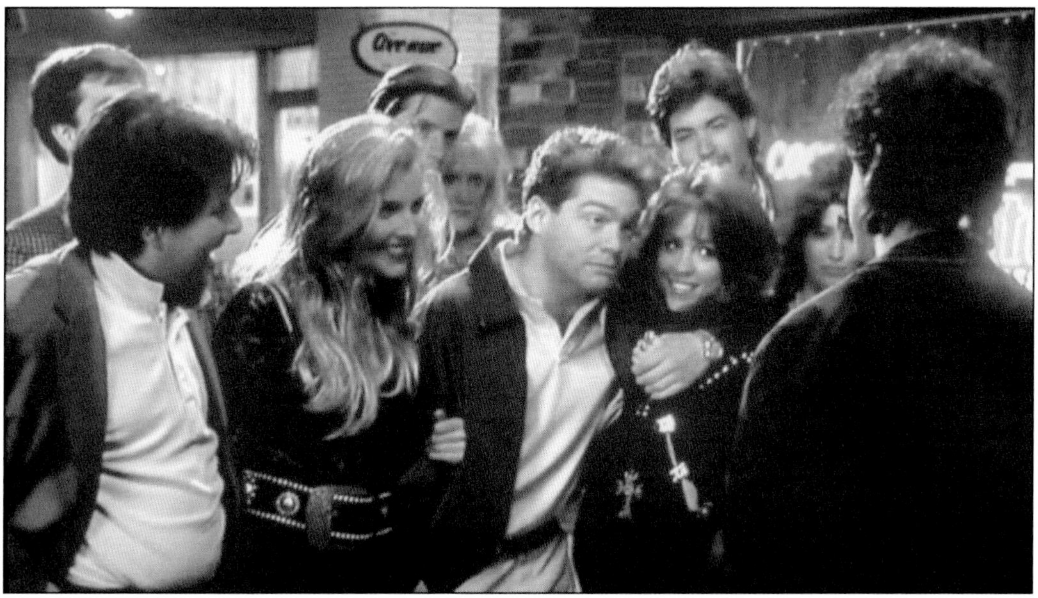

In the 1998 Adam Sandler movie *The Wedding Singer*, there were several sequences filmed in Montrose, including the wedding cake sequence at the Montrose Bakery and Adam Sandler drinking at Avignone's Cocktails. In this scene, Sandler (far right) is confronting Drew Barrymore's fiancé (Matthew Glave) and friends outside the bar. Montrose Bakery is in the background. The location for this sequence is visible in the photograph on page 67. (Courtesy of New Line Cinema.)

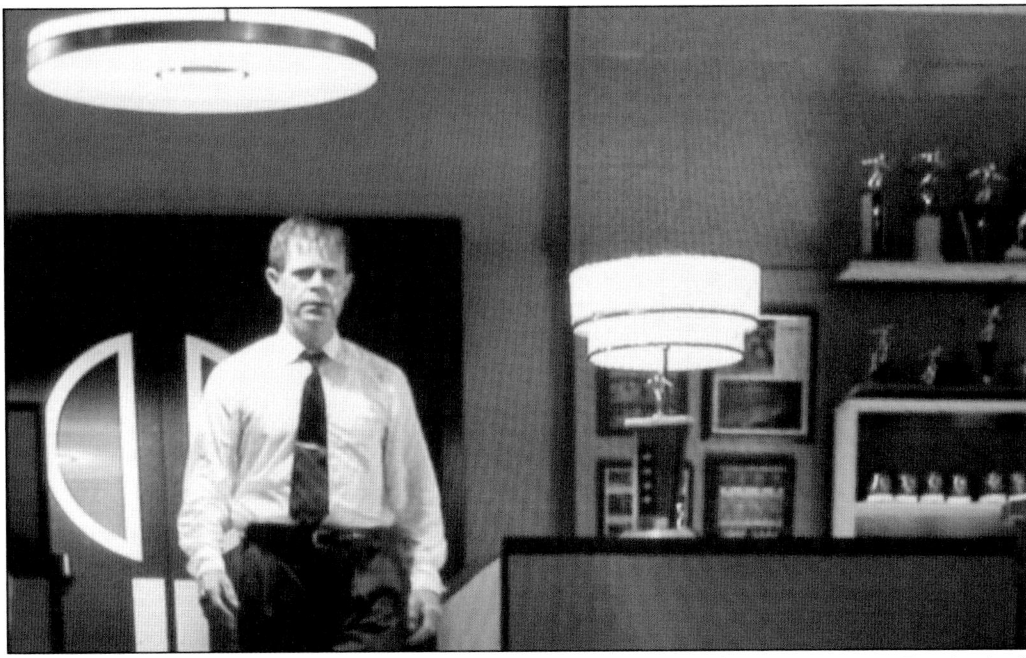

In 1998's *Pleasantville*, there is another extended scene that takes place at Montrose Bowl, which was heavily modified for the film. (The current paint job is a leftover from it.) J.T. Walsh tries to calm William Macy and friends with the line, "We're safe now. Thank goodness we're in a bowling alley." Interestingly, the exterior of the bowling alley was recreated on a studio lot as part of Pleasantville. (Courtesy of New Line Cinema.)

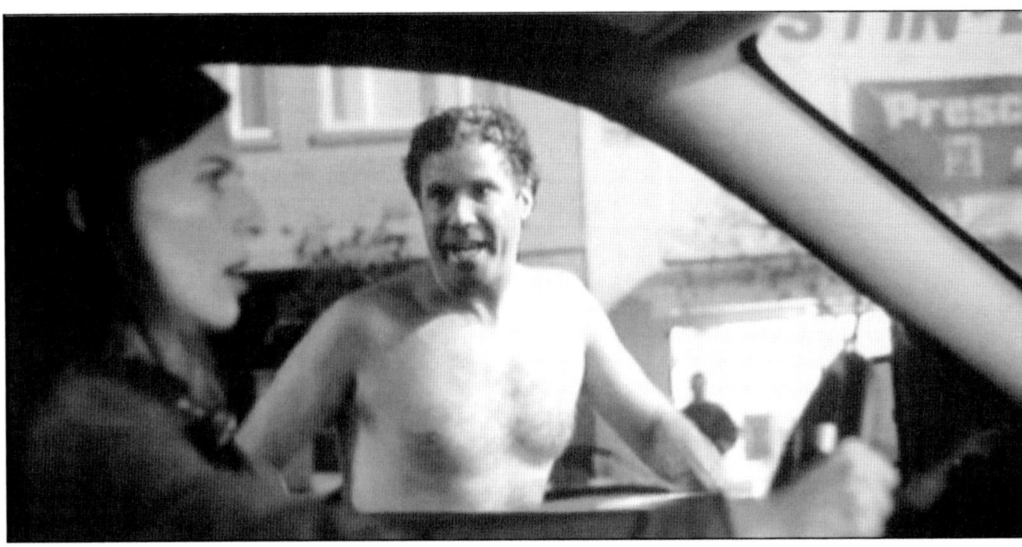

There are several scenes in 2003's *Old School* that were filmed in Montrose, but the most famous is Will Ferrell streaking down Honolulu Avenue. The former Austin Drugs (now Bluefish) is behind Ferrell in this shot. Mary and Dale Dawson tell the story of walking down Honolulu Avenue that cold February night and being asked to stop for a moment for a film shoot. A minute later, Ferrell streaked past them. (Courtesy of Dreamworks.)

Five

Gone to Seed
Remnants of Old Montrose

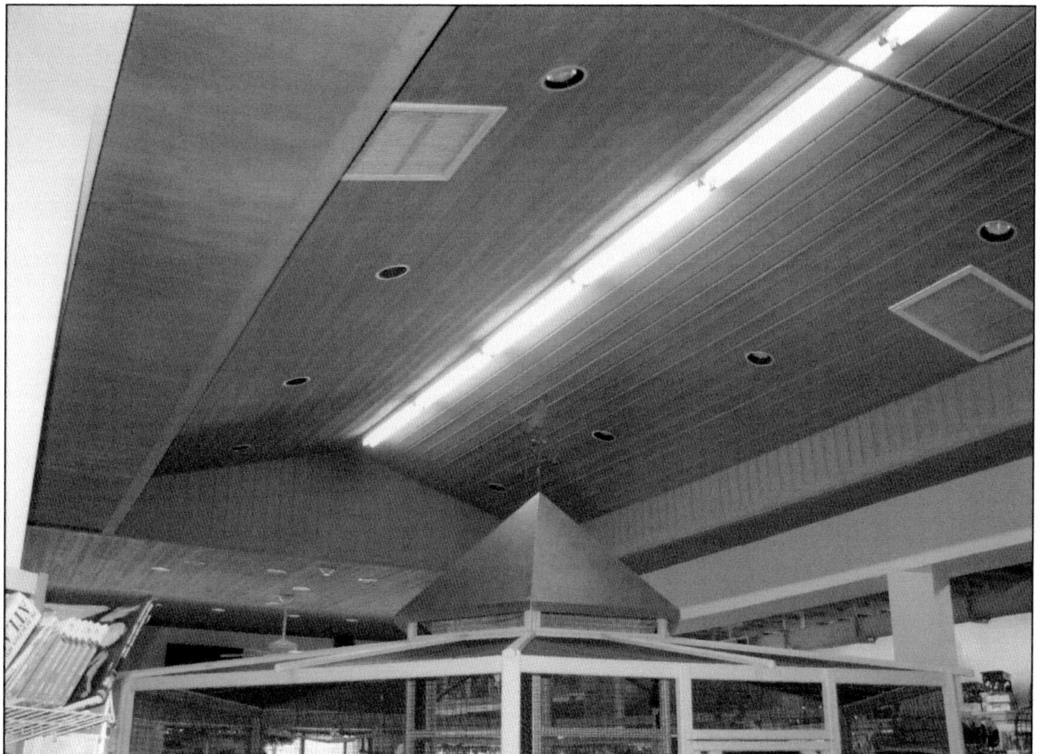

While many of the buildings from days past are still standing and in plain view, there are some remnants of old Montrose that are not so obvious. The Montrose Hotel used to have a glass-ceilinged atrium in the lobby. It was boarded up at some point, but the frame of it is still visible in the ceiling at Andersen's Pet Shop. (2218)

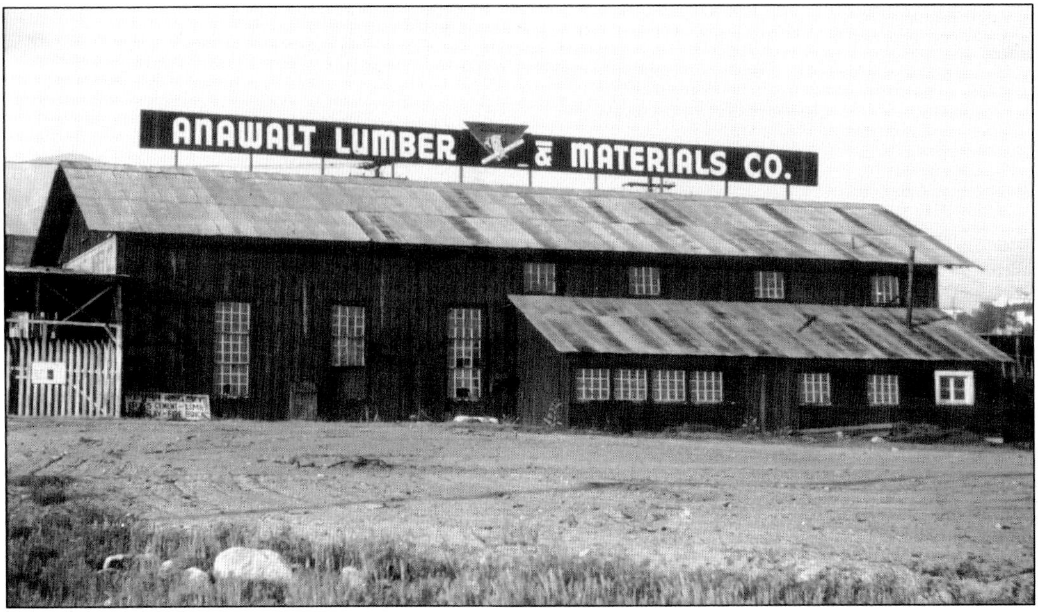

It is probably not surprising that the oldest continuously run business in Montrose would have two remnants on its property. The top photograph is the trolley barn for the Glendale & Montrose Railway from the early 1920s. When the G&M went out of business in 1930, Anawalt's bought the barn and has used it for storage ever since. In the right light, some of the tracks are visible under the asphalt in front of the barn. The bottom photograph is of Anawalt's in 1967, with the large pole sign in front. The sign had to come down, so the pole is now used as a flagpole and the elephant part of the sign hangs in a prominent spot in the former trolley barn. (Above, courtesy of Mike Morgan.)

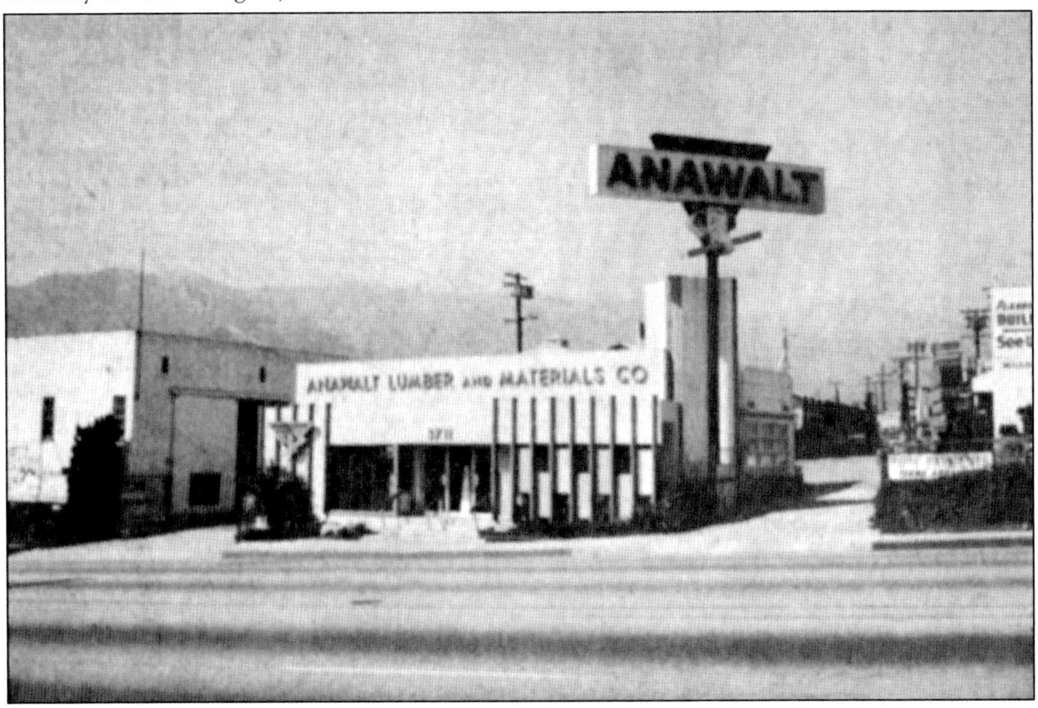

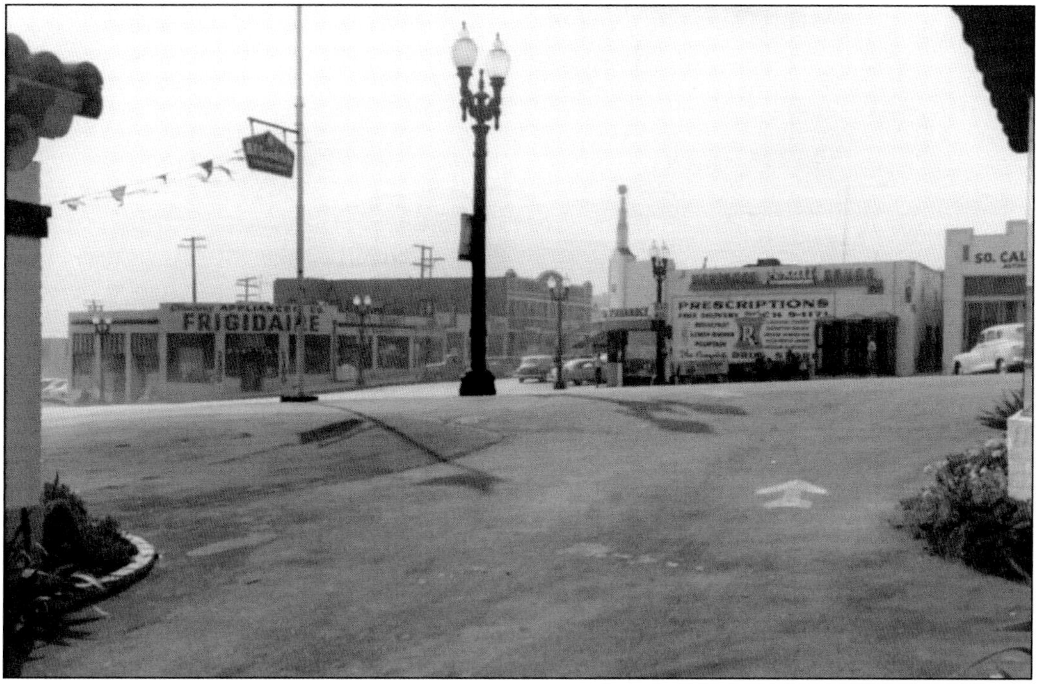

When Robert Cooke bought the Montrose Pharmacy, he expanded it by buying the building to the north and connecting them. This unusual view of Honolulu and Montrose Avenues, from the sloping drive of the service station on the northeast corner, shows clearly that the pharmacy and the building to the north of it were separate structures. But the new building was at a higher grade so Cooke added a small staircase between the new and old space. Today, it looks like one building, but that same staircase connects the main room of Rocky Cola to the back, upper room.

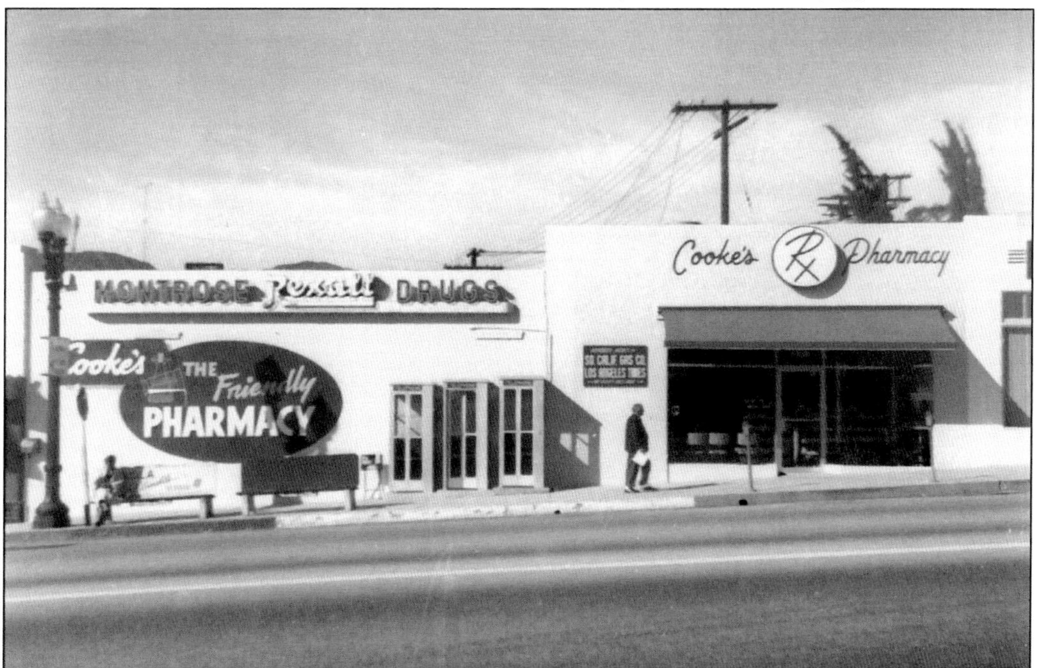

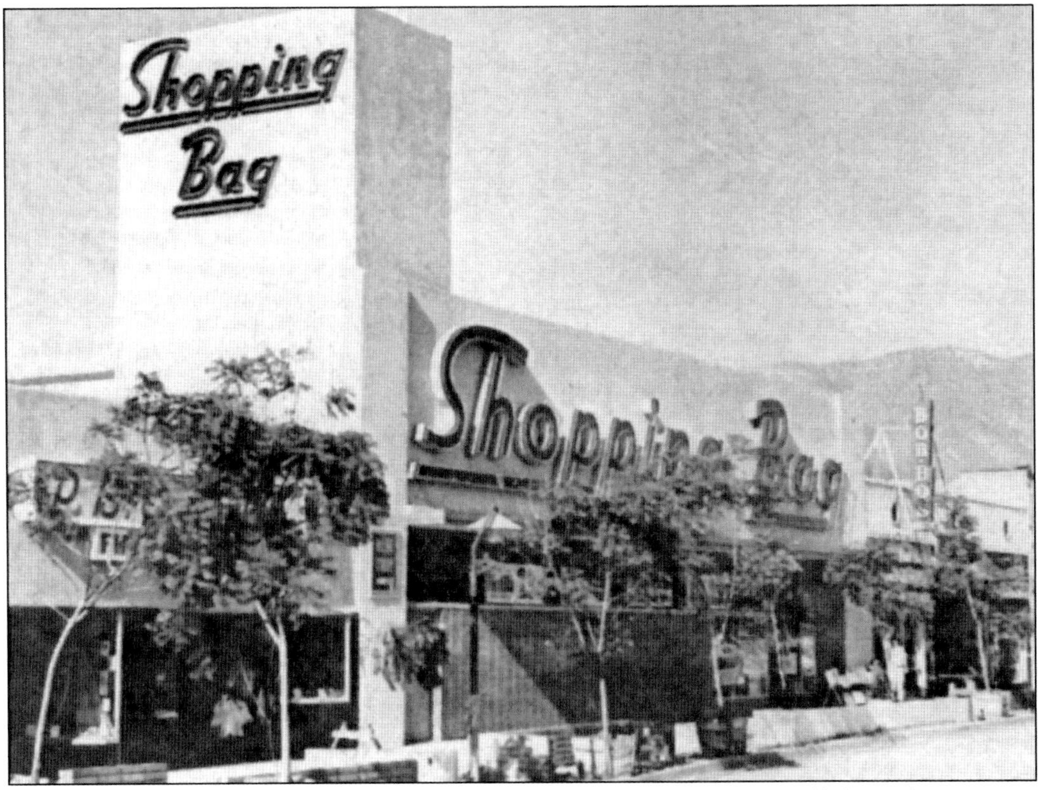

Local historians suspect that the neon Shopping Bag sign remains on the wall above the entrance where it is in this photograph. No one seems to know for certain, but the top part of the current building sticks out a yard or so and does not look particularly attractive or fitting with the building. It looks like the sign was simply boxed in, which would have been cheaper and easier than removing it.

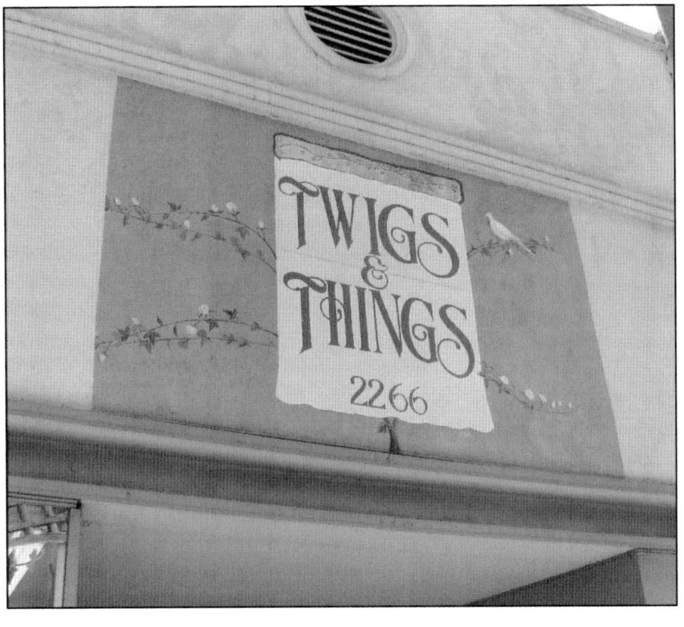

The sign for Twigs & Things is actually the sign for the previous tenant, the Little Place Boutique. When Cynthia Redden moved her business from the Village Square into this location, she did not have a lot of money so she tracked down the artist who had originally painted the sign and had her replace the name with Twigs & Things, leaving the rest of the sign the same except for adding the dove.

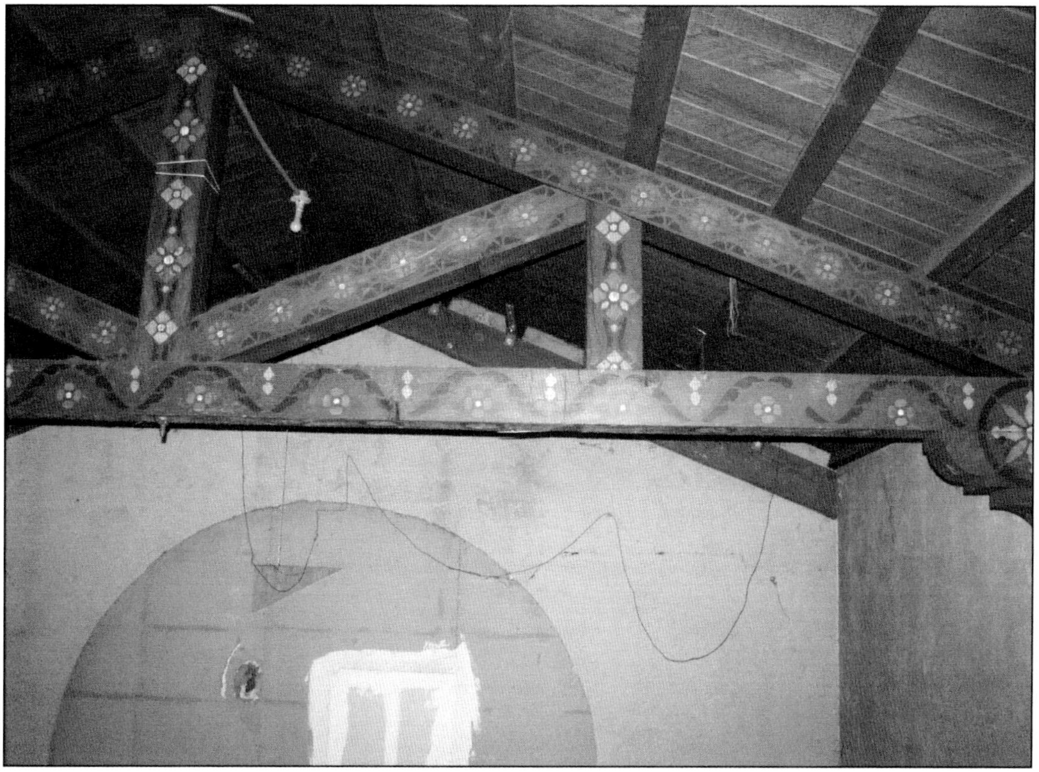

When the Crescenta-Cañada bank opened at the southeast corner of Honolulu Avenue and Ocean View Boulevard, it featured a large arched window and hand-painted wooden beams in the open-beamed lobby. The window was removed and the beams hidden by a drop ceiling when the building was converted to retail space, but the beams (and plywood covering the hole where the window was removed) are still there in the storage space above what is now a Starbucks.

The great neon sign from Ebmeyer's Bakery is . . . well, we don't know what happened to it, but the corrugated wall on which the pieces hung is still visible at 2287 Honolulu Avenue under the awning. The spots around the signs have been sun-bleached and are easily seen by looking straight up while standing close to the wall.

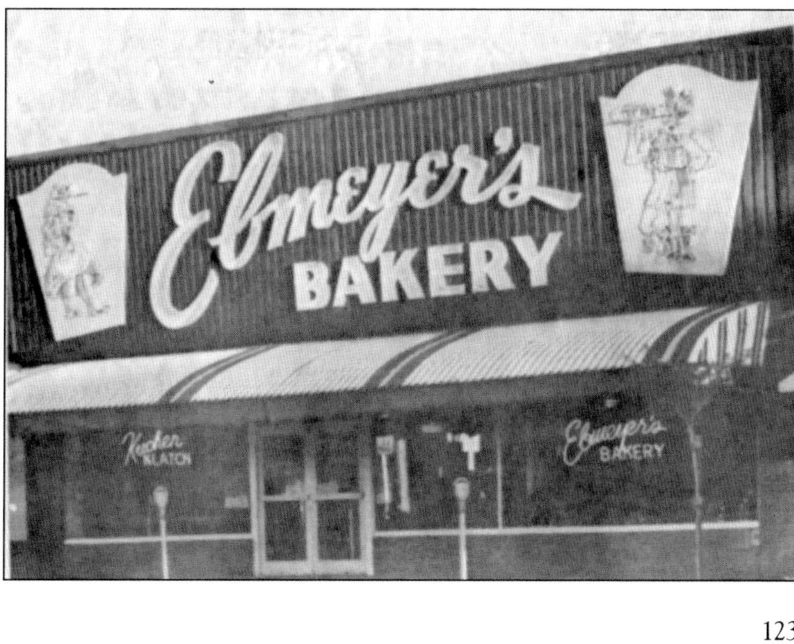

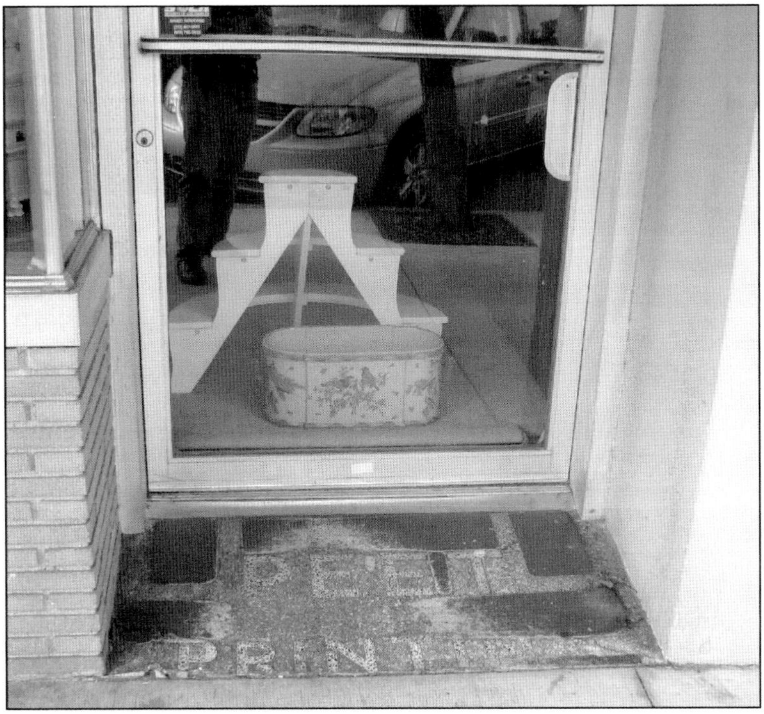

Peet Stationers was a Montrose staple at 2311 Honolulu Avenue for close to 60 years. The first business that Floyd Peet ran was a print shop, and he inlaid the name of it, Peet's Printing, in the tile in front of the door. It is still there, in front of Holiday Hats and Gowns.

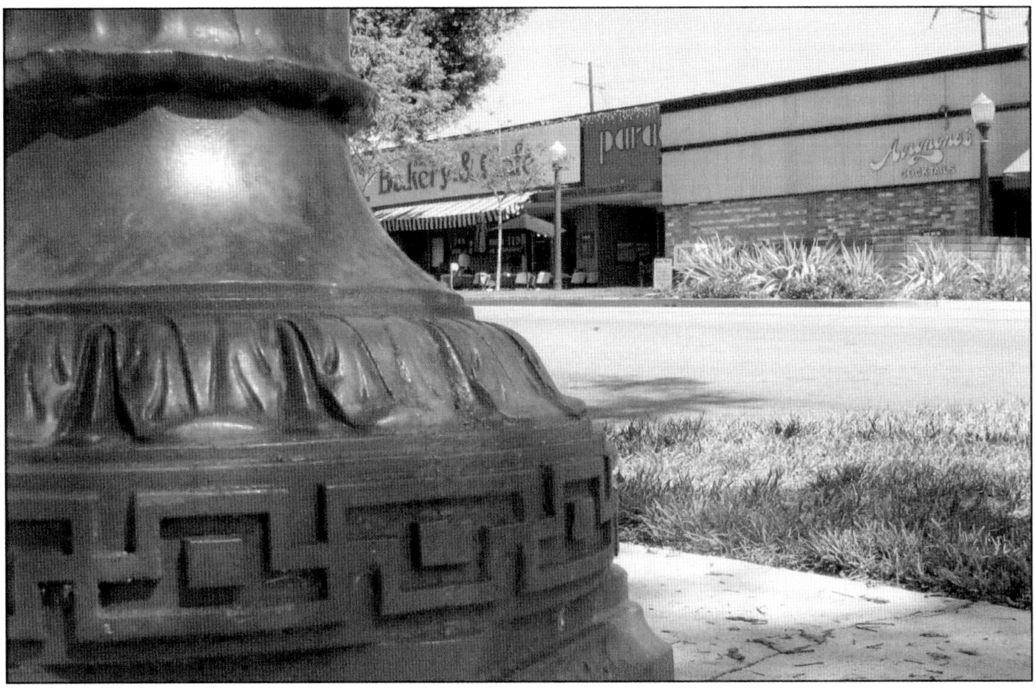

The current lampposts were erected in 2005, but, amazingly enough, were created from the same molds that were used to make the original Montrose lampposts in the 1920s. A swastika is part of the design element around the base, which sometimes startles people when they discover it, but the swastika symbol has been around for over 3,000 years and had a positive meaning until the Nazis adapted it as the symbol of their party.

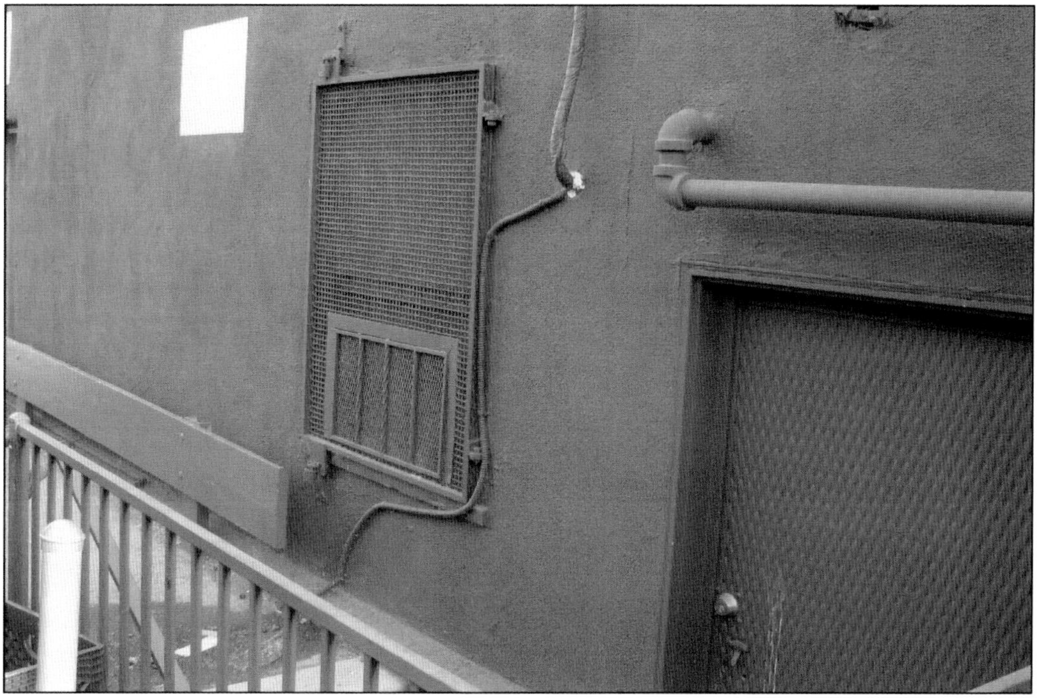

The sheriff's department on Ocean View Boulevard had two jail cells, with this pass-through window for delivering food. When prisoners were housed here, staff members from the City Hall Coffee Shop would cart meals down the street and hand them through this opening. The jail cells are still in the back of the building and are currently being used for dog grooming.

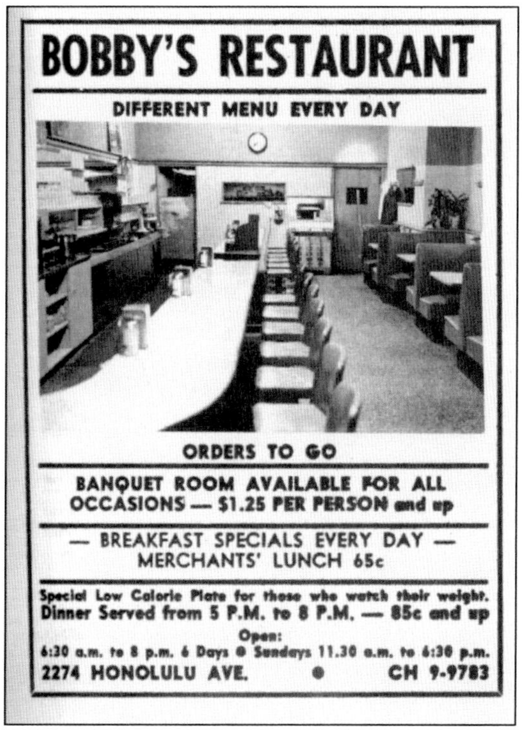

When Edie moved her coffee shop from 2272 to 2327, she seemed to have taken the whole shebang with her. This advertisement from the 1957 phone book shows Bobby's Restaurant (one of the previous owners), but it looks almost identical to the City Hall Coffee Shop even today. The counters and booths have been updated, but the layout is the same. (Courtesy of Mark Havlik.)

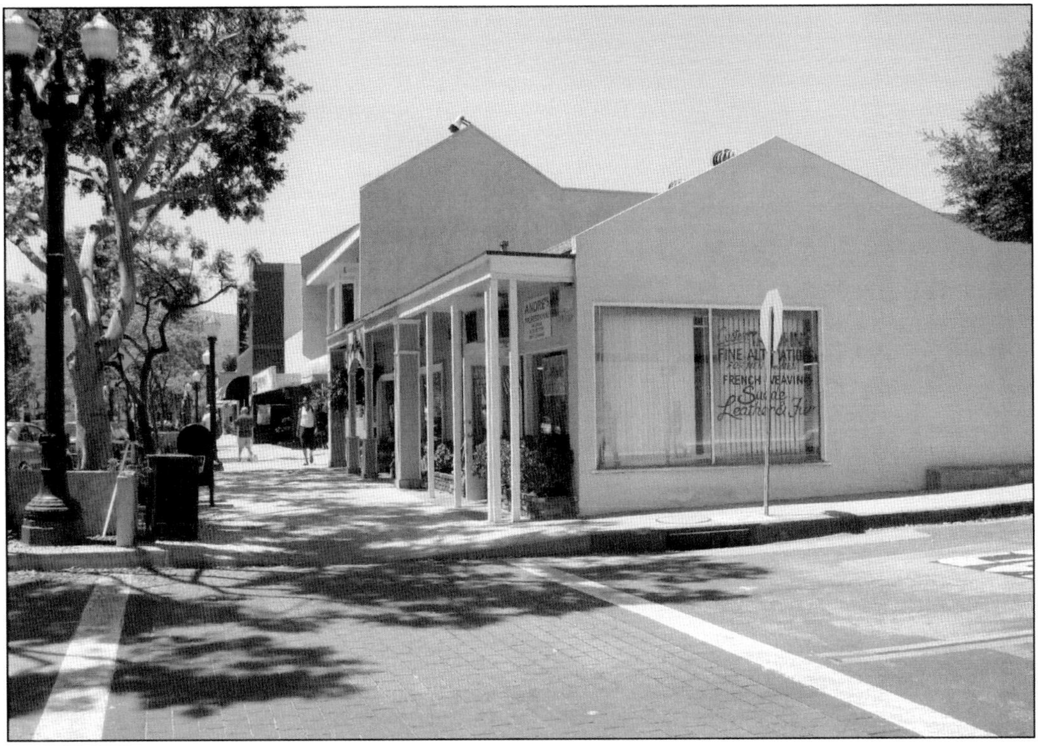

Since Montrose Avenue was the intended main business "stem," houses were built along Honolulu Avenue west of Ocean View Boulevard. As the business district instead expanded west, homeowners found themselves surrounded by retail shops. Some sold, some started businesses in their homes, and others simply remained as long as possible. There are two houses remaining in the shopping park, this one at 2405 and the other at 2341.

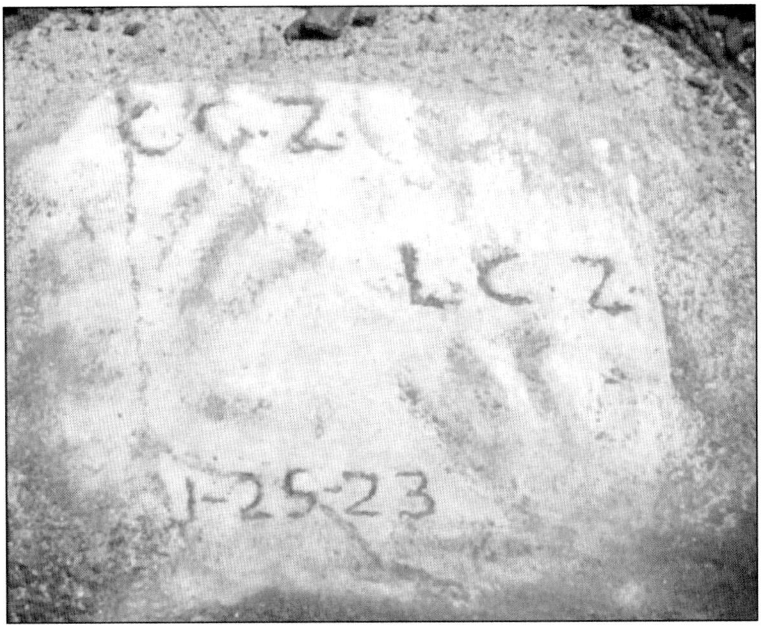

The Zwick family was one of the last holdouts and lived in their house at 2331 Honolulu Avenue until the late 1950s. The family had been struck by tragedy during World War II as their two sons were killed within a month of each other. Out of respect for the family, the new owner kept the family name on the plaza and preserved the blocks of cement containing handprints of the Zwick children in the plaza.

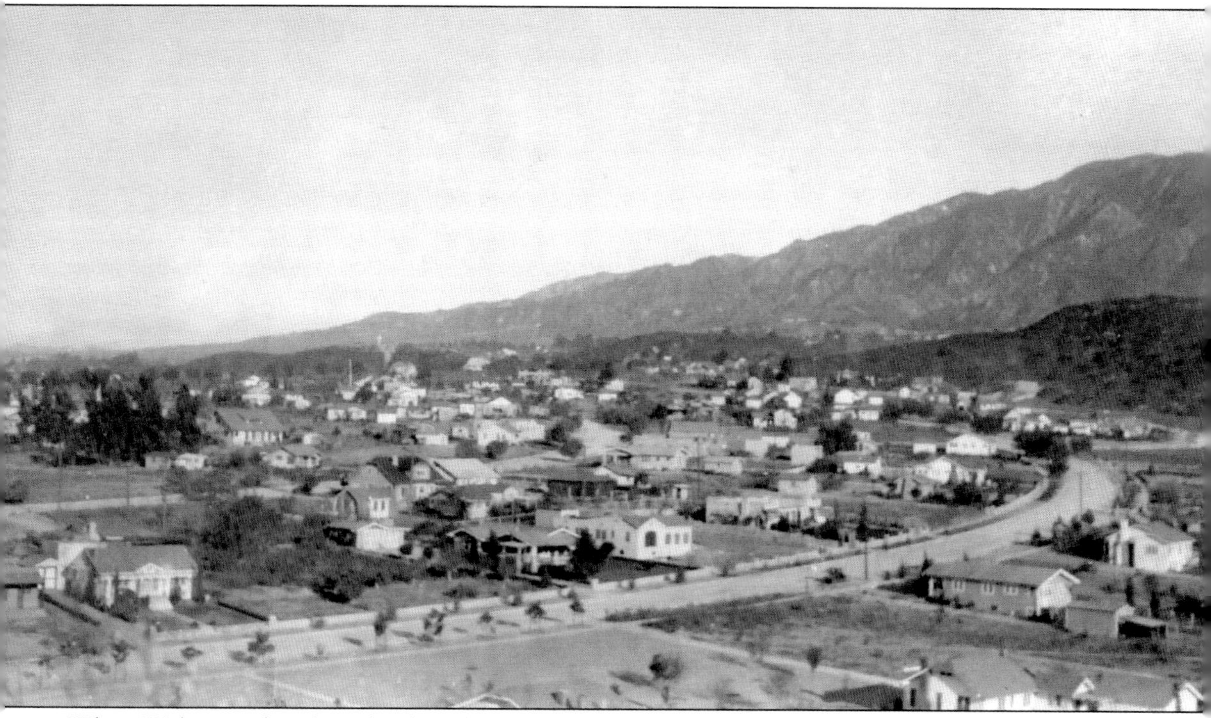

When Walton and Walters developed Montrose, they intended it to be a suburban neighborhood more than the rural farming community La Crescenta had been. Nevertheless, because the lots were large and for many years remained empty, there were some small farms here. This view looks northwest towards Waltonia Drive, just north of Park Place, in about the late 1920s. The 210 Freeway left this part of the rose intact, passing over Waltonia on the right side of this photograph, but pruned the rest of the top petals on its way west. The barn on Glenada Avenue and the house next to it on Waltonia still stand today (below). (Above, courtesy of Mark Havlik.)

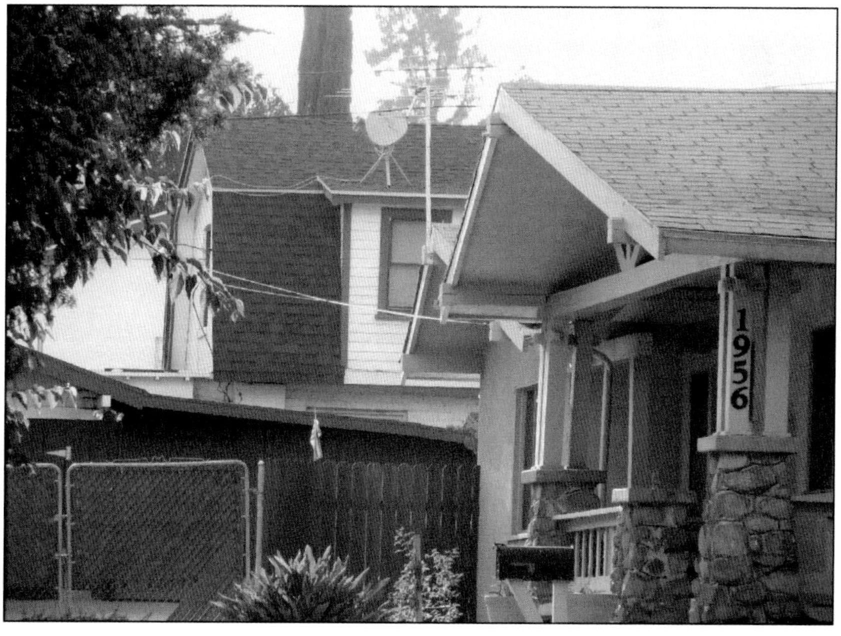